NATIONAL TRAUMA

AND

COLLECTIVE MEMORY

NATIONAL TRAUMA

AND

COLLECTIVE MEMORY

EXTRAORDINARY EVENTS IN THE AMERICAN EXPERIENCE

SECOND EDITION

ARTHUR G. NEAL

M.E.Sharpe
Armonk, New York
London, England

ATLANTA
INTERNATIONAL
SCHOOL

Library of Congress Cataloging-in-Publication Data

Neal, Arthur G.
  National trauma and collective memory : extraordinary events in the American experience /
Arthur G. Neal.— 2nd ed.
     p. cm.
  Includes bibliographical references and index.
  ISBN 0-7656-1581-9 (cloth : alk. paper)
  1. United States—History—20th century. 2. United States—Social conditions—1933–1945.
3. United States—Social conditions—1945– 4. Crises—Psychological aspects—United
States—History—20th century. 5. Memory—Social aspects—United States—History—
20th century. 6. National characteristics, American. I. Title.

E741.N43 2005
973.91—dc22   2004027365

Printed in the United States of America

The paper used in this publication meets the minimum requirements of
American National Standard for Information Sciences
Permanence of Paper for Printed Library Materials,
ANSI Z 39.48-1984.

∞

BM (c)   10   9   8   7   6   5   4   3   2   1

Contents

List of Symbolic Events

Preface

This new edition emerged from the events set in motion by the terrorist attack of September 11, 2001. The distinctive features of the first edition are retained, and the revised book still covers the major traumas of the nation over the past hundred years. The basic design of the first edition is followed through refining and extending the concept of national trauma as it impinged on the personal lives of individuals. The book focuses on both the individual and collective responses of Americans to some of the most memorable events of their time and place. In a variety of ways, these responses work their way into perceptions of society as a moral community and into the collective memories of the nation.

The terrorist attack of September 11, 2001, became deeply etched into the memories of Americans as another day of infamy. It was on this day that nineteen men, armed only with box cutters and a willingness to die, changed the world. This day provided a reference point for Americans to organize their memories into "before" and "after." It was on this day that Americans experienced a trauma that unified the nation just as the Japanese attack on Pearl Harbor had done. It was on this day that the previous edition of *National Trauma and Collective Memory* became out of date and a new edition was needed.

The new chapter on the terrorist attack of September 11 focuses on the intense sadness, fear, and anger generated by media reports on the tragic events. Assumptions were shattered with the loss of a sense of safety and security, and Americans struggled to find plausible explanations of how and why the attacks occurred. The sense of unity and solidarity immediately after the attack gradually dissipated as the nation became more highly divided than at any time since the Vietnam War. Restrictions were placed on the civil liberties guaranteed by the U.S. Constitution in an attempt to promote a greater sense of homeland security. If the primary objective of the terrorists was to instill fear within the general population, they could not have been more successful.

The volcanic effects of 9/11 should not obliterate the fact that our nation has been exposed to recurrent episodes of homegrown terrorism in recent years. I was a little uncomfortable in leaving out a chapter on the Oklahoma

City bombing in the first edition. But at the time, it did not seem to be a national trauma of the same magnitude as the others in the book. Since then, however, it became significant as an advanced indicator of subsequent tragedies. I have now included a new chapter to remind readers that domestic terrorism is deeply embedded in the nation's history as well as in recent troubles. The school shootings at Columbine, the burning of black churches, and the bombing of abortion clinics are among the many episodes of domestic terrorism in the recent history of the nation.

Several features of the new edition are designed to significantly improve the book for classroom use. The previous text was modified out of a recognition that traumatic events take on new meanings as narratives are told and retold in the history of the nation. For this reason, I incorporated new references and added new perspectives on the major traumas of the past century throughout the book.

In this new edition, a specific symbolic event has been highlighted for each chapter. Through the many forms of mass media, traumas become epitomized by episodes of symbolic meaning that eventually become incorporated into the social and political life of the nation. The symbolic events are either major happenings as the trauma was unfolding or subsequent consequential events in the mass culture of remembrance. The sources of the symbolic events include radio broadcasts, newsworthy events, scholarly studies, popular movies, photographic images, and other types of modern technology for informing a nation about itself.

Discussion questions have been added at the end of each chapter to engage students in the subject matter for study. The discussion questions are designed to tap unresolved issues, to promote critical thinking, to examine ethical issues, and to permit students to evaluate their own understanding of consequential events. The discussion questions have flexible uses. They may be used to organize classroom discussion, to provide content for either take-home or in-class exams, or to promote discussion between students and their parents and grandparents.

An effective pedagogical assignment may very well consist of having students prepare a report to present in class or write a research paper based on interviews with parents or grandparents. Having lived through the Cuban missile crisis, the Vietnam War, the Great Depression, or World War II has emotional consequences that cannot be duplicated by the younger generation, who only hear or read about these events. Discussing these experiences becomes meaningful to parents and grandparents as well as to the younger generation that comes to recognize linkages between the lives of family members and the unfolding of historical events.

There are many people to whom I am indebted for many of the ideas incorporated into this book. My deepest appreciation goes to the reviewers of both the first and the second editions for their helpful comments. These include Helen Youngelson-Neal, Mike Marsden, Charles Smith, Ray Browne, Dena Eber, Ridwan Laher Nytagodien, Jan Hajda, Bernard Sternsher, Joe Perry, Lorna Gonsalves, Harold Vatter, Jack Fried, Ken Dvorak, and Kim Steele. Many useful suggestions came from several of my students in social psychology, American society, and mass communication classes. I am especially grateful to Niels Aaboe for calling my attention to the need for a second edition and for his critical insights. Finally, I would like to express my appreciation to the many strangers in airports, coffee shops, shopping malls, and doctors' waiting rooms who shared with me their personal experiences of our national traumas.

1 • Collective Sadness, Fear, and Anger

The concept of trauma is applied primarily to extraordinary experiences in the personal lives of individuals. Trauma involves an element of shock, such as the shock of being stung by a bee, touching a live electrical wire, undergoing emergency surgery, or being in a serious automobile accident. These examples represent the essence of the trauma experience in the sense that an adverse happening that is unexpected, painful, extraordinary, and shocking has interrupted an ongoing activity. A trauma has an explosive quality about it because of the radical change that occurs within a short period of time.

Many of the most severe personal traumas grow out of abrupt changes in the quality of social relationships. Perceptions of danger, chaos, and a crisis of meaning replace previous feelings of safety and security. Such traumas include, for example, confronting the sudden death of a child or a spouse, being raped by a friend or an acquaintance, or being diagnosed as having the AIDS virus. These are traumatic events in the sense that a fracture has occurred in the lives that men and women have built. The rape victim becomes traumatized through a diminished sense of social value and personal integrity. The person diagnosed as having the AIDS virus is traumatized by the isolating effects of the disease and by the reduced opportunity for living a normal life. The magnitude of such traumas frequently makes people feel that they have become "damaged" or permanently changed.

The psychiatric components of trauma involve the many maladaptive responses that follow an encounter with a deplorable event. These include such symptoms as intrusive recollections of the event, recurrent nightmares and other sleep disturbances, eating disorders, feelings of detachment and estrangement from other people, impaired memory, difficulty in concentrating on everyday tasks, a sense of emptiness, and psychological numbing. In effect, the psychological and physiological responses to traumatic events add up to feelings of helplessness and a crisis of meaning in the personal lives of individuals. Restructuring a self-identity and reestablishing one's place in the broader scheme of human affairs become necessary.

The concept of trauma may also be applied collectively to the experiences of an entire group of people. Here conditions of trauma grow out of an injury, a wound, or an assault on social life as it is known and understood. Something terrible, deplorable, or abnormal has happened, and social life has lost its predictability. Initial responses to a traumatic event are shock, disbelief, and incredulity. Chaos prevails, and people become uncertain about what they should or ought to believe. Individuals lose confidence in their ability to see the interrelatedness of events, and disturbing questions are raised about the linkage of personal lives with historical circumstances.

A national trauma differs from a personal trauma in that it is shared with others. A rape victim or a person diagnosed as having the AIDS virus experiences some degree of stigma and is thrown back on his or her own resources. The trauma of the victim is an individualized experience that occurs within a context of otherwise normal and happy people. The victim runs the risk of being rejected, developing a sense of estrangement from others, and losing the support of significant others. In contrast, a national trauma is shared collectively and frequently has a cohesive effect as individuals gather in small and intimate groups to reflect on the tragedy and its consequences. Personal feelings of sadness, fear, and anger are confirmed when others express similar emotions.

The enduring effects of a trauma in the memories of an individual resemble the enduring effects of a national trauma in collective consciousness. Dismissing or ignoring the traumatic experience is not a reasonable option. The conditions surrounding a trauma are played and replayed in the national consciousness in an attempt to extract some sense of coherence from a meaningless experience. When the event is dismissed from consciousness, it resurfaces in feelings of anxiety and despair. Just as the rape victim becomes permanently changed as a result of the trauma, the nation becomes permanently changed as a result of a trauma in the social realm.

Responses to national trauma involve elements of fear and a sense of vulnerability. The fear response reflects a sense of danger and feelings of personal insecurity. For example, the Japanese surprise attack on Pearl Harbor evoked intense levels of fear that the attack was simply a forerunner of a planned invasion of California. People living on the West Coast conjured up images of living in an occupied country. The Cuban missile crisis was accompanied by a fear of nuclear war. Mass destruction and death were seen as possible outcomes. The terrorist attacks on the World Trade Center and the Pentagon were seen as forerunners of additional calamities. Thus, national trauma evokes imagery of living in a dangerous world that is unresponsive to personal needs and interests.

Under conditions of national trauma, the boundaries between order and chaos, between the sacred and the profane, between good and evil, between life and death become fragile. People both individually and collectively see themselves as moving into uncharted territory. The central hopes and aspirations of personal lives are temporarily put on hold, replaced by the darkest of fears and anxieties. Symbolically, ordinary time has stopped: the sun does not shine, the birds do not sing, and the flowers do not bloom.

The collective sadness of a national trauma grows out of the death symbolism that is involved either directly or indirectly. For example, the unexpected deaths of President John F. Kennedy and Martin Luther King Jr. evoked intense sentiments of grief, mourning, and loss. The feelings of sadness were intensified by reflections on the loss of significant leaders and the manner in which the deaths had occurred. For employees at the World Trade Center on 9/11, the journey to work became associated with a journey to death and destruction. With continuous news coverage, the sadness of Americans intensified as they identified with victims and their families. The sadness of such events is collective in the sense that it is shared with other people. On these occasions, the individual does not stand alone.

When collective sadness is accompanied by anger, a volatile situation frequently develops. For example, following the Japanese attack on Pearl Harbor, collective anger was directed toward Japanese Americans living on the West Coast. The Japanese Americans were the most readily available target for venting a collective sense of rage and hostility toward the Empire of Japan. After the assassination of Martin Luther King, collective anger took the form of widespread destruction and looting in American cities. The actual sources of the stress were not clearly identifiable, while at the same time there seemed to be a need for some kind of action in response to a sense of outrage. Proximate symbols were substituted in order to vent the aggressive impulse. The facade of harmony and tranquillity in the social realm broke down as collective resentments became expressed in violent action.

It is primarily because of the blending of national identities with personal identities that individuals are drawn into the political arena during times of crisis. Through attachment to the United States as a society, Americans are set apart from all other peoples of the world. A distinction is sometimes made between "insiders and outsiders," between "friends and enemies," and between "those who are with us and those who are against us." An assault or challenge to national integrity taps into basic values and the moral foundations of society itself.

A national trauma involves sufficient damage to the social system that discourse throughout the nation is directed toward the disruption and the repair work that needs to be done. The disruption may take the form of a threat of foreign invasion, a collapse of the economic system, a technological catastrophe, or the emergence of rancorous conflicts over values, practices, and priorities. Whatever form the trauma takes, a significant and deplorable departure from the normality of everyday life is in process.

While traumas become transitional events in the life of a nation, some traumas have more lasting effects than do others. Permanent changes were introduced into the nation as a result of the Civil War, the Great Depression, and the trauma of World War II. The shock of these events touched the entire fabric of the nation. Other traumas have intense emotional effects at the time of the crisis, but tend to have less enduring effects on the social system. For example, the trauma of President Kennedy's assassination elicited one of the most intense emotional responses in the history of the nation, but very few changes in national priorities or public policies grew out of the event.

The degree to which a nation dwells upon a trauma depends on the degree of closure that is achieved. For example, a few days in October 1962 were the most terrifying moments in the history of the nation. We were on the brink of nuclear war. However, the Cuban missile crisis subsided with the removal of the Soviet missiles from Cuba. The case was closed, and most people were able to put the episode behind them. In contrast, the lack of closure to the conditions surrounding the assassination of President Kennedy resulted in continued preoccupation with what happened in Dallas on November 22, 1963. Although this date is alive in the memories of many Americans, it was not an event that was associated with any clear policy implications or any line of action other than the quest for setting the historical record straight.

The emotions that are tapped by a national trauma grow out of what it means to be human. Universally, the ingredients of trauma include some form of bafflement, some level of suffering, and perceptions of evil in human affairs. The bafflement grows out of an encounter with chaos and an attendant loss of a sense of coherence. Perceptions of evil reflect the frustrations of human effort and the awareness that others do not share one's sense of morality and decency. Because of the suffering associated with trauma, individuals are unable to remain emotionally detached or indifferent. Traumatic experiences suggest that to be human is to be vulnerable and that efforts directed toward mastery and control over the outcome of events are limited in their effectiveness.

A national trauma frequently has enduring personal consequences of a highly disturbing nature for those who experience the event directly. For example, psychiatric studies have revealed that those who directly experienced the Japanese attack on Pearl Harbor continued to suffer from flashback memories and recurrent nightmares. Although the attack itself lasted less than two hours, the experiences of fear, terror, and helplessness were of sufficient intensity to persist and to recur sporadically throughout the lifetime of the survivors.

On the fiftieth anniversary of the D-day invasion of Europe, interviews with survivors received a great deal of attention in the news media. Personal stories were told in a variety of ways about confronting the probability of one's own death, the sadness of seeing comrades killed, the feelings of survivor guilt, and the moral conflicts growing out of being required to kill others. The trauma of the event had a permanent impact on the thousands of men who participated in the heroic undertaking.

The traumas of the past become ingrained in collective memories and provide reference points to draw upon when the need arises. Hearing or reading about an event does not have the same implications as experiencing an event directly. However, as parts of the social heritage, events from the past become selectively embedded in collective memories. For example, following the opening of the U.S. Holocaust Memorial Museum in Washington, DC, an extraordinary number of people came. Museum officials found it necessary to request that people stay away or postpone their visit to a later date. The people came because the traumas of the past are important for reflections on the human condition. The horrors and atrocities inflicted upon human beings by other human beings in Nazi Germany became ingrained in historical memories as one of the major traumas of all times. In reflections on the Holocaust, it becomes clear that the range of worlds that humans are capable of creating is very vast indeed.

Social Disruption

An event becomes a collective trauma when it appears to threaten or seriously invalidate our usual assessments of social reality. Under such conditions, doubts emerge about the future as an extension of the present, and social events are perceived as discontinuous. Forces are operating that can be neither clearly understood nor controlled. It becomes difficult to integrate the problematic event with perceptions of the orderliness of social life. A deplorable condition has surfaced in the social realm that requires some form of remedial action. The integrity of the social fabric is under attack, and some form of repair work is needed to promote the continuity of social life.

The crises precipitating a national trauma are of two types. One consists of an acute crisis that impinges upon the normal course of events in an abrupt and dramatic fashion. The acute crisis is an unscheduled event in the sense that it falls outside the range of harmony and order within the social system. Acute crises include such events as the firing on Fort Sumter by Confederate forces at the beginning of the Civil War, the assassination of President Abraham Lincoln, the Japanese attack on Pearl Harbor, and the assassination of President Kennedy. Although these were abrupt disruptions of the social order, they were not isolated events. A great deal of collective stress and tension preceded each of them. However, each was generally perceived as "a bolt from the blue."

The second type of crisis is chronic, enduring, and long-lasting. A chronic crisis lacks the dramatic beginning of an acute crisis, but builds in intensity with the passing of time. This is the type of crisis that grows out of persisting contradictions within a social system. Conditions become deplorable, and problems emerge that require the attention of the nation. Rather than a volcano-like intrusion into an otherwise orderly system, a chronic crisis grows out of enduring conflicts within a social system and the emergence of a crisis of authority. The Great Depression and the Vietnam War are prime examples of a chronic crisis in the social realm.

While the stock market crash of 1929 is typically regarded as the beginning of the Great Depression, it was not in and of itself a national trauma. Certainly the collapse in the price of stocks was traumatic to many investors, but not to the entire nation. The stock market has a volatile quality to it, and the fluctuation of prices was widely recognized as a market characteristic. What was different about the early 1930s, however, was the scope and severity of the economic decline that ensued. As banks began to fail with increasing frequency and as levels of unemployment escalated, the nation confronted one of the most severe traumas in its history. Economic hardship took its toll on all major sectors of the economy. Capitalism was in a state of crisis, and the free enterprise system failed to work. Economic hardships translated into fear, vulnerability, and a sense of despair. The trauma of economic failure had an indelible imprint upon the consciousness of the entire society.

The trauma of the Vietnam War grew out of conflicts over American foreign policy. The nation became more highly divided than at any time since the Civil War. The government was committing troops and resources to a war that a significant number of Americans regarded as immoral and unjust. The combat veterans in Vietnam became unclear about the purposes of the war and what the United States was trying to accomplish. Before the war was over, several million American men and women served in Vietnam but failed to achieve any major victory. It became increasingly evident that it was a war we could not win. After the fall of Saigon, most Americans wanted to forget about the war and put the nightmare behind them. Many veterans returning from Vietnam were unable to make a smooth reentry into civilian life and continued to suffer from post-traumatic stress disorders. The enduring pain and suffering experienced by the veterans commanded the attention of the nation.

It is not the scope of human injuries, deaths, and suffering alone, however, that makes an event a national trauma. For example, the American fatalities in the Korean War were only slightly less than those suffered in Vietnam or in all of the Pacific during World War II. Much of the fighting for the hills in Korea was fierce, and many American lives were lost. The war in Korea was certainly traumatic for the men who fought in it, but we do not think of the Korean War as a national trauma in the same way we think of the Vietnam War as a national trauma. Public opinion was polarized over U.S. involvement in Vietnam in ways in which it was not regarding the commitment of troops to Korea. We did not win the Korean War in the usual sense of winning a war, yet it did result in a stalemate that succeeded in stopping the spread of communism. Our national objectives had been achieved. The military effort was never officially designated as a war, but only as "a police action" under the auspices of the United Nations. The military engagement was perceived as proper and just not only by the policy makers but also by the American public generally.

Several of the major collective traumas of the 1960s and 1970s grew out of the problems of political and criminal violence. Attention came to be focused on the causes, conditions, and consequences of violence in American life. The fear of personal victimization and the rhetoric of law and order were evident in public discourse and debate. Many Americans were shocked at the violence directed toward participants in the civil rights movement. Others were shocked at the scope of violence in urban riots and looting following the assassination of Martin Luther King Jr. One of the most intense emotional experiences in the history of the nation followed the assassination of President Kennedy. Concerns about violence in the public sphere were subsequently extended to include concerns about such intimate forms of violence as rape, child abuse, and spouse abuse.

The major traumas of the twentieth century led to recognition that the orderliness of society is a human creation. Serious and unexpected problems emerge regardless of how well a society is organized. For example, the spectacular technological achievements of the twentieth century were accompanied by extraordinary tragedies. The ingredients of trauma were embedded in such technological accidents as the sinking of the *Titanic* in 1912, the explosion of the *Hindenburg* in 1937, and more recently the explosion of the space shuttle *Challenger* in 1986. Each of these events dramatized the dangers inherent in the modern world. To adequately understand the place of trauma in the human experience, it is necessary to examine the conditions that give rise to catastrophes that no one actually intended or wanted.

A collective trauma grows out of the shared experience of a deplorable event that falls outside the range of ordinary human experiences. This form of trauma is evident in such natural disasters as earthquakes, volcanoes, hurricanes, floods, and tornadoes. Such natural disasters result in the loss of human life, demolished homes and property, and the destruction of community. Humans are reminded that their life plans are subjected to disruptions in unintended ways when the forces of the physical world become hostile and unfriendly. Yet natural disasters are less the subject for analysis in studies of national trauma than those disruptive events that grow out of the social worlds that humans have created.

An extraordinary event becomes a national trauma under circumstances in which the social system is disrupted to such a magnitude that it commands the attention of all major subgroups of the population. Even those who are usually apathetic and indifferent to national affairs are drawn into the public arena of discussion and debate. The social fabric is under attack, and people pay attention because the consequences appear to be so great that they cannot be ignored. Holding an attitude of benign neglect or cynical indifference is not a reasonable option.

Newsworthy Events

Calamities and tragedies in the social realm provide the core ingredients of a newsworthy event. Extraordinary disruptions gain attention and arouse widespread public responses. The news that is reported daily tends to emphasize dramatic events, unusual happenings, and moral disorders. The activities of ordinary people are seldom reported unless they are engaging in social protest or acting in opposition to some established institution. Rather, it is the disruption of everyday life that constitutes the newsworthy event. Something unexpected has occurred and adjustments to changing circumstances are required. Disruptions of the social order become prominent in conversations throughout the country.

Such shocking developments as the mass suicides at the People's Temple in Guyana, the school shootings at Columbine High School, and the bombing of the Alfred P. Murrah Federal Building in Oklahoma City command the attention of the nation for an extended period of time. Such episodes intrude into everyday life and serve to define the moral boundaries of society. These events are significant primarily because of the large number of people that respond to them and because of the opportunities they provide for examining selected aspects of social life.

Disruptive events become a national trauma only when the very institutional foundations of society are subjected to a challenge. For this reason, the criminal conduct of Richard Nixon as president of the United States was a national trauma in a way in which crimes embedded in Olympic competition or the mass suicides in Guyana were not. Deviance and criminal conduct, wherever it occurs, is disturbing to a social system. However, it becomes a national trauma only when it shakes the basic structure of society and the orderly progression of social life as it is generally known and understood.

A unique feature of news in modern society derives from the fact that the activities of a small number of people are observed selectively by millions of spectators. Messages that originate at some central location are disseminated over a large geographical area. People pay attention to news events because of their need for living in a meaningful cosmos. The millions of people who watch the evening news and read a daily newspaper are seeking information for linking personal lives with an ultimate set of values. In this process, news events provide stimulants for reflecting on social norms and deviancy, on public attitudes and behavior, and on social trends and unusual developments. Awareness of societal happenings serves to modify and clarify everyday assumptions and thus establish a firmer link between oneself and the broader scheme of human affairs.

The selective task of individuals in responding to the news is separating the genuine from the spurious, the illusion from the reality, and the authentic from the inauthentic. Routinely, the pronouncements of government officials are disproportionately reported as newsworthy events. Both the Red Scare of the 1920s and the fear of communism during the McCarthy era were intensified by the credibility the news media gave to the outrageous claims of public officials. Both public officials and the news media may misinform the public because of incomplete information about the topics of concern. Yet in some cases, misinformation may stem from the ideological and economic conditions under which the news media operate.

Audiences respond not only to the basic facts being transmitted by the news media, but also to the special meanings that people as individuals give to events. The construction of reality is a continuous process in our everyday lives, and in this respect we are all news makers. Through reading or listening to the news we extend our awareness beyond the range of experiences available in our immediate environment. Remote events become part of our general understanding of social relationships, life in our society, and what it means to be human.

Events in the broader society are of practical importance in establishing references for orienting our lives. One illustration of this process is the social game in which individuals recall the routine activities of their lives when they were interrupted by some major event of societal importance. This game takes the form of a question such as "Where were you when you heard about the Japanese attack on Pearl Harbor?" This question could easily be asked about the death of President Franklin Roosevelt, the assassination of President Kennedy, the resignation of President Nixon, or the terrorist attack of September 11.

Such games reveal more than interesting topics of conversation. We tend to draw on news events as benchmarks for linking the past with the present in our personal lives. Important occurrences are useful in marking social time in much the same way that birthdays, anniversaries, getting married, getting a job, becoming a parent, changing place of residence, and attending a funeral are used by individuals as reference points for assessing the quality of their lives. Such events are used creatively for constructing the meaningfulness of past experiences and anticipating the future.

When a trauma intrudes into our lives, ordinary time seems to stop, and our everyday pursuits are put on hold. Our equilibrium has been upset and our engagement in a continuous flow of events has become problematic. The tragic occurrence is replayed over and over in our minds as we seek to understand what has happened and why it happened. By becoming a marker in the lives of individuals, it provides a framework similar to the way in which primitive peoples measured time without clocks or watches. Events that occurred in the personal lives of individuals prior to a trauma become mentally separated from the events that occurred after the trauma. This is especially the case when the trauma is of the magnitude of the Japanese attack on Pearl Harbor, the bombing of the federal building in Oklahoma City, or the terrorist attack on the World Trade Center. Turning points occurred in the social life of the nation and in the personal lives of individuals.

If the official news sources are perceived to be inadequate or if the news converage is regarded as untrustworthy, individuals pool their intellectual resources in attempts to make the event coherent. Imagine, for example, the Japanese Americans living in the San Francisco Bay area on December 7, 1941, who suddenly found themselves suspected of being enemy agents, or the confusion of residents of Japan after the world's first encounter with the atomic bomb on August 6, 1945. These are examples of dramatic events that cannot be understood in terms of past experiences. Under these conditions, individuals react not as separate entities but in collaboration with others in the quest for understanding and action. Through deliberation on the event in question, a pattern of agreement tends to emerge for the construction of plausible explanations of events and their implications.

The communication patterns associated with trauma at the individual level differ from the communication patterns associated with trauma at the national level. At the individual level, many people are particularly reluctant to communicate negative information to the persons who may be affected by it. The uncertain outcome of transmitting undesirable information was evident long ago in ancient Sparta, where the messenger who brought bad news was sometimes put to death. The stigma associated with such forms of trauma as rape or being diagnosed with the AIDS virus leads to withholding information from friends, relatives, and coworkers. Because of this tendency to keep bad news of a personal nature to themselves, individuals are frequently cut off from the social supports that otherwise may be available.

Box 1
Symbolic Event: The Invasion from Mars

Vague perceptions of personal vulnerability and the dangers of the world in which we live were evident in 1938 when Orson Welles's broadcast of a fictitious invasion from Mars precipitated a mass panic. The radio broadcast was structured to have interludes of music interrupted by news reports from New Jersey on the landing of the Martians. As on-the-scene reports of "the invasion" came in, the level of hysteria mounted in the New York City area. Approximately 6 million people panicked in response to the broadcast.

Many people fled the area. One man drove all the way to Cleveland before he discovered that the broadcast was a hoax. It was a time in which it was difficult for the individual to know what to believe. Anything and everything seemed possible. Hundreds of people dropped to their knees to pray, thinking that the end of the world had come. Grown men wept and college students trembled. Perhaps no other episode in modern times has so completely terrorized so many people.

The announcement that the program was a dramatization of *The War of the Worlds* by H.G. Wells was either not heard or ignored by a large number of listeners.

Tensions stemming from the unemployment of the Great Depression and the seriousness of the war crisis in Europe had produced a susceptibility to suggestion. The panic was intensified by individuals responding to the fear exhibited by others.

In contrast, news of a national trauma tends to be communicated very rapidly, not only by the news media but also by the exchange of information at the personal level. Telephone lines frequently become overloaded with a large number of calls as individuals reach out for support and personal reinforcement. Serious disruptions of the social order are shared collectively and become associated with the need to talk about their meanings and implications. In this respect, national traumas tend to have cohesive effects within interpersonal networks in ways in which traumas of a highly personal nature do not.

Under conditions of serious social disruption, individuals frequently desire more information than the news-gathering agencies can make available. This especially occurs during times of crisis and may be noted in reactions to urban riots, natural disasters, or unsolved mass murders. Social life becomes disrupted and people make collective attempts to arrive at some adequate understanding of the events in question. Individuals verify and modify their assessment of events by engaging in conversations with others. Because of the pervasive ambiguity surrounding a national trauma, individuals reach out to others for social support and reinforcement. The major task, individually and collectively, is integrating the traumatic event into the fabric of social life in order to make it less threatening.

Causal Explanations

It is through causal explanations that the dynamics of the social world are constructed into coherent patterns. We make assumptions about cause and effect because we must if we are to live in a world that is understandable. Without the assumption of causality, events would appear to be random, haphazard, and chaotic. In this respect, we construct the world through our perceptions of it. Especially important in constructing a predictable world are notions about how human intentions, decisions, and actions are linked in shaping the course of events. Causal explanations promote an understanding, even if erroneous, of the social world and reinforce a sense of management both in the social realm and in personal lives.

Beneath the appearances and facades of everyday life, there are necessarily plans, strategies, and plots that are not available for public scrutiny. Sociologists describe this aspect of modern life in theatrical terms by observing that there is a "backstage" and a "front stage" to public performances. Under conditions of national trauma, the mystery and secrecy surrounding backstage areas result in perceptions of devious plots and conspiracies. Through conspiracy theory it is assumed that most of the news that is reported reflects only the tip of an iceberg. Only a small part of what is happening is made visible through the news of the day. When the news media are defined as untrustworthy, or when the news is regarded as incomplete, people fill in the information gaps by imposing their own structure on the situation. Meaning is attributed to senseless events, order is imposed upon chaos, and simplistic explanations are constructed from complex and contradictory information.

For example, in 1865 it was widely assumed that Lincoln's assassination was the result of a Confederate plot. The war was over, but resentment and hostility still ran high. The assassination of President Lincoln was seen as a form of revenge. Although the South had been defeated, it could still retaliate through an assault on a major national symbol. A crisis of meaning occurred with Lincoln's death, and individuals became unclear about what they ought to believe. Much more was assumed to be involved in Lincoln's death than had been brought out into the open. Many believed that the Civil War had not really ended. While no supportive evidence was ever found, conspiracy theories persisted for several decades after the war.

While individuals at the periphery of modern society are ready-made targets for suspicion and distrust during times of crisis, there is also a tendency among Americans to impute conspiratorial motives to those at the center of power and influence. American history has seen both a clamor for strong and effective leadership and a fear of too much concentration of power at the center. The ambivalence about power is reflected in both admiration for political leaders and the belief that politics is a dirty business. Many Americans see schemes and plots as basic to the way the system works.

The negative images of public officials go beyond their involvement in devious plots surrounded by secrecy. The more pervasive form of political negativism grows out of perceptions of inefficiency, waste, and mismanagement. Many citizens think that public officials are not evil but rather incompetent. Why were we so disastrously unprepared for the Japanese attack on Pearl Harbor? Why did the space shuttle *Challenger* explode shortly after launching? Ready-made responses to such questions draw upon perceptions of incompetence and dereliction of duty. Those in positions of power and authority are seen as having failed to do the things that should have been done under the circumstances.

The fear of religious conspiracies has been prominent in American history. The early witchcraft trials were based on the notion that human beings had entered into an alliance with the devil and that a conspiratorial, demonic order had been organized to shape the course of events. In colonial America, each of the thirteen colonies had enacted laws defining the practice of witchcraft as criminal conduct. The linkage of religion with evil frequently occurs in public perceptions of those groups whose beliefs and practices stand in opposition to the dominant values of a society. Such dramatic episodes as the mass suicides at the People's Temple at Guyana and the tragedy at Waco, Texas, generated a fear of new religions as satanic or demonic cults. National trauma is frequently associated with evil in human affairs, and perceptions of demonic conspiracies are regarded by some as plausible explanations.

The sadness and tragedy of traumatic events prevent most people from remaining indifferent. The quest for news is great and the amount of information that can be made available is limited. It is for these reasons that plausible explanations are offered individually and collectively. The psychological tensions of national trauma require individuals to reflect on the ways in which a fine-tuning of everyday assumptions can be accomplished. Such a concern is directed toward the implications of traumatic events for the personal lives of individuals and for the future of society.

Psychological Modernity

Through mass communications, the millions of people constituting large viewing and listening audiences become aware of much more than they could experience directly. Happenings in faraway places are brought into the homes and lives of millions of people. Instead of local areas being isolated, self-contained units of meaning, they are influenced by decisions and events occurring in society at large. Through developing an awareness of broader events, the individual seeks a firmer link with the totality of modern social life.

Most people believe that the conditions that prevail in their own time differ from those of any previous century. Such beliefs about psychological modernity include perceptions by individuals of the historical uniqueness of their time and place. The concept embraces notions about the dominant types of men and women who prevail, the defining characteristics of society, the primary agencies of social change, and the direction in which history is moving. Such conceptions, typically held by all adults, represent constructions of the social world from individual vantage points. The content of such ideas shapes the moods and motivations of the general population.

Within this context, responses to national traumas have meaning for individuals through the creation of links between personal thought and action and the historical dimensions of their time and place. Accordingly, the time dimension of psychological modernity is reflected in perceiving how we got to where we are now, where we are now, and where we are headed as we move into the future. Coping with changing conditions in society, responding to the changes that are occurring within us, and elaborating on the meaning of social events are among the many elements of modern awareness. In effect, modernity is the social setting in which we enact the drama of freedom and control as we seek to invent our futures.

Focusing attention on symbolic events reduces the complexity of living in the modern world. It is for this reason that national traumas become endowed with extraordinary meanings in the heritage of the nation. Such events as the Japanese attack on Pearl Harbor, the Cuban missile crisis, the bombing of the federal building in Oklahoma City, and the terrorist attack of September 11 provide contexts for reflecting on the dimensions and contours of contemporary society. The symbolic event does not speak for itself and cannot be taken as self-evident. While the event is initially structured by the news media as attention getting, the meaning of the event is subsequently refined and elaborated as it works its way into our collective consciousness.

The symbolism of traumatic events grows out of the ambiguous forces and remote dimensions of a social system. In any given case, reflection is required in order for an extraordinary event to be understood and made coherent. The consequences as well as the causes of the trauma must be evaluated. Is the event an advanced indicator of additional calamities that are to follow? Or is the event simply an ephemeral occurrence that will pass in significance as the general population returns to business as usual? Immediate responses are oriented toward juxtaposing the abnormal event against the normality of everyday life.

Several variations in styles of thought surface as individuals assign meaning to traumatic events. The least complicated style of thought is reflected in strong moralistic judgments of right or wrong, good or bad, true or false. Such simplicity overlooks the intricacies and complications of human tragedy while providing for an immediate resolution of an encounter with chaos. Such a response reflects only a superficial awareness of events and a tendency to place extraordinary events within such preexisting frameworks as religious fundamentalism or a political ideology.

The emergence of a crisis in the social realm provides a ready-made framework to justify a social cause among those who perceive the main drift of society as moral decay. Routinely, new lifestyles and new moralities challenge cherished beliefs and values. These sentiments frequently develop into what sociologists describe as a "symbolic crusade." Symbolic crusades select specific symbols to indicate the degenerate character of modern social life. Alcoholism, pornography, and abortion are frequently topics of concern that provide a basis for condemning the erosion of traditional, patriotic, religious, and moral values. Crisis events permit crusaders to wax eloquent about the need to uphold moral mandates, restore traditional values, and restrain the forces of evil. These moral crusaders tend to insist strongly that their own conceptions of right and wrong be accepted and applied by the rest of society.

Others recognize the complexities of a national trauma but tend to be overwhelmed by it. These individuals respond to the conflicts and competing explanations by taking on the role of a neutral observer. This perspective essentially holds that we must wait for more information or until the event can be placed into a historical perspective. Some disinterested segments of the population are unwilling to probe beneath the surface of public events. The emergence of a national trauma confirms their ready-made notions about living in a chaotic and unpredictable world. Such views are reflected in the failure to become informed about the consequential happenings in society. Unfortunate events just happen, and there is nothing we can do about it.

A more rational response to complex events consists of a high degree of receptiveness to available information and accepting the challenge of integrating information into a coherent position for oneself. Alternative explanations are weighed and evaluated. Different points of view are examined and synthesized. This is the rational decision-making model growing out of scientific, technological, and economic approaches. This approach also reflects the ideals of court proceedings and investigative committees. The ideals of official reports, however, can seldom be met under conditions of incomplete information, high levels of emotional involvement, and competing constraints and demands on time and energy.

The appointment of commissions to investigate the conditions surrounding national traumas (such as the assassination of President Kennedy, the lack of preparedness at Pearl Harbor, and the explosion of the space shuttle *Challenger*) serves multiple purposes. Making such appointments gives recognition to the importance and the complexity of the issues involved. By seeking authoritative explanations, the government devotes a great deal of time and effort to the fact-finding process. However, appointing an investigative committee also becomes a way of buying time to take pressure off public officials for some immediate line of action. Given the complexity surrounding a national trauma, an investigative committee is frequently unable to bring closure to the case. The causes, conditions, and consequences of most national traumas become topics for debate and argumentation for many years to come.

National traumas build upon and intensify the overriding anxiety, stress, and vulnerabilities that are implicit in the pluralism of modern social life. The United States as a pluralistic society is divided by race and ethnicity, by age categories and gender roles, by educational and income levels, and by religious and political affiliations. There are many specific frames of reference by which individuals are linked to modern society. America is not the same society for the superrich as for those caught up in conditions of poverty. The experiences of American life are not the same for men as for women, nor for racial minorities as for the white majority. The perceptions of America are not the same for the aged as for young adults, nor for the college-educated as for those with only a high school education or less. The multiple linkages to society suggest that the system is not experienced in a uniform way by all segments of the population. Instead, what we encounter as the defining characteristic of modern social life depends upon our own location within the system and on the perspectives we bring to bear on the events in which we are engaged.

A national trauma frequently has liberating effects on a social system. Older ways of doing things are called into question, and new opportunities for change and innovation surface. The very fact that a disruptive event has occurred opens up the possibility that the social system will be perceived as defective in some way or another. In the confrontation with the danger implied in a crisis event, new opportunities for innovation and change emerge. For example, the Great Depression provided new opportunities for governmental involvement in solving problems that previously had been neglected. The Japanese attack on Pearl Harbor provided opportunities for elaborating military institutions and developing new forms of technology. Such crises as those growing out of economic failure, the threat of a foreign attack, or the breakdown of law and order generate a need for new forms of public policy initiatives.

Social order is always a fragile creation. Regardless of how men and women construct their world, it cannot endure for long. Changes are always occurring within the outside world and in themselves. A great deal of repair work is required in the maintenance of social order because both societies and individuals always remain unfinished products: people pursue self-interests at the expense of the group's well-being, human efforts lead to frustration and failure, people sometimes make mistakes and do stupid things. In that fragile structure called civilization it sometimes seems that hardly a brick touches the ground. Under conditions of national trauma, aspects of the foundation seem to be crumbling or to rest on quicksand. If the trauma is of sufficient severity, all things appear possible. A basic human problem is that of imposing order on chaos and making sense out of the conditions of existence. The study of trauma in its collective form has a special relevance for an understanding of our time and place.

Discussion Questions

1. What are some of the major ways a personal trauma differs from a collective trauma? How are they similar?
2. What role do the news media play in orchestrating collective emotions following the occurrence of a national trauma?
3. How does a natural disaster (flood, hurricane, volcano, etc.) differ from a national trauma? How are they similar?
4. Why is there a tendency to draw upon conspiracy theory in explanations of a national trauma?
5. How is our perception of time affected by an encounter with trauma? Why does time seem to stop? How are national traumas used as markers of time in the personal lives of individuals?
6. How does a personal experience of a national trauma differ from only hearing about it many years later?
7. To what extent has your personal life been affected by a national trauma? What about your parents or grandparents? (Note: you may wish to interview them to find out.)

2 • Society as Moral Community

The social edifices that bind men and women together into a system of meaning frequently are thought of as imperishable. Social order, however, is always a fragile entity. Through the unfolding of traumatic events, social landscapes may be disrupted by upheavals of volcanic proportions. Cracks in the system may continue to widen until internal and external pressures can no longer be contained. Under these conditions, the social order is replaced by chaos, and a great deal of repair work is required. Social systems may then be seen as recurrently undergoing a process of collapse and rebuilding. Crises are replaced by new sacred meanings that seek to restore continuity in the social realm.

While the responses of individuals to national traumas are highly varied, collective responses tend to become standardized through the elaboration of myths and legends for defining the moral boundaries of society. Stories are told about extraordinary events, noteworthy accomplishments, and unusual tragedies. Such accounts provide ingredients for the creation of a sense of moral unity among any given group of people and permit linking personal lives with historical circumstances. Notions about "who we are" and "what we are to become" are shaped to a large degree from the shared identities that grow out of both extraordinary difficulties and extraordinary accomplishments in the social realm.

Perceptions of the greatness of a nation are confirmed by historical memories of how resources were pooled in times of trouble. For example, during the American Civil War, a deep fracture threatened the unity of the nation. Whether the United States would continue as one nation or be divided into two became an issue that could be resolved only through armed conflict. The thousands of books that have been written, and still are being written, about the Civil War serve as a reminder of the epic struggles growing out of the deep divisions within the nation. Although the coercive powers of the state had sealed the fracture, the healing process was long and tedious.

The collective suffering, sadness, and anger growing out of social disruptions provide the raw materials for the re-creation of society as "moral community." The notion of society as moral community is selectively embellished through the creation of a body of sacred symbols. The role of trauma in the creation of these symbols is evident. Arlington Cemetery, the Vietnam Veterans Memorial, the Washington Monument, the Lincoln Memorial, and the Tomb of the Unknown Soldier are among the sacred symbols that shape the national identity of Americans. Each in its own unique way reflects the personal sacrifices that have been made individually on behalf of the nation.

Under conditions of national trauma, the moral underpinnings of a society are subjected to close scrutiny. Volcano-like disruptions call into question the qualities and attributes of social life. Men and women strive for new ways to relate to each other, and everyday hopes and aspirations are temporarily put on hold. Restoring a sense of order and coherence becomes a necessary societal response to conditions of trauma. Insofar as traumatic events result in a fragmented community, a great deal of repair work may be necessary to discover new forms of social glue for binding people together into a shared form of membership and belonging.

Shaping a National Identity

The cumulative effects of national traumas are of central importance in forging the collective identity of any given group of people. Among Americans, there are three events that stand out above all others in shaping a national identity. The epic struggles of the American Revolution, the trauma of the Civil War, and the heroic undertakings in winning World War II required extensive personal sacrifices and permanently changed the content of what it means to be an American. Taking an active approach toward mastery and control over events through the pooling of collective resources became embedded in national consciousness. The creation of heroic and legendary figures to symbolize the aspirations of the nation provided sources of inspiration for future generations.

The trauma of the American Revolution helped to shape the identity of Americans as separate from the British. The Revolution is remembered as a time in which the colonists were oppressed by the British, who ignored pleas for the redress of grievances. Some of the more militant colonists came to the conclusion that nothing short of a revolution was a viable alternative. Of the many events of the Revolution, few are remembered as vividly as the suffering at Valley Forge and the signing of the Declaration of Independence. Through the Declaration of Independence, the moral basis of the Revolution was grounded in the notion that any given group of people have an inalienable right to alter or abolish a government that is perceived to be unjust. Government, it was argued, exists for the benefit of the governed. The revolutionary ideology held that the right to "life, liberty, and the pursuit of happiness" permitted overthrowing an alien and tyrannical government. The suffering at Valley Forge became emblematic of the long, difficult struggle from which our Founding Fathers emerged victoriously.

While the Declaration of Independence established the revolutionary identity of Americans, it was the development of the Constitution that permitted an opportunity for a fresh start in building a new nation. The Constitution built upon collective sentiments about what a government should be like after the revolution was over. Guaranteeing certain liberties to all citizens and giving all men the right to vote downplayed elitist values and social class privileges. The new nation emphasized the personal dignity of the individual, the integrity of the common man, and permitted popular democracy to play a major role in shaping the policies of the nation. The pride of Americans in their new nation provided the foundations for a new national identity built upon revolutionary and democratic principles.

The American Revolution led to the creation of two separate countries in North America, not just one. Canada was created as a country that was separate from the United States. Several thousand colonists who did not share the revolutionary fervor of the day resolved their discontent by moving to Nova Scotia or Ontario. Those who wished to retain their British heritage rejected the ideologies surrounding the American Revolution. Evolution, rather than revolution, became the preferred way to approach the problems of social change. In the absence of the type of heroic struggles that characterized the Revolution and the American Civil War, Canadian national identity is less sharply defined. It has been said that Canadian national identity is built primarily around the assertion "we are not Americans."

In creating a new system of government, Americans were bent on demonstrating that they were a distinctive group of people separable from the rest of the world. While the Constitution created a new social contract by which Americans were to be governed, the Declaration of Independence provided Americans with a clear conception of their genesis as a separate nation. July 4, 1776, is a date deeply etched in American consciousness as the beginning of a new nation that was clearly distinguishable from all other nations of the world. We became independent at the moment that we announced we were, at the moment we developed a clear justification for revolution, at the moment we committed ourselves to overthrowing the yoke of British rule. In the absence of any similar type of historical experience, Canadians do not agree or seem to care when they became a separate and independent nation.

For more than 200 years, the speeches delivered on the Fourth of July have served to rejuvenate the values associated with American society as a moral community. The annual commemorations of the Revolution permit a blending of secular and sacred values, linking personal sacrifices with promoting the collective good and expressing devotion to the Founders. While the speeches vary from year to year, all are directed toward promoting the notion that there is a source of unity in American consciousness that cuts across the multiple groups and vested interests within the nation. In view of the heterogeneity of the United States in terms of race, ethnicity, social class, and religion, many foreign observers have been puzzled by the depth of the American belief that there is a national consensus, of an almost sacred nature, that binds Americans together. In the absence of a similar genesis myth among Canadians, pluralism and cultural differences tend to be given priority over a national consensus. Canadians lack any form of commemoration comparable to the Fourth of July for solidifying a sense of collective identity.

The second major event in shaping the American national identity was the Civil War. The nation became deeply divided over the issues of slavery, state rights, and its revolutionary heritage. The firing on Fort Sumter represented the beginning of an insurrection that would eventually result in one of the bloodiest wars the world had ever known. The emotionality surrounding the issues of the Civil War became so intense that the war became a sacred crusade both for the North and the South. The crosses at Arlington, Gettysburg, Antietam, and many other cemeteries serve as a grim reminder of what can happen when mass armies meet on the field of battle. It was the Civil War in its many phases and consequences that constituted the dominant historical experience of Americans during the nineteenth century. It was through the coercive powers of the state that the unity of the nation was confirmed and elaborated.

Following the conclusion of the Civil War, the assassination of President Lincoln provided the nation with one of its major heroic figures. The sanctification of Lincoln placed his image on par with that of the first president. While Washington had played a major role in shaping the identity of Americans, Lincoln came to symbolize the leadership of a coherent, organic nation that could not be torn asunder by insurrection. Notions of America as "a confederacy of nations" or as a "league of nations" were firmly rejected. As a result of the protracted struggles of the Civil War, Lincoln's presidency came to symbolize heroic sacrifice, emancipation, and military victory in affirming the unity of the nation. In the creation of Presidents' Day as a national holiday, Lincoln stands alongside Washington as a major president to be remembered. The traumas and the triumphs of the Revolution and the Civil War remain at the forefront of the collective identity of Americans.

Memorial Day was created to stand alongside the Fourth of July as both a "holy day" and a holiday. Shortly after the end of the Civil War, Memorial Day was established to show respect for the Union solders who were killed in the war. As a result of the increased sophistication of the technology for waging war and the lack of modern medicine for treating the wounded, there had been enormous casualties. Over time, the ceremony of remembrance was extended to include the American military dead of all wars. The symbolism of Memorial Day simplified the complexities of the conditions promoting involvement in warfare and permitted Americans to reflect on the common values that unify them.

Although Canadians never had anything like the American Civil War, internal conflict and fragmentation have persisted historically as a defining characteristic of their society. The development of a unified identity has been precluded by the sharp divisions between the French Canadians and the English Canadians. The French, who were in Canada first, developed a large population that was geographically based. The position of the French Canadians in the power equation has been sufficiently strong that English Canadians were prevented from imposing their own language and other aspects of culture on the total population. Attempts to designate Canada as a "bilingual" or "multicultural" society continue to generate considerable controversy and dissension. As a result, the success of developing a national unity that all Canadians can identify with and draw upon has been limited. Canadians repeatedly remind themselves of the forces that divide them, such as region and language, while the sources of unity have a much lower profile.

The third major trauma for shaping the national identity of Americans grew out of the Japanese attack on Pearl Harbor. The integrity of the United States had been assaulted, and the effects were electrifying in the transformation of American society into a moral community. The collective sharing of a sense of sadness and a sense of anger produced nationally unprecedented feelings of cohesion, membership, belonging, and community. Now that we were at war, we were involved in a struggle to defend the integrity of our country. The nation was militarily unprepared and uncertain about the outcome. Previous opposition to American involvement in World War II vanished, and virtually all Americans reflected on the part they would play in the national objective of winning the war. Group differences that had divided the nation disappeared, or were suspended, as all segments of the population became engrossed in the historical undertaking. National symbols came to be endowed with special sacred meanings. Chills ran up the spines of many Americans as Kate Smith sang "God Bless America." The nation became unified with an unprecedented level of intensity. The war effort had indeed become a moral crusade.

The national identity of Americans was permanently altered by the trauma of the war experiences. While other countries suffered greater fatalities and greater damage to their infrastructure, Americans believed that it was their contribution to the war effort that resulted in the decisive defeat of Nazi

Germany and the Empire of Japan. The United States came out of the war militarily and economically strong. The other countries of the world did not. The United States had been thrust into a position of world leadership. The problems of the world had become our problems. The psychological separation of the United States from the rest of the world had vanished. We had provided the resources that were necessary for winning World War II, and we had the resources for rebuilding the postwar world. The world had become more interdependent, and we had found a new place for ourselves among the nations within it. Advances in technology had made all areas of the world accessible, and Americans had come to occupy center stage on the world scene. It was no longer a viable option, nor seen as desirable, for the United States to maintain a position of isolation from the rest of the world.

The effects of World War II have been profound in shaping the national identities of the defeated nations. Both Germany and Japan were required to struggle with the evil and banality of their conduct during the war. In Germany, a separation is frequently made between "the Nazis" and "the Germans" in discussions of the atrocities of the war. Many Germans claimed that they were mostly spectators or that their cooperation with the Nazis was based on necessity and coercion. What are seen as the best qualities of the German social heritage were frequently separated from the aberrations of the Nazi regime. Japan was also faced with the problem of dealing with a difficult and traumatic past. The scope of the atrocities committed by the Japanese army in the countries it occupied included not only inhumane medical experiments on thousands of captives, but also the brutal slaying of about 15 million Chinese civilians. At the end of the war, the people of each country drew a sigh of relief as they began the challenge of rebuilding a seriously damaged infrastructure and a seriously damaged national identity.

At the conclusion of the war in the Pacific, feelings of surprise, relief, and apprehension spread throughout Japan when the emperor went on radio to announce an unconditional surrender to the American forces. The Japanese had been prepared psychologically to give their lives if necessary for the defense of their country. The immediate sense of relief stemmed from the freedom of no longer being obligated to die for a national cause. The level of apprehension was subsequently diminished by the recognition that the Japanese people would not be brutalized by the army of occupation. Given the rights of self-determination in building a new social order, the Japanese were provided with an opportunity to reinvent their society. New social institutions were elaborated, and older institutions underwent extensive reforms that were generally recognized by the Japanese people as essential.

The economic and technological development of Japan is one of the major success stories of the twentieth century. The rebuilt society selectively retained positive values from before the war, while discarding those that had resulted during an intense trauma for Japan as a nation. Such traditional values as personal discipline, commitment, and group loyalty facilitated the development of one of the world's strongest economies. Traditional Japanese values were incorporated in a modified form in several institutional areas. For example, the Samurai emphasis upon discipline and loyalty is very much evident among employees in business corporations today. The disciplined approach to life was also reflected in the sense of duty among children and young adults to put forth their best efforts in preparing for the competitive examinations of their educational system.

The numbing effects of the American bombings of Hiroshima and Nagasaki more than offset any sense of national shame or humiliation resulting from Japan's decisive defeat. While Hiroshima became permanently ingrained in the collective memories of the entire world, it had a special salience for the national consciousness of the Japanese.

While the relationships between Japan and the United States have been positive over the past several decades, residual elements of the trauma of the war remain. The destinies of the two countries became linked not only through the conduct of the war but also in the process of building a new world order once the war was over. The critical battles of the war became too firmly etched into the living memories of older Americans to be completely swept aside. The Japanese, however, have a special sensitivity to the ways in which Americans publicize the historical events of the war. As a result, the recognition Americans now give to decisive battles at such places as Iwo Jima, Guadalcanal, and Okinawa has been tempered by a reluctance to intensify any latent sentiments of humiliation and shame in the Japanese over their conduct during the war. The younger generations in contemporary Japan feel that they bear no direct responsibility for the atrocities of the past.

Japanese officials, however, have issued many apologies over the years for the atrocities that were committed by the Japanese during World War II. The apologies have had a dramatic impact on the modern national identity of Japan. The serious mistakes that were made in the past have served as a major referent for what to avoid in the future. The dominance of their society by the military had calamitous effects for both the Japanese people and the peoples of the Pacific Rim nations. Renouncing war as a means for resolving international disputes, Japan built a new national identity around economic development. A stratified view of the nations of the world, which was deeply embedded in the social heritage of Japan, took the form of striving for excellence in technological development and becoming a major force in international trade and commerce. The repair work in developing a new national identity provided the Japanese people with a new source of pride in them-

---

Box 2
Symbolic Event: Remembering Hiroshima

Both the United States and Japan had difficulties with the question of how to properly remember Hiroshima on the fiftieth anniversary of the bombing. The event had such a lasting impact on each of the countries, indeed upon the rest of the world, that some form of historical recognition seemed necessary. The trauma of the nuclear holocaust for Japan had become ingrained in collective memories, superseding any feelings of humiliation and shame that may have otherwise resulted from losing the war. Americans had their revenge for the surprise attack on Pearl Harbor, while the Japanese were made keenly aware of the negative consequences of permitting the military to gain control of their society.

A storm of protest emerged in Japan in response to plans by the U.S. Post Office to issue a stamp portraying the mushroom cloud over Hiroshima. The stamp had disturbing implications and was regarded as an insult to modern Japan. It commemorated a glorious American victory without raising serious moral questions about the appropriateness of using such a weapon of destruction on a civilian population. When many Americans agreed with the Japanese, the Post Office canceled plans to issue the stamp.

Plans at the Smithsonian Institution in Washington, DC, for commemorating the fiftieth anniversary of the bombing of Hiroshima were designed to develop a reflective attitude on the atomic bomb and the use of nuclear weapons as instruments of war. The planned exhibit was to include emphasis on the Manhattan Project in developing the bomb, how the decision was made to drop the bomb, the plane and crew that delivered the bomb, photographs of the burn victims at Hiroshima and Nagasaki, and the implications of the bomb for the cold war. Members of Congress and veteran groups protested vehemently against the exhibit, and as a result the Smithsonian terminated its plans. People objected primarily to the emphasis on Japanese burn victims and the moral issues that were involved. Veterans maintained that the planned exhibit detracted from the heroic sacrifices that Americans had made in the war. Older Americans have vivid memories of the war and believe that the actions of Americans in vaporizing two Japanese cities were both appropriate and necessary.

---

selves and in their place among the nations of the world. Compensations for the mistakes of the past were achieved through building a new position of respect in the economic sphere among the nations of the world.

National identity has been much more problematic for Germany in the postwar years. The place of the atrocities of the Holocaust in national consciousness continues to be surrounded with controversy and uncertainty. What happened at such places as Auschwitz, Dachau, Buchenwald, and Treblinka still defies adequate explanation. How was it possible for a nation that produced some of the world's finest contributions to philosophy, music, and literature to also produce Adolf Hitler? Why did the German people comply with the mandates of the Nazi Party when it was not in their own best interest to do so? Most Germans would prefer to forget about their recent past, leaving explanations of what happened to professional historians. The lessons of the Holocaust are of such a magnitude, however, that selectively forgetting is not a reasonable option. The issue continues to surface and resurface in intellectual discourse both in Germany and in the rest of the world.

When the news was released that President Ronald Reagan planned to celebrate the fortieth anniversary of V-E Day by placing a wreath to honor the German military cemetery at Bitburg, an unanticipated storm of protest surfaced. Reagan had intended the ritual as an act of reconciliation. Instead, it tapped into continuing resentments over the traumatic events of the Third Reich and World War II. Recriminations were clearly evident in the United States and elsewhere. Veteran groups, Jewish organizations, and several other constituencies expressed indignation at Reagan's ceremonial act. The Holocaust had such a dramatic impact that the world is ready neither to forgive nor to forget. Instead, in the absence of other more pressing issues, the ending of the cold war has provided a time for serious reflections on the recent social heritages of many nations of the world.

The debates over the Holocaust frequently center around whether this event was unique among the atrocities in human history or whether it was simply a reflection of the type of event that had occurred at many other times and places. Those who relativize the Holocaust by seeing it simply as another case of atrocities in human affairs tend to downplay its lasting significance for German national identity. In contrast, those who perceive the banality as unique in human affairs maintain that Germany must confront in some major way the significance of the event for a national identity. In the absence of an adequate historical resolution, some degree of collective guilt is likely to remain. What continues to remain uncertain is what form of atonement would be appropriate for remembering such a difficult past.

The biblical notion "let he who is perfect throw the first stone" is implicit in the responses of many Americans who believe that as a nation we have failed to give adequate recognition to the atrocities of our own past. Our own history includes the systematic annihilation of American Indians by settlers bent on confiscating tribal lands, the brutality directed toward captives transported from Africa for the American institution of slavery, and the vigilante activity of the Ku Klux Klan. In recent years, controversy has surfaced over appropriate ways to remember Columbus's discovery of America and the American bombings of Hiroshima and Nagasaki. The sense of collective guilt has become muted in the new generation of Americans, who claim that "we were not alive at the time," "we had nothing to do with such practices," and besides, "we don't do that kind of thing anymore." Yet the issues continue to surface among subgroups of the population who see themselves as disadvantaged by the ways in which the past is selectively remembered. Confronting a painful past can never be easy, even for those who are young enough to bear no direct responsibility for what happened. The sense of a society as a moral community must necessarily take into account the full scope of its social heritage.

The ending of the cold war has required several countries of the world to rethink their national identities and what they are to become in the years ahead. The disillusionment in the Soviet Union with the communist experiment has led to widespread chaos and uncertainty both about its recent past and what the future holds. Americans think of themselves as having won the cold war, but are also faced with uncertainty about what their future holds. International affairs were more coherent when the United States had the Soviet Union as an archenemy. The struggle between the forces of good and evil had a unifying effect on the nation that is now missing. While images of another world war have grown dim, few Americans believe that the world has become a less dangerous place with the breakup of the Soviet Union. As a result, such questions as who we are collectively and what we are to become are now subjected to new forms of reflection. The new generation is necessarily faced with the task of refining and clarifying our recent social heritage.

Once traumatic events become embedded in the political culture of a nation, they may be drawn upon for elaboration and embellishment in a variety of ways. The freedom of expression in modern society permits people-in-general to have their say about the events transpiring in their society. In barroom conversations, in the pulpits of the nation, in newspaper editorials, and in television commentaries, traumatic events become an ongoing basis for discussion and reflection. In these deliberations, people attempt to integrate the tragic event into the hopes and fears of their personal lives and to refine their understanding of the changes occurring in their society.

Disturbing a National Identity

All collective traumas have some bearing on national identity. While in some cases national trauma results in enhancing a sense of unity within a society, in other cases collective traumas have fragmenting effects. Feelings of alienation depend in some measure on the predictions that are made about the outcome of events. For example, during the early years of the American Revolution, the outcome was by no means evident. Had the insurgency been suppressed by the British, the heroic figures that now loom larger than life would have been designated as criminals and punished accordingly. Had the American Civil War resulted in a stalemate or a victory for the Confederacy, we would now have two nations rather than one. The implications are clear that there are few inevitabilities in the outcomes of historical events. Through the epic struggles of the American Revolution and the American Civil War, we came to recognize more clearly what it means to be an American.

The social heritage provides us with an everyday blueprint and a sense of social continuity. A serious crisis of meaning surfaces when we can no longer make assumptions about the continuity of social life as it is known and understood. Such was the case with the trauma of the Cuban missile crisis. For a few days in October 1962 there was a disturbing possibility that human life on this planet would be extinguished within a matter of days. There had been no previous episode in the history of the world in which the stakes were so high and the fate of the world in so few hands. The moral fiber of society itself was called into question with the possible use of nuclear weapons for the destruction of civilization. The crisis intruded into everyday consciousness and temporarily brought into focus unthinkable prospects for the human condition. The continuity of social life from one generation to the next seemed doubtful. The desire for peace and tranquility came to be temporarily juxtaposed against the possibility of annihilation.

Of all disruptions of the social system, few events in the history of the nation matched the emotional intensity of collective responses to the assassination of President Kennedy. While we usually think of the political process as falling within the realm of the secular and profane, under conditions of trauma our usual way of thinking is changed. Extraordinary events border on the sacred rather than on the mundane. It is not the event itself that conveys a sense of the sacred, but our responses to events that bestow upon them a sense of awe. Sacred events are extraordinary, there is something mysterious about them, and they command our attention and respect.

The assassination of President Kennedy became a sacred event to Americans. Analogies were drawn between the death of Kennedy, the assassination of President Lincoln, and the crucifixion of Jesus Christ. Each constituted a human sacrifice in cementing the bonds of society as moral community. Through bloodshed, suffering, and death, the sacred character of social life became rejuvenated. For a few days following Kennedy's assassination, the nation was totally engrossed in the news media coverage of the event and in the collective mourning process. The sadness of specific individuals became linked with the sadness experienced by others.

Quiet reflections were directed toward the meaning of society, its sacred values, and what it was to become. At both conscious and latent levels, the assassination tapped into hopes and aspirations for the nation as well as into the underlying fears and anxieties. Kennedy, in effect, became sanctified, looming larger than life as a sacred symbol of tragedy and heroism in American life. Few events in the history of the nation had such unifying effects through a collective mourning process.

As one of the primary living symbols of the nation, the presidency and its occupant are important ingredients of society as moral community. The president speaks on behalf of the nation, represents the nation on ceremonial occasions, and occupies a primary position of trusteeship. While Americans have a legal right to say negative things about their president, he is the symbolic leader of the nation. It is perhaps because of the central place of the presidency in the sacred pantheon of the nation that a great deal of disbelief and denial accompanied the criminal charges that were brought against President Richard Nixon.

While the House of Representatives charged President Nixon with "high crimes and misdemeanors," many Americans had difficulty in dealing conceptually with what they were hearing. The importance of the presidency to the affairs of the nation was of such a magnitude that efforts were made to neutralize the effects of criminal conduct. Defects both in individual officeholders and in the social system were evaluated in attempts to restore a sense of moral community. The orations given at Nixon's funeral emphasized his contributions to the nation. Few references were made to the Watergate affair and the obstruction of justice. Selective inattention to the higher immoralities helped to sustain and reinforce the image of society as moral community.

Some level of deviance and criminality may be necessary within a social system for establishing the boundaries around acceptable conduct. However, if the perceptions of deviancy take the form of widespread beliefs about hidden conspiracies, the society itself is in trouble. This occurred with the widespread fear of hidden communists in our midst during the 1950s. Political demagogues built their careers around unsupported allegations against American citizens. The allegation that many Americans were withdrawing their allegiance from the United States and promoting the communist cause resulted in mass hysteria that resembled the witch hunt of an earlier time. The latent fears of the cold war allowed high levels of suspicion and distrust to be directed toward American citizens. Tranquility in the social realm was disrupted by the political preoccupation with determining who was or was not a communist or a communist sympathizer. Democratic principles were compromised as hundreds of Americans lost their jobs on the basis of nothing more than the claim that they were communists, communist sympathizers, or a security risk to the United States.

The emergence of social turmoil and collective violence conveys disturbing implications for the moral conscience of society. For example, the civil rights movement called into question the contradictions inherent in American racial policies and practices. The traditional forms of racial segregation and discrimination stood in sharp contrast to the political values of freedom and equality and to the constitutional guarantee of civil liberties for all citizens. Such contradictions now took the form of a contested struggle. Americans watched television with sadness and dismay as police violence was directed toward peaceful demonstrators. The millions of television viewers constituted a type of judiciary whose attention became focused on issues of racism and social justice. Few Americans were able to remain indifferent to the issues that were dramatized. The moral conscience of society had been turned upon itself through the confrontations growing out of the civil rights movement.

The complex interdependency of the many parts of a modern society greatly increases the probability of its disruption. Technological accidents and the failures of the economic system reflect the process of historical drift toward unwanted and uncontrolled outcomes. If our field of symbolic meanings is suddenly plowed up by tremendous changes in the social order, the firmness of our grasp of reality is weakened and our sense of connection grows fragile. The intrusion of traumatic events into the fabric of social life requires a great deal of remedial work in the maintenance of society as moral community.

As societies have grown in size and increased in complexity, they have become increasingly vulnerable to disruptions by those who are angry and hostile toward the established social order. Terrorists are well aware of this complex interdependency and are able to disrupt the orderliness of social life with only a limited amount of resources. Exploding bombs in public buildings, releasing poisonous gases in subways, serial murders, political assassinations, and placing explosives aboard aircraft are attention-getting strategies that provide recognition for the disenchanted, highly alienated members of a society. Thus, deviants and social misfits play an important role in the creation of traumatic events in the social realm.

The scope of the conditions promoting serious disruptions of everyday life are thus wide-ranging and unpredictable. The shock effects of the many ways in which a modern society can be disrupted point toward the complex role that custodians of the social order are required to play. It is for this reason that authority figures become the focus of attention in the collective desire for circumventing future occurrences of the types of trauma that have surfaced in the recent past.

Trusteeship

Under conditions of national trauma, the performance of authority figures is subjected to close scrutiny. This is because authority figures are entrusted with the task of maintaining society as a moral community. As custodians of the social order, those in top positions of power and authority are assumed to be competent and are expected to make decisions for the common good. Because they are granted the right to make decisions that bind others, authority figures incur obligations for the conduct of societal affairs and trustee responsibilities for the effective management of group resources. The sense of comfort provided by living in a society is grounded to a large degree in respect for authority and the belief that leadership decisions and actions are directed toward the best interests of the country.

The trauma of the Japanese attack on Pearl Harbor was intensified by the failure of our military commanders to take the measures that were necessary in view of the threat of war and the mounting political tensions between the United States and the Empire of Japan. Had the military commanders in Hawaii exercised sound judgment, they would have recognized the need to disperse our Pacific fleet, rather than concentrate it at Pearl Harbor. Some form of surveillance of the surrounding area should have been undertaken to give advance warning of any impending enemy attack. In military training exercises in Hawaii, war games had routinely focused on developing a response to a surprise Japanese attack on Pearl Harbor. The irony of these rehearsals is that such an attack was not regarded as a realistic possibility, and our military forces were caught completely off-guard when the attack did occur. The military commanders in Hawaii had failed to exercise properly the authority that had been delegated to their command.

The incompetence of authority figures may not grow out of their personal qualities and attributes so much as from evaluations of their performance. For example, during the Great Depression the public viewed President Herbert Hoover as cold, uncaring, and cynically indifferent to the problems of those who were suffering. While this imagery may not have been warranted, it did grow out of the worsening of economic conditions during his tenure in office. As president, he had failed to exercise the authority of his office to stem the economic deterioration. Hoover was evaluated not on his moral character or his good intentions but on his lack of effectiveness in producing desired results.

The crisis of authority becomes evident with the occurrence of a colossal blunder. As a case in point, we may note Kennedy's authorization of the Bay of Pigs invasion. The Central Intelligence Agency during President Dwight D. Eisenhower's administration had initiated plans for the invasion of Cuba by refugees from Fidel Castro's regime. Kennedy had been assured by his advisers that any attempted invasion would precipitate a mass uprising in Cuba that would result in the overthrow of Castro's regime. All his advisers endorsed the plan to go ahead with the invasion. Some individuals on Kennedy's staff had serious reservations about the plans, but remained silent. The subsequent assault on the beaches resulted in a disaster. Castro had advance information and was prepared for a slaughter of the invaders. The United States was not in a position to follow through with an air strike without running the risk of a war with the Soviet Union. The fiasco became a major source of embarrassment to Kennedy and to the United States. A crisis of authority had resulted from a faulty decision-making process.

Authority figures tend to surround themselves with subordinates and advisers who are like-minded individuals. The affairs of state are assumed to run more smoothly if subordinates endorse and support the lines of action recommended to them. Very often, however, the emphasis on group consensus becomes so great that the critical abilities of advisers and subordinates recede into the background. Through positive reinforcement of each other, an inner circle of political advisers may develop a sense of invulnerability and believe in the infallible correctness of the decisions that they are making. Apparently, it was such a faulty form of decision making that resulted in the quagmire of our involvement in Vietnam and the tragedy of the *Challenger* explosion.

The failure of those in top positions of authority to consult with experts who were opposed to the Vietnam War resulted in a serious crisis of authority in the social realm. Those who early opposed the war, maintaining that it was a war we could not win, were never admitted to the central circle of decision makers. Instead, they were negatively stereotyped as unpatriotic, disloyal, and soft on communism. The deep divisions within the society over the war reflected a lack of public support for what had been designated as a national priority.

Twenty years after the fall of Saigon, Robert McNamara, secretary of defense during the Vietnam War, published a memoir admitting that serious mistakes were made in the conduct of the war. His sense of remorse was a result of the fact that, although he recognized that it was wrong to continue the war, he did nothing to stop it. At the time, there was strong opposition both in Congress and among the military to any critical assessment of our policies in Vietnam. Only those who were team players were allowed to participate in the decision-making process. Thousands of American lives were lost in Vietnam long after McNamara and other senior leaders at the center of power realized that the war was a mistake. The use of deception and misrepresentation in continuing the war made a major contribution to the loss of confidence in political authority in our society. Those entrusted with managing the affairs of state had failed to reflect the integrity that was necessary for effective leadership.

A loss of confidence in political authority also grows out of the excessive use of force in attempts to maintain law and order. The violence directed toward peaceful demonstrators during the Democratic Convention in 1968 was seen as unnecessary by many Americans who were opposed to the Vietnam War. Rather than restoring order, the use of police violence during an urban riot frequently intensifies the disturbance. Attempts to suppress a demonstration protesting the bombing raids in Cambodia during the Vietnam War resulted in the slaying of students at Kent State University by the Ohio National Guard. Such excessive use of the coercive powers of the state becomes problematic in view of the rights of democratic participation and social protest in an open society.

When those in positions of authority become intolerant of public demonstrations or dissent, society tends to lose its coherence as a moral community. Officials frequently attempt to uphold and reinforce traditions and vested interests long after they have outlived their historical usefulness. For example, a great deal of the trauma surrounding the civil rights movement grew out of the police violence that was directed toward those engaged in peaceful demonstrations. Attempts were made to prop up a system of special privilege for white Americans at the expense of racial minorities.

In the social heritage of the nation, traumas are drawn upon in shaping collective identities, in setting national priorities, and in providing guidelines for what to do or not to do in any given case. We negotiate between the past and the future through our concern about historical repetitions. Serious disruptions of the tranquility of everyday life tend to be remembered and to become embedded in collective perceptions of society as moral community. Such perceptions provide a close link between self-identity and national identity. Some people hold a strong sense of integration and correspondence between self and society, while others develop a sense of estrangement from society and the culture it manifests. The comfort of living in modern society is shaped to a very large degree by perceptions of collective mastery over the challenges that emerge in unexpected ways.

We live in a time period in which heroes are out of favor. Our preoccupation with scandalous behavior may very well grow out of a crisis of authority and the creation of moral boundaries that are not attainable by public figures. Well-known and famous people are subjected to humiliating and debunking allegations by the press and a receptive readership that takes pleasure in reducing the gap between "us" and "them." Our constitutional guarantee of freedom of speech gives us the right to say scandalous things about public figures, all the way from the member of the local city council up to the president of the United States.

Discussion Questions

1. Why do collective traumas play such an important role in shaping the national identity of any given country?
2. Is the Fourth of July primarily a "holy day" for Americans, or is it primarily a holiday? Please justify your answer.
3. How did the outcome of the Civil War result in a selective repudiation of America's revolutionary past?
4. Why are there so many new books published on the American Civil War each year?
5. Why is national identity more of a problem for Canadians than it is for Americans? How did variations in the historical experiences of the two countries shape their separate identities?
6. In your view, was it immoral for Americans to drop the atomic bomb on the Japanese cities of Hiroshima and Nagasaki? Why or why not?
7. What are some of the major ways trustee responsibilities fail to be met in modern society?
8. How was the national identity of Americans altered or modified by the terrorist attack of September 11, 2001? Please clarify your answer.

II
Case Studies of National Trauma

3 • The Great Depression

The Great Depression of the 1930s was the most severe trauma the nation had experienced since the Civil War. The severity of the collapse of the economic system caught most Americans by surprise. The stock market crashed, banks failed, industrial production was severely curtailed, and unemployment rates escalated. Personal fortunes were lost and millions of Americans faced near starvation. The economic system had failed to work, and levels of helplessness and hopelessness reached unprecedented levels within the general population.

The economic trauma grew not out of a single episode, but out of a series of shock waves that had cumulative effects on the social system. The Great Depression had its beginning with the stock market crash of 1929 and ended with mobilization of the nation for waging World War II. During the interval between these two events, American capitalism was in a state of crisis. The economic euphoria of the 1920s came to be replaced with unprecedented economic hardship. While all major segments of society were affected, the severity of the economic decline was experienced unevenly among subgroups of the population.

The shock effects of the economic collapse devastated the millions of Americans who had experienced a rough time even before the Depression. Damaged lives were becoming increasingly evident. But even the more privileged members of the American middle class were frequently faced with cuts in pay and required to manage with diminished resources. Before the Great Depression ran its course, all major sectors of society confronted adversity and the system became permanently changed.

The business cycle was very much a part of the American experience. Many economic expansions and times of prosperity had been followed by economic contractions. President Herbert Hoover optimistically designated the economic downturn as a "depression." In his view, the term "panic," which had been used previously to describe deteriorating economic conditions, was unwarranted in the early 1930s. He persisted in the view that the economic downturn was a normal, natural process. The base building that occurs during a recession was seen as providing the foundation for even greater prosperity in the future. As the depth and severity of the Depression became clear, however, few could remember economic conditions that were worse, and there was little evidence for the view that the future would be better any time soon.

The initial jolt to the economic system came with the stock market crash on October 24, 1929. Prices dropped sharply, and thousands of individual investors found their personal finances in shambles. The initial trauma of the Great Depression fell disproportionately on the privileged members of society who had overextended themselves in the financial markets. The reversal of fortunes among investors symbolically represented the beginning of the hard times that were to follow.

The crash of the stock market in 1929 was not followed by a turnaround in prices, as some of the leading experts on the stock market had predicted. Instead, stock prices continued their precipitous decline. The losses that were initially defined as "paper losses" subsequently translated into "real losses" from the panicked selling that followed. The failure of the stock market to recover from its catastrophic collapse contributed to a sharp reversal in public attitudes. Greed and economic euphoria were transformed into fear. Brokerage houses were swamped with sell orders as investors attempted to cut their losses. Before the bear market of the early 1930s ran its course, the Dow Jones Industrial Average dropped to a low of 41, down from a high of 381 on September 3, 1929. The 90 percent decline in stock prices translated into severe economic losses for investors. About $30 billion in assets had vanished, a sum approximating the total cost of World War I to the United States.

The second wave of the economic collapse occurred in the banking industry. Banks failed at an alarming rate during the early 1930s. The banks got into a lot of trouble because they had failed to maintain adequate cash reserves, made risky investments, and loaned money to people who could not repay. The use of banks for depositing personal savings and weekly paychecks had been based on the assumption that funds would be available when there was a need for them. Individual depositors responded with shock and alarm as banks failed and checking and savings accounts vanished. The scope of the bank failures generated an atmosphere of panic. There was a run on banks as depositors scurried to get their money back. The available resources in the banks were quickly exhausted, and the banks became insolvent. Banks became the object of a great deal of anger as a result of the foreclosures on mortgages, the loss of depositors' savings, and the worsening of economic conditions.

By 1933, industrial production fell to about one-third of its 1929 total, and the U.S. gross national product was trimmed to half of what it had been four years earlier. A dark cloud descended over a nation that had control over vast natural resources, with an agricultural system unsurpassed in its capacity for food production and an industrial base for producing vast quantities of consumer goods and services. The business sector cannot sustain a high level of production for very long under conditions of falling prices, falling demand, and escalating corporate losses. American consumers no longer had prosperity-level resources for purchasing the products of industry. Production was curtailed, plants were closed, and thousands of employees received layoff notices.

Reasonable estimates place the overall unemployment rate for the nation at about one-fourth of the civilian labor force by 1933. Out of a civilian labor force of 51 million, about 13 million workers found themselves unemployed. Thirty-seven percent of nonfarm workers were unemployed. In several metropolitan areas, the unemployment rates were more than 50 percent. Employment opportunities were vanishing, and for millions of those who were employed, the rate of pay was severely cut. The income levels for about three-fourths of those who were employed fell below the minimum necessary for maintaining a decent standard of living. The families of several million workers had no income of any kind.

The American dream had turned into a nightmare. Life plans were shattered, families were disrupted, and several million Americans became homeless. The collapse of the economic system caused widespread suffering and unhappiness in the personal lives of individuals throughout the country. Men and women who had thought of themselves as self-sufficient found themselves standing in bread lines and making use of soup kitchens to alleviate their hunger. Many of those who took advantage of the limited relief available did so with a personal sense of embarrassment and shame.

One of the many dramatic episodes of the Great Depression was the veterans' march on Washington, DC, in the late spring of 1932. More than 20,000 veterans came to demand payment of the bonus that had been promised to them for military service in World War I. The cash bonus for the veterans had not been authorized for payment until 1945. The poverty-stricken veterans hoped to get about $500 each, which would provide temporary relief from their personal suffering and the suffering of their families. The veterans camped out with their wives and children in city parks, dumps, empty stores, and warehouses. A sense of desperation was written across the faces of those who participated in daily marches around the White House. While the veterans marched to call attention to their plight, they were met with a governmental response that seemed to be cold and indifferent. President Hoover was embarrassed by what he saw happening in the nation's capital and maintained that the demonstrators were "communists" or "criminals," rather than veterans.

Out of a sense of despair, the veterans persisted in their demands and refused to obey orders to move out of Washington. A military unit under the command of General Douglas MacArthur was dispatched to disperse the demonstrators. Veterans who had served their country in the trenches of World War I were now faced with tanks, gas grenades, machine guns, and rifles with fixed bayonets. More than a hundred demonstrators were injured in the forceful dispersal. The coercive powers of the state had been employed to suppress public expression of discontent. The veterans were bitter as they left Washington. All evidence pointed to the conclusion that the nation was ungrateful for the personal sacrifices they had made. The nation had failed to respond to their needs in a time of trouble.

Even the forces of nature seemed to be conspiring against human hopes for a secure world and a better life. Contributing to the depth of the Depression, a prolonged drought resulted in the most devastating agricultural disaster in American history. The drought, which was frequently accompanied by unprecedented heat waves, lasted throughout the 1930s. Overplowing and overgrazing of the Great Plains were man's contributions to what became known as "the dust bowl." The affected area extended from the Mississippi River to the Rocky Mountains and from North Dakota to Texas. The topsoil became airborne when the high winds came. Clouds of dust covered the landscape, entered houses around windows and doors, and made breathing difficult. The shifting sands altered the landscape and made a vast land area uninhabitable.

Farm populations dependent on the annual crop yield encountered food shortages and, in many cases, near starvation. Even under the best of circumstances, making a living by farming in desertlike conditions is difficult. Thousands of families were forced off the land when crops were destroyed by dust storms, loans could not be repaid, and banks foreclosed on farm mortgages. Farm laborers lost their jobs as a consequence of the government policy of removing land from production in order to prop up farm prices.

A mixture of hope and despair was associated with the mass migration of hundreds of thousands to other parts of the country. The pathos of the mass migration was captured in John Steinbeck's novel *The Grapes of Wrath*. The quest for new beginnings and a more favorable life stood in sharp contrast to the reality shock of transient camps and temporary work at very low wages. Feelings of bitterness and disillusionment grew out of the recognition that hard times had affected all areas of the country.

An increasing proportion of Americans saw themselves as living in an environment that was unresponsive to their personal needs and interests. Those in positions of political authority were seen as failing to provide adequate leadership and as being indifferent to the suffering that was occurring throughout the country. Under existing conditions, society could fulfill neither the economic nor the spiritual needs of the general population. Many intellectuals embraced communism as the only viable system for alleviating the deep troubles the country was facing. People came to believe that capitalism was in a state of crisis. Those pressing for remedial action encountered resistance from those who wished to maintain the status quo. The impact of the Great Depression on American society was of volcanic proportions.

The Crisis of Capitalism

A crisis of capitalism grew out of the failure of the economy to provide for either the needs of individuals or the needs of the social system. All the markets of the American economy were out of alignment and in serious trouble. The financial markets were in a state of turmoil, the labor markets failed to provide employment, and the commodity markets were faced with surpluses that could not be sold. The contradictions of capitalism were evident in the agricultural sector. Farmers were producing food that could not be sold, while millions of Americans suffered from hunger. Impersonal forces were operating that were understood neither by business leaders nor government officials.

In contrast to the public view that President Hoover was indifferent to economic hardships, he had taken an active role in appealing to business corporations to take voluntary measures for alleviating the crisis. For example, he called for a voluntary freeze on wage reductions. He argued that business corporations would benefit in the long run if they undertook voluntary measures to stem the tide of economic deterioration.

The Ford Motor Company responded to the president's appeal by announcing that wage levels would not be reduced, but instead would be increased to $7 a day for production workers. The role of the Ford Motor Company in stemming the tide of economic deterioration, however, was short-lived. The annual sales of automobiles dropped from more than 5 million in 1929 to slightly more than 1 million in 1932. Economic hardships had caused consumers to make drastic cuts in their discretionary spending. Ford followed the general trend in industry by seriously curtailing production and laying off thousands of workers to reduce payroll costs. In Detroit, Toledo, Cleveland, and other industrial cities of the Midwest, more than half of the labor force joined the ranks of the unemployed.

President Hoover attempted to reassure the nation that all was well. He asserted that in the long run the nation would benefit from the present difficulties. Adversity, in his view, would contribute to strong moral character. Individuals should show more initiative and try harder to solve their own problems. In his view, governmental initiatives in the area of welfare would only lead to chronic dependency. The government, particularly the federal government, should minimize its role in the lives of private citizens. His political agenda included an emphasis on protective tariffs (which intensified the economic crisis worldwide), an emphasis on tight money policy when there was a need for easier access to credit, and an emphasis on governmental economies when there was a need for economic stimulus. Many Americans saw Hoover's political measures as the source of the problem rather than the solution.

Hoover maintained that unemployment relief should be the primary responsibility of charitable organizations and local governments, not the federal government. He strongly held the conviction that voluntary cooperative action at the local level could not only relieve the distress but also reinforce national values by promoting an ethic of social responsibility. The ethic of social responsibility called for the more prosperous members of society to provide help for the less fortunate who were in need. Many local officials initially agreed with President Hoover. Serious efforts were directed toward implementing the tradition of private philanthropy to meet the needs of the suffering.

The cities of New Orleans, Minneapolis, and many others made a concerted effort to draw upon local resources for dealing with the emergency. All the efforts were destined to fail. The local resources that were mobilized turned out to be far too limited to deal with economic problems that were increasing in severity. The increasing number of unemployed men, homeless families, and hungry schoolchildren quickly exhausted all available local resources. Unemployment and homelessness were increasing at the same time that tax revenues were decreasing at both the local and the federal levels. Hoover's orthodox emphasis upon an annually balanced federal budget stood in contrast to the growing need for government assistance in the general population. Voluntary forms of relief could not keep pace with the accelerated economic deterioration. Families in serious trouble were required to do the best they could with the limited resources they had available.

The conclusion became inescapable that only the federal government had the resources necessary for dealing with the emergency. Voluntarism on the part of business corporations and charitable organizations had failed to deal adequately with the emergency. As a result, the crisis of capitalism became a crisis of authority in the political realm. Those holding positions of power and trusteeship had failed to act when action was necessary. It was not so much that the president and the Congress were indifferent to the problems that were developing; rather, the crisis stemmed from an intellectual failure to recognize that old ideologies and historical precedents were not adequate for dealing with the seriousness of the economic collapse. Viewing the emergency as only a temporary one that would eventually correct itself was not good enough. Such views subsequently came to be regarded as reflecting attitudes of benign neglect and cynical indifference.

In the final analysis, the crisis of capitalism produced a loss of confidence in the economic system. Business corporations responded by initiating retrenchment policies. Banks responded by foreclosing on mortgages when homeowners were unable to repay. With plant closings and layoffs, the unemployed were required to fend for themselves. There were no provisions for unemployment compensation or transitional measures for relocating workers. Those looking for work confronted a labor market in which no jobs were available. Individuals faced scarcities and shortages in their personal lives, while corporations and farmers were confronted with surplus production. In effect, neither corporate America nor the American government was able to deal effectively with the problems of economic failure.

The many oral histories of the Great Depression and the pathos in the letters written to Eleanor and Franklin Roosevelt revealed symptoms of trauma resembling those of combat veterans. Sleep disturbances, eating disorders, feelings of detachment and estrangement from others, and a sense of emptiness were evident. The letters to the Roosevelts, disproportionately from women, appealed for help out of feelings of desperation. The letter writers revealed a sense of having no other place to turn and a conviction that the president and his wife were sympathetic to their suffering and would be willing to provide personal help.

Economic Hardship

Throughout most of the human past, deprivation and hardship were the normal state of affairs for most people. Industrialization and urbanization changed that. In the decade following World War I, the purchasing power of the American family was increasing, the overall standard of living was improving, and people were living longer. The types of goods and services now available to the masses had previously been limited to only the very rich. While not shared uniformly, the overall prosperity in the United States during the 1920s produced a state of euphoria. The production and distribution of automobiles, telephones, radios, refrigerators, and other consumer durable goods pointed toward a future that would be even better. Materialistic values were given free rein by mass advertisers who encouraged people to want more, to spend more, and to consume more. The system no longer was concerned with simply meeting the survival needs of the population; it now placed an emphasis on generating desires for commodities that did not exist previously.

The American values of individualism and consumerism were counter-productive during the economic setback of the 1930s. A large number of Americans had come to want and expect a type of lifestyle they could no longer have. The success theme in American culture had always emphasized the correspondence between merit and reward, between what people deserve and what they actually get. While pockets of poverty persisted throughout the 1920s, there was a general belief in the United States as a land of opportunity: Any man or woman with a lot of initiative and hard work would be able to make it within the system. Subscribing to these values contributed to the anguish of the millions who blamed themselves for their troubles, rather than seeing hardship as a result of a system failure.

The economic hardships of the Great Depression fell disproportionately upon the family unit. The family has always been one of the primary organizational units within a society. When the family is functioning properly, it provides a major source of life satisfaction, a place to retreat from the world, and a place to pursue central life interests within a context of security and intimacy. The effective link of the family to the larger society, however, is dependent upon some minimal level of financial resources. Conditions of crises surface when parents lack the resources to serve adequately as providers and caretakers for their children and for each other.

At the time of the Great Depression, families were organized along more traditional lines than they are today. It was the husband's primary responsibility to be the breadwinner, while the wife stayed home to do the chores and raise the children. As a result, most households had a single wage earner. When the husband was laid off, no other source of income was available. If the unemployment continued for very long, the family's savings were soon exhausted, insurance policies were cashed in, and furniture and other possessions were sold or pawned to obtain the money needed for survival. Families frequently used credit for buying food or paying rent and sought loans from friends and relatives. Debts piled up, obtaining food became more difficult, and conflicts within the family intensified.

Many of the conflicts within the family grew out of the psychological effects of unemployment on the breadwinner. In a society that places a positive value on work, the self-esteem of men was heavily dependent upon success in performing the provider role. The meaning of work went beyond providing the paycheck for paying the family bills. Having a paid job served to validate social worth and to establish a social identity. The routines associated with keeping work schedules, completing assigned tasks, and meeting family financial needs were important sources of personal stability and order. Then as now, employment served as a psychological stabilizer in the lives of individuals.

A social vacuum often developed with the loss of occupational status. The loss of a job required developing a new self-identity, which was in part forced on the unemployed by the responses of others. Children frequently looked upon their fathers as failures, and wives frequently complained that their husbands were not trying hard enough to find work. Many of the unemployed tended to withdraw from others. They saw less of their friends, they went to church less frequently, and they interacted less with neighbors. Within the family, husbands became gloomy, detached, and unable to communicate effectively with other family members. A sense of apathy and despair grew as the unemployed came to see themselves as "damaged" or "defective" because of their inability to find work. They were thrown back on their own coping resources at a time when these resources had become fragile.

The unemployed men were disproportionately unskilled and semiskilled workers who had limited experiences with job hunting. The skills required in mining, steel mills, and automobile plants were not skills that could be transferred to other lines of work. The inability to find work was accompanied by the men's feeling that their skills and abilities had little value in the labor force. Standing in long lines with others seeking work frequently resulted in feelings of futility. Previously, a job had been thought of as primarily something offered by an employer. Such was not now the case. Working at odd jobs at a very low rate of pay was the very best that many workers could do. It was not a matter of not putting enough effort into looking for work. The jobs simply were not available.

The unemployed had time on their hands, but it was not time that was suitable for the pursuit of hobbies, sports, or other creative and meaningful uses of leisure. It was coerced leisure accompanied by the lack of a sense of connectedness. Having husbands around the house all day added to the daily stress of their wives. Couples' interactions frequently became hostile as arguments surfaced over money, childrearing, and relationships with relatives. While some couples were able to maintain the coherence of family life under conditions of economic adversity, most were not. Family relations were seriously affected by husbands who had developed attitudes of fatalism and helplessness, by children who had lost their respect for parental authority, and by wives who attempted to manage a household with diminishing resources.

Some husbands and fathers abandoned their families and joined the army of those drifting around the country in search of work. Without any means of financial support, wives gathered up their children and moved in with parents or other relatives. Being unable to support oneself or to care for one's children was associated with attitudes of despair. Households became overcrowded and levels of stress increased when limited resources had to be shared with needy relatives. Something was wrong with the system when some households be-

---

Box 3
Symbolic Event: Riding the Rails

About 250,000 of the homeless wanderers were adolescents and young adults who traveled the country in search of work, adventure, and subsistence. Under normal conditions, young adults would enter the labor force after the completion of schooling. Then as now, there was a low tolerance for young adults who are neither in school nor in the labor force. Both male and female adolescents whose families could not support unproductive members joined the homeless nomads. The availability of food was associated with gluttonous eating only to be followed by near starvation when food was not available. The transient population, having lost the safety and security of their previous lives, confronted serious threats of victimization. Hungry people fought over access to garbage pails that were placed in alleys in back of restaurants. For many, life had become harsh and brutal.

The primary mode of travel among the poverty-stricken was hopping freight trains and riding in empty boxcars. Hopping a freight train was a dangerous, risk-taking activity. Several hundred were killed or seriously injured in the process. Initially, the railroads attempted to stop the practice by arresting the transients for trespassing. When the number of transients reached several hundred thousand, the railroads became somewhat sympathetic to their plight and, out of a sense of futility, stopped the practice of arresting and prosecuting them.

Attitudes were ambivalent in the communities that became hosts to the transients. Many towns showed some degree of generosity in making food available while having an interest in getting the transients out of town as soon as possible. Many relief stations provided only two meals a day, which frequently consisted of no more than weak soup and a limited amount of bread. In some communities, the soup kitchens were made available for no more than three days for any given person and then he or she was expected to move on. The strangers in town were frequently perceived as undesirable and of questionable character.

---

came seriously overcrowded at the same time that there were empty apartments and houses because of the inability of potential tenants to pay the rent.

Without places to live and with no jobs available, several hundred thousand Americans were required to take to the road. Many of these were families who packed up their belongings in an old automobile and sought greater opportunities elsewhere. The poverty-stricken nomads were seeking escape from intolerable conditions in their present environment. Usually, migration is associated with optimism about greater opportunities elsewhere and hopes for a better life. There were little grounds for optimism, however, among rural families uprooted from their homes by dust storms or urban dwellers who confronted homelessness and near starvation. The nomads of the Great

Depression were forced to move, and the quest for a better life was limited primarily to the need for subsistence.

A new vocabulary surfaced for describing the homeless and the unattached who were drifting. The term "tramp" described individuals who were seen as unwilling to work and simply looking for a handout, while the term "hobo" was used for men who were willing to work when work was available. The hobos were frequently accepted as men who were down on their luck, and they sometimes were willing to share the limited work available. The tramps, by way of contrast, confirmed the stereotypes of the underprivileged. They were seen as lazy, shiftless con artists. Thus, in any given case, the widely used phrase "brother, can you spare a dime" was met with judgments about the validity of the need for help relative to the probability of being taken in by an operator. The beggars frequently referred to "having a bad run of luck" and "having children who were hungry." Only a few people defined the problem as a system failure, rather than in terms of the perceived qualities and attributes of the unfortunate.

The transients became aggregates of individuals who settled in empty lots, city dumps, or some other vacated land space within communities. These hobo jungles were composed of an assortment of people who had no ongoing relationships with each other and who would prefer to be someplace else. All major cities had such areas in which the homeless congregated. These areas, known as Hoovervilles, were characterized by makeshift shacks that had been constructed from whatever materials were available to provide protection from the wind, cold, and rain. The newspapers that were used as sources of warmth became known as Hoover blankets. Many of the homeless survived only through begging or scrounging through garbage cans or garbage dumps in search of food.

When the severity of the Great Depression reached its peak in the early 1930s, there was no other major subgroup of the population as severely affected as African Americans. In all areas of the country, the level of economic deprivation was consistently greater for blacks than for whites. Unemployment had reached 50 percent among blacks by 1932, and among those who were employed, there was a sharp drop in wages. Routinely, blacks faced a labor market in which whites had received preferential treatment in hiring and job security. African Americans were among the last hired and among the first to be dismissed when layoffs became necessary. At the outset of the Depression, the majority of blacks in the United States lived in rural areas. Several hundred thousand of them were sharecroppers, who in 1930 had an average annual income of only $295 per year. With the sharp drop in farm prices during the 1930s, the economic hardships increased dramatically for black families that were dependent on farm labor as the source of income.

Blacks in urban areas had routinely fared better than their rural counterparts in terms of income. With the onset of the Depression, however, there was a reversal in the sense of well-being. The unemployment rates for blacks in urban areas were 30 to 60 percent higher than for whites. As jobs became scarce, blacks and ethnic minorities were least likely to find employment, and when payrolls were reduced they were among the first to join the ranks of the unemployed. The health of many black families became seriously impaired as a result of the reduced expenditures for food. Disproportionately, black families were reduced to the subsistence level. The jarring effects of the Depression were severe for most of the population, but among those routinely underprivileged the effects were catastrophic.

The American middle class was also confronted with economic deprivation during the Great Depression. While its level of suffering did not match that of the lower socioeconomic classes, many did face wage cuts and sporadic work opportunities. Several adaptive responses emerged as coping mechanisms. People reordered their priorities, downplaying the importance of money and emphasizing the intrinsic rewards of social relationships. Particularly prominent along these lines were the themes of positive thinking and the importance of getting along with people. The best-selling book of the decade was Dale Carnegie's *How to Win Friends and Influence People*. Movies became increasingly popular; people turned to them for vicarious thrills. Identification with the celebrities of popular entertainment served as compensation for what was missing in people's personal lives. The many forms of diversion reflected ways of coping with problems that could not be confronted and solved directly.

Remedial Action

Serious problems of social inequality surfaced with the unfolding of the Great Depression, and discontent was expressed in organized protest. In Chicago, riots broke out in protest against landlords who had evicted tenants because of their inability to pay the rent. Labor turmoil and strikes became widespread in response to deplorable working conditions and cuts in pay. Hungry people seeking food looted stores in Oklahoma City and Minneapolis. Farmers in Iowa organized to protest falling farm prices by pouring out milk and withholding their products from the market. Pigs by the thousands were floated down the Missouri River to dramatize the plight of farmers in producing a product that could be sold only at a loss. Unemployed men and women marched on city hall in Los Angeles, Cleveland, Philadelphia, and other cities to call attention to their plight and suffering. In Madison, Wisconsin, unemployed workers took over the state capital and for several days enacted mock legislation to reform the system. Suffering at the grassroots level led to a clamor for remedial action at the political level. Never before had so many Americans suffered from hunger or lived under such wretched conditions.

The hard times were seen by some as confirming what the socialists had been saying for a long time about the contradictions of capitalism. The writings of Karl Marx and Friedrich Engels had predicted that a revolution would grow out of a cataclysmic depression and an intensification of misery for the masses. Although the American communists saw conditions as ripe for revolution, the unfolding of historical events suggested that revolution was not the only response to economic misery. There was no widespread call for revolution, although one-third of the population was, in Roosevelt's terms, "ill-fed, ill-clad, and ill-housed."

Most Americans wanted not a revolutionary overthrow of the system, but only access to those resources that were needed to relieve their suffering. The attention of most people was directed toward the troubles of everyday life. Wearing handed-down clothing, buying day-old bread, eating less meat, growing gardens, and canning were typical of the economies initiated in the management of daily affairs.

The American Communist Party made a concerted effort to recruit members of the working class and racial minorities into its movement. These efforts turned out to be a dismal failure. Blacks were unsympathetic to the communist cause, in large measure because they saw the movement as an attempt to exploit them for ends that were not their own. The classical theories of Marx and Lenin had failed to address the issue of race in their condemnations of the capitalist system. The members of the working class were less concerned with political ideologies than with getting a fair share of the rewards that modern industry had to offer. The aspirations of industrial workers were believed to be better served through labor negotiations than through a revolutionary overthrow of the system.

The turmoil of the 1930s was of a sufficient magnitude that all things seemed possible. The growing levels of discontent combined with the political activities of extremist groups to produce a potentially volatile situation. In the presidential election of 1932, Franklin Roosevelt responded to the voices of discontent. His campaign was constructed around the promise that the federal government would take an active role in addressing the problems of the Great Depression. A concerted effort would be made to restore confidence in the country through direct action at the center of power.

In his inaugural address, Roosevelt observed, "The only thing we have to fear is fear itself." He noted the vast resources of the country, maintained that a great deal of repair work was needed in the social realm, and called for collective and cooperative efforts in addressing the serious problems of the nation. Roosevelt's subsequent "fireside chats" made full use of the radio as a medium of communication and conveyed to the nation a personal sense of warmth, closeness, and caring. As is frequently the case in times of crisis, a charismatic leader had emerged to symbolize the hopes and aspirations of his constituents. Many Americans soon came to regard Roosevelt as standing alongside Washington and Lincoln in providing the greatest leadership the nation ever had.

During the first few months of Roosevelt's administration, extensive executive and legislative initiatives were undertaken. These included creating policies for regulating banks and insuring deposits in order to restore confidence. The rights of labor unions to organize and to engage in collective bargaining were recognized. Federally funded emergency projects were initiated to provide employment. The explosion of collective reforms replaced what had previously been defined as "defects of individuals" by a recognition of "systems defects." Roosevelt drew upon the notion of a crisis as both danger and opportunity. The crisis provided an opportunity to initiate changes that had long been needed. The political process, however, became increasingly rancorous as the initiatives for change collided with strong vested interests.

Among the initiatives undertaken through New Deal legislation, few matched the symbolic significance of the Social Security Act. Some saw the social security measures that called for unemployment compensation and old-age pensions as the beginnings of a welfare state and argued that too much power was being concentrated in the federal government. Support and opposition came to be crystallized along social class lines. Deficit spending to support New Deal legislation was seen by some as undermining the foundations of the American economy. In effect, "capitalists" did not want social security. However, in retrospect, several historians have noted that it was Roosevelt and the New Deal legislation that saved the capitalist system. According to some historical analyses, "It was social security or the barricades." Without major reforms, the integrity of the private property system was in jeopardy. Stemming the tide of economic collapse served to circumvent the discontent and turmoil that was developing at the grassroots level.

The remedial measures initiated under the New Deal legislation did not solve the basic problems of the Great Depression. At the time neither Roosevelt nor his advisers could see the full scope of the efforts that would be required for economic recovery. Some conservatives were outraged in 1938 when the president succeeded in getting $3.7 billion from Congress for public spending. We now recognize that even this amount was far too little to get the job done. The civilian unemployment rate was still 15 percent as late as 1940. It was not the New Deal that brought an end to the Great Depression, but the Japanese attack on Pearl Harbor. Gearing up for wartime production provided the type of stimulus that was needed for economic recovery. Full employment was not achieved until about 15 million Americans were in uniform and $50 billion was spent annually for the war effort. Unemployment vanished as men and women previously on the margin of the labor force found themselves at the center of the war effort. Economic hardship and despair came to be replaced by renewed optimism and a new set of opportunities.

The Legacy of the Great Depression

While no one yet understands the precise reasons for the severity of the economic collapse, we can now see some of the measures that the government can take to avoid the type of catastrophe that occurred in the 1930s. There are now procedures in place for drawing upon professional expertise in regulating the American economy. The creation of the Council of Economic Advisers was a direct outgrowth of the Great Depression. Macroeconomic theories became more fully developed, and we now have more dependable knowledge for reducing the severity of economic recessions. The Federal Reserve Board now plays a central role in fine-tuning the American economy. Interest rates may be reduced, or the money supply increased, to offset the severity of a recession swing. It is now recognized that an increase in government spending or a reduction in taxes can have a stimulating effect on the American economy. Thus, we now have a much clearer understanding of the macroforces that are operating and how to offset some of the serious problems that developed during the Great Depression.

The central role of the federal government, speaking in the name of society about the economic affairs of the nation, became well established. The scope and functions of the federal government came to be legitimated and elaborated. What previously had been defined primarily as personal troubles were increasingly seen as public issues. Taking steps to promote stability within the economic realm became one of the major responsibilities of government. No modern government can afford to ignore sharp increases in the rates of unemployment or sharp drops in the standard of living in the general population. Meshing the needs of individuals with the needs of the social system has become an overriding political challenge.

Such measures as unemployment compensation and social security are now perceived as necessary and as forms of entitlement. The taken-for-granted provisions of social security have greatly altered the ways in which individuals build their life-worlds. For example, young married couples of today seldom plan to have children in order to have someone to look after them in their old age. This was a major reason for having children prior to the Great Depression. Adult children do not regard it as a personal responsibility to provide for the economic needs of their aging parents. Private pension plans and social security benefits have made a substantial contribution to personal independence and to the quality of life among the aged. Access to desired resources provides a greater sense of personal dignity in the later years than was the case when aged parents were more heavily dependent upon their children.

Collective memories of the Great Depression became muted during the economic prosperity of the postwar years. Experience of the economic hardships of the 1930s became frozen in the past, and the nation came to be caught up in consumer-oriented lifestyles. From the many oral histories of the Great Depression, it becomes clear that collective memories take a selective form. In reflections on the 1930s, there is a certain amount of denial of economic hardship among those who made it through with limited psychological scars. Most individuals thought they had fared pretty well in comparison to others they knew who had suffered more. While painful memories tend to be downplayed over time, they are sufficiently embedded in collective consciousness that they may be drawn upon when the need arises. The Great Depression serves as a major reference point for making evaluations when there is a sharp drop in stock market prices, an increase in bank failures, an increase in unemployment rates, or a deep recession swing in the business cycle.

The trauma of the Great Depression conveyed the message that individual initiatives and motivations were not enough, in and of themselves, for a fulfillment of the American dream. The structure of opportunities is a property of a social system. Whether solving basic social problems or promoting acquisitive individualism is to become the national priority is currently subject to political debate. Attitudes of cynical indifference toward social problems are likely to result in unintended consequences. High rates of crime, an increase in personal pathologies, and the recurrence of civic disorders are likely outcomes of the failure of a social system to provide for the basic needs of its members. The legacy of the Great Depression serves as a reminder of what happened in the past and of the type of collapse and calamity that could happen again.

In summary, the impact of the Great Depression on American society was extensive. An entire generation continued to bear what Caroline Bird called "the invisible scar." The lives of individuals became closely linked with historical circumstances. By confronting hard times and moving beyond them, an entire generation of Americans came to hold a special appreciation for the material abundance of the postwar years. While few looked upon increased income as increased increments of human happiness, there was an overall appreciation for the advances that had been made in the economic realm. For the generation seriously scarred by the Great Depression, economic prosperity was not taken as self-evident. Knowing what both hard times and prosperity were like contributed to a keen awareness of the limitations and prospects of the human condition.

Discussion Questions

1. To what extent was the leadership style of President Hoover responsible for the Great Depression? How did the crisis of capitalism become a crisis of authority?
2. What were some of the reasons that the Great Depression had a more severe impact on African Americans than on the rest of the population?
3. What were some of the reasons that the unemployment of husbands had such negative effects on family relations?
4. What accounts for the popularity of movies during the Great Depression?
5. Why was the Great Depression more intense for urban dwellers than for those living in rural areas?
6. How close did the nation come to a revolutionary overthrow of the system during the Great Depression? Please justify your answer.
7. How would you account for the harsh treatment the veterans received during their march on Washington? Does the treatment they received suggest that the nation was ungrateful for their service during World War I? Why or why not?
8. Please describe, in your own words, the problems most likely to be confronted by the thousands of young adults who were riding the rails.
9. What was meant by Roosevelt's statement "The only thing we have to fear is fear itself"? Does this comment have any relevance for the terrorist attack on September 11? Why or why not?

4 • The Japanese Attack on Pearl Harbor

Americans encountered one of the most traumatic and consequential events in the history of the nation on December 7, 1941. The millions of Americans who were listening to their radios were shocked by the news that interrupted their regular programs. Suddenly and without warning, military forces from Japan had launched an aerial attack on the American naval base at Pearl Harbor. The integrity of the United States as a nation had been violated; the orderliness and security of everyday life had been disrupted. The damage was extensive and fatalities were high, including civilian as well as military personnel. It was clear that a serious national emergency existed.

The attack occurred early Sunday morning in Hawaii and the initial responses were shock, disbelief, and denial. Japanese aircraft carriers supported by heavy cruisers had moved secretly and inconspicuously across about 2,000 miles of ocean to assemble in a wedgelike formation for the assault on Hawaii. The attack was an outgrowth of planning that had been in process for several years. As dawn was breaking at Oahu, wave after wave of Japanese assault planes pounded the naval base at Pearl Harbor. The meticulous preparations for the attack could not have been more successful. The easy targets and the complete surprise of the Americans resulted in a military victory for the Japanese that exceeded their expectations.

The peace and tranquility that Americans enjoy on Sunday mornings had contributed to their vulnerability. The relaxed atmosphere that prevailed in Hawaii seemed far removed from any immediate threat of war. When the scope of the damage was assessed, it was clear that a large part of the American Pacific Fleet had been destroyed or incapacitated. Nineteen ships were sunk or seriously damaged, including six battleships. Additionally, 188 of the planes on the ground at Hickham Field were destroyed. More than 2,000 American sailors, soldiers, and civilians were killed, and more than a thousand were wounded. Aerial and naval assaults had been launched simultaneously against American bases in the Philippines, Guam, and Midway.

The news of the Japanese attack intruded into the daily lives of Americans and had a dramatic impact. Very few Americans who were alive at that time have difficulty in remembering the activities in which they were engaged when they heard about the attack on Pearl Harbor. The event became a marker in the personal lives of men and women. A reference point had been created for separating the past from the present and from the events that were to follow. The world had undergone drastic change and could never be the same again. Social worlds and personal lives had been exposed to a shock of volcano-like proportions. Subsequent memories of life events were to be organized around what happened before Pearl Harbor and what happened afterward. Personal biographies were linked with the unfolding of historical events.

The level of shock and disbelief among Americans was comparable to what it would have been had the invasion been from Mars. The trauma to the nation was intensified because the attack came from Japan. The attention of Americans had been riveted to the German blitzkrieg in Europe—within two years the German army had invaded and conquered not only Austria, Czechoslovakia, Hungary, and Poland, but also the Netherlands, Belgium, and France. All had fallen to the onslaught of the German army, and England appeared to be next. Americans had thus followed with interest and anxiety the developments in Europe, while giving less attention to the expansionist policies of Japan in China and Southeast Asia.

The emotional shock of the attack was followed by intense feelings of sadness. The immediate feelings of sadness grew out of the loss of lives at Pearl Harbor and the conditions under which the deaths had occurred. The news media played upon the tragedy by elaborating accounts of experiences in Hawaii, with particular emphasis on the acts of heroism on the part of both the men who had died and those who had lived. Attention was also given to the impact of the casualties upon their surviving family members, their hometowns, and their close friends.

The sense of shock and feelings of sadness within the American population were accompanied by intense levels of fear. The world had lost its predictability, and people felt uncertain about the possibility of additional calamities to follow. Some people expected the attack on Pearl Harbor to be followed by an invasion of the American West Coast. Many expected bombing raids on American cities and towns. The fear bordered on mass hysteria as thousands of people from Southern California to Alaska scanned the skies for approaching Japanese aircraft. Assumptions about the probability of an invasion or the eventual outcome of the war could not be made with any reasonable degree of certainty. The nation had been militarily and psychologically unprepared for the emergency that it now confronted.

The anger of Americans was intensified by the perception that the attack was unprovoked and had been launched without warning. There was no formal declaration of war. The Japanese ambassador had received instructions to announce to the State Department that Japan was breaking diplomatic relations with the United States. However, the Japanese ambassador was unable to get an appointment at the State Department on a Sunday morning. He did not succeed in delivering the message until about an hour after the attack had occurred. His message was received with a cool and hostile response. The entire nation was outraged. An assault on the integrity of the United States as a nation had occurred. Images of the Japanese as devious, cowardly, evil, and unpredictable were elaborated.

To everyone it was apparent that the United States could neither remain isolated from world affairs nor sustain the role of a neutral observer. Isolationism was dead, never to return. The wars in Europe and Asia had become worldwide in scope, and the United States was involved. Beyond this fact, it was difficult for individuals to know what they should believe. Anything and everything seemed possible. For many Americans, the idea of war conjured up images of chaos and carnage. The attack on Pearl Harbor was seen as a forerunner of the shocks and suffering that were soon to be encountered.

Millions of lives had already been lost in Europe and Asia, and millions more would be lost before the war was over. Many Americans would now be required to join the ranks of the military dead. The trauma was especially great for the families of those going off to war. Husbands were separated from their families, and the continuity of family life was broken for an extended period of time. Emotional intensity ran high in families who clearly recognized the dangers and the absurdities of war. Parents saw their sons and daughters depart for a war from which they might never return.

People listened to the news with a degree of desperation and helplessness that was evident throughout the country. The crisis was intensified by the speed with which the Japanese army invaded and occupied such widely dispersed geographical areas as Manila, Guam, Hong Kong, Shanghai, and Singapore. All of this was accomplished by the end of February 1942. The early tide of the war favored the Japanese, and levels of panic and hysteria mounted. Would the Japanese invade and conquer the continental United States? If so, millions of lives would be lost, and Americans would live in an occupied country.

The generalized anxieties about the war and its eventual outcome soon crystallized into sets of specific concerns. These included questions about our lack of preparedness, what to do about the Japanese Americans living on the West Coast, and how to mobilize the resources of the nation for bringing the war to a decisive, expedient, and dramatic end. In addressing these concerns, the United States as a nation would be permanently changed. In response to its lack of preparedness for World War II, the United States would assemble the most awesome military arsenal the world had ever known. In response to the mass hysteria over Japanese Americans living on the West Coast, the civil rights of American citizens would be violated. The development of the atomic bomb that ended the war meant that the conditions of war and peace were permanently changed. The events set in motion by the jolt of Pearl Harbor thrust the United States into a position of world leadership, and American lifestyles were permanently altered.

Lack of Preparedness

The trauma of the Japanese attack on Pearl Harbor was intensified by the fact that the United States had been caught unprepared. As a nation we had failed to develop an adequate awareness of the importance of the wars in Europe and Asia for our own national security. The lack of military preparation now contributed to a collective sense of vulnerability.

Before the attack on Pearl Harbor, the conflict between Japan and the United States over supremacy in the Pacific had escalated following the Japanese invasion of China and Japan's announcement of plans for increasing its influence in Asia. Peacefully inclined officials in Japan were replaced by those with a military bent as Japan prepared for war. The Japanese saw the military presence of the United States in the Pacific as a major obstacle to the attainment of their national objectives. The United States embargoed the shipment of scrap metal and oil to Japan to slow down its military momentum. Yet the threat of Japan to the security of the United States had been underestimated.

Many of the overriding anxieties of the day were still directed toward the problems of the Great Depression and the extremely high levels of unemployment and economic hardship that the nation recently had encountered. While there was a great deal of uneasiness about what was happening in Europe, this uneasiness was not linked to planning for the heroic undertaking that was to follow. Apparently humans have a great deal of difficulty in identifying the most appropriate things to worry about. Ambivalence about world events and the lack of public support for the buildup of the machinery of war resulted in inactivity when circumstances called for decisive action.

The lack of preparedness at Pearl Harbor was a single episode in the lack of preparedness for a war that many saw as inevitable but hoped would never occur. The trench warfare and heavy casualties of World War I were still vivid in the memories of many Americans. Thousands of veterans had returned to their communities only to continue suffering from the carnage and futility of trench warfare and from the devastating effects of exposure to chemical warfare. The mental anguish and physical pain engendered by the war had not ended for many American veterans with the formal end to the war itself. Many Americans had seen our involvement in World War I as a senseless undertaking, and many veterans believed that the nation was ungrateful for the sacrifices they had made. Some resolved that never again should the United States become involved in "someone else's war." In the presidential campaign of 1940, Franklin D. Roosevelt promised that if he were elected "American boys would not have to fight on foreign soil."

The unbelievable lack of preparedness at Pearl Harbor was partially an outgrowth of the deep-seated isolationism in American thought. Very early, President George Washington in his Farewell Address had advised the nation against becoming involved in foreign wars. Our geographic isolation from Europe had provided us with the opportunity to develop our own national identity with its own distinctive qualities. The general mood of the country was a desire for stability and a wish not to become involved in the rancorous conflicts of Europe and Asia.

The lack of military preparedness at the time of Pearl Harbor was thus an outcome of the mood of the country. Neither the American people nor their representatives in Congress had favored the financial costs that would be required for a military buildup. Given its geographical separation from Europe and Asia, the wars in those parts of the world did not constitute an immediate threat to the national security of the United States. The attack on Pearl Harbor changed all of that. Many Americans saw the lack of preparedness as the collective responsibility of the entire nation. There were still serious questions to be raised about why U.S. military commanders in Hawaii had been caught so completely off guard by the Japanese attack.

Military officials had known that a crippling attack on U.S. naval forces in the Pacific had been a standard part of Japanese strategic planning for more than a decade. "How would you carry out a surprise attack on Pearl Harbor" had been a standard examination question for the cadets graduating from Japan's naval academy. Signal Corps intelligence had established that top naval officers in Japan were engaged in planning for a major attack on Pearl Harbor and deliberating on the most feasible way of doing it. As diplomatic relations between the United States and Japan reached the breaking point, every major American commander should have known of the impending danger. Why were between one-third and one-half of all naval officers on shore leave? Why was there no surveillance of Hawaii's perimeter? Why was such a large part of the U.S. Pacific Fleet concentrated in a single location? Several investigative commissions and more than forty volumes of documents have failed to come up with rational answers to these questions.

On January 26, 1942, a commission investigating the disaster at Pearl Harbor found both Admiral Husband E. Kimmel, the commander of the U.S.

Pacific Fleet, and General Walter C. Short, the commander of the army unit in Hawaii, guilty of a dereliction of duty. Each was guilty of not having done what a prudent military commander should have done under the circumstances. While each commander had advance military information on an impending Japanese attack, neither believed the attack would occur at Pearl Harbor. After the war, several retrospective evaluations pointed to the conclusion that Kimmel and Short had been used as scapegoats. They may have failed to do what they should have done, but many issues of responsibility remained unresolved. Foremost among them was why officials in Washington who knew of an impending attack had not relayed this information to the commanders in Hawaii.

Officials in both the State Department and the War Department had been well aware of the possibility of a military assault following the deterioration of diplomatic relations with Japan. Intercepted messages sent to envoys from Tokyo indicated the intent to break off diplomatic relationships, and this was generally understood to mean war. Nevertheless, despite the advance knowledge of an impending attack, top military and diplomatic officials expressed shock and surprise along with the rest of the nation when the attack did occur. Wishful thinking had generated both an unwarranted optimism and a culpable state of unpreparedness.

A major conspiracy theory that surfaced after the war implicated both Franklin Roosevelt and Winston Churchill. According to the theory, both knew of Japan's plans, but wanted Japan to strike first in order to arouse public indignation and support for the war. If it was indeed true that Roosevelt knew of Japan's plans and waited for events to unfold as expected, the scheme could not have been any more successful. Americans were outraged by the attack, and opposition to American involvement in World War II vanished immediately. Allegedly, a relaxed but jubilant Churchill called Roosevelt shortly after the attack and then went to bed and slept soundly. America's future was now linked with that of Britain in the pursuit of the war effort. The question of responsibility for unpreparedness quickly receded into the background as anger and hostility toward Japan mounted.

Internment of Japanese Americans

Hostility toward people of Asian background living in the United States and in Hawaii provided the raw material for a great deal of speculation about how and why the Japanese attack on Pearl Harbor occurred and what was likely to happen next. Hundreds of rumors initially surfaced about the part local Japanese residents had played in the success of the attack. The attack was obviously well planned and based on accurate information about the position of American military units in Hawaii. How could the Japanese have known so much if local residents had not been involved in treachery and sabotage? Rumors also spread among the Japanese themselves that the American army planned to kill all residents of Japanese ancestry. While these rumors quickly subsided in Hawaii because of the lack of confirming evidence, additional rumors persisted on the mainland and contributed to the incarceration of a large number of American citizens.

About 110,000 Japanese Americans lived on the West Coast at that time, and most of them had been born in the United States. They thought of themselves primarily as Americans, but like other ethnic groups, they had retained their social heritage and aspects of lifestyles associated with their country of origin. Many had become successful in business and farming and had believed in the American dream. Although many were moving toward the American mainstream and shared the sense of indignation over the attack on Pearl Harbor, sinister characteristics were imputed to all of them. Their Japanese ancestry was taken as evidence of obvious and collective guilt.

For several weeks following the attack on Pearl Harbor, the outrage and hostility toward Japan became directed toward the Japanese Americans living on the West Coast. They were here, living as aliens in our midst, and symbolic of what had surfaced as manifestations of evil. General John L. DeWhitt, the commanding general of the Western Defense, was vehement in his view of the primary loyalty of Japanese Americans to Japan. He saw them as constituting a vast espionage network that would aid the enemy in any planned invasion of California. The newspapers on the West Coast also drew upon and sensationalized public sentiment against those of Japanese ancestry. Even the distinguished journalist Walter Lippmann defined the Japanese Americans as a menace and urged "mass evacuation and mass internment." The nation wanted revenge.

The deep-seated racial prejudice against Asian Americans that had existed before the war now became conspiratorial and perceived as justified. The combination of extreme racism with anger and fear produced a highly volatile situation. Out of a sense of outrage and anger, banks in California froze the funds of Japanese American depositors and refused to cash their checks. Japanese American doctors lost their patients, Japanese American business owners lost their customers, and Japanese American lawyers lost their right to practice law. Grocery stores refused to sell food to Japanese Americans, and business establishments refused to provide basic services. In effect, Americans of Japanese descent were abused and stigmatized with accusations of disloyalty.

By executive order of President Roosevelt, "military camps" were authorized for the removal of Japanese Americans from the West Coast. The executive order was consistent with the prevailing sentiment of political and military leaders throughout the country. Even the Supreme Court ruled that the rights guaranteed to American citizens by the U.S. Constitution could be suspended under conditions of war. Given the devious attack on Pearl Harbor, an invasion of the West Coast was perceived as a realistic possibility. The government ordered that all precautions should be taken to ensure that the spies and saboteurs who were living there would not facilitate an invasion. Doubts about the loyalty of Japanese Americans and the hysteria of the times resulted in the suspension of constitutional guarantees of due process and the most serious violation of civil rights in the history of the country.

General DeWhitt issued a military proclamation setting a curfew for Japanese Americans and restricting their travel to within a five-mile radius of their homes. Shortly afterward, all Japanese Americans living in California, Oregon, and Washington were ordered to report to assembly points for evacuation. The order included all Americans with any trace of Japanese ancestry, including Japanese women who had married American men and orphan children who had been adopted by American parents. The forced relocation of Japanese Americans was the first time the U.S. government had "imprisoned" such a large group of people in barbed-wire enclosures on the basis of nothing more than their ethnicity. There were no formal charges against them, there was no trial by jury, and there was no direct evidence of subversive activity.

The Japanese Americans were notified to report to assembly points on a given day for relocation. They had between twenty-four hours and two weeks to report to the assembly point. They were permitted to keep only the personal property they could carry with them. Homes and businesses were sold for whatever price anyone was willing to pay. In some cases, neighbors took advantage of the situation, acted like scavengers, and offered outrageously low prices for homes, cars, household furniture, and other private property. The Japanese Americans salvaged what they could, but suffered enormous economic and personal losses. A great deal of personal and family archival materials were trashed or burned. The loss of jobs and personal property resulted in a great deal of confusion for the people involved.

After being held in temporary camps, in some cases up to six months, the Japanese Americans were loaded into boxcars that would provide transportation to places unknown to them. Armed guards with fixed bayonets were herding American citizens. The relocation movement was, in effect, a form of incarceration. The internment camps were located in desolate areas far removed from the West Coast. The camps, hastily constructed by the Army Corps of Engineers, were like concentration camps. The temporary housing consisted of overcrowded barracks, and few of the amenities associated with normal living were available. Entire families were frequently housed in a single room. There was little protection from winter storms and the scorching summer heat. Dual barbed-wire fences surrounded the camps, and the guard towers were manned by soldiers with machine guns. American citizens found themselves in the absurd position of being held as prisoners of war within their own country.

As the tide of the war changed and it became apparent that the Allies would eventually win, there was an official recognition by the federal government that a mistake had been made. The Supreme Court, reversing itself, declared the evacuation and internment of Japanese Americans to be an illegal act. The Japanese Americans were now free to go. But where could they go? They had been deprived of their jobs, their homes, and their property. The negative sentiment directed toward them had not diminished. Those released from the internment camps had very little to return to. They now confronted the problem of rebuilding a life for themselves in a hostile world.

War Mobilization

The Japanese attack on Pearl Harbor produced an unprecedented level of cohesion in American society. News accounts of heroism and personal sacrifice at Pearl Harbor tapped a responsive chord. The intensity of the national trauma extinguished any hopes for a better world anytime soon. The nation was at war and the level of emotionality ran high. The sadness inspired by the casualties at Pearl Harbor was accompanied by high levels of anger and hostility toward Japan. The United States had been cravenly attacked and was now engaged in an epic struggle, not of its own choosing, between the forces of good and evil.

In the days and weeks following the attack on Pearl Harbor, patriotic music was given a prominent place in radio programming. The multiple themes of the music were directed toward building up hatred for the enemy and bolstering courage, bravery, national commitment, and self-sacrifice. Popular war heroes were celebrated and commemorated in ballads, linking them with heroic figures from the past. Maintaining morale on the home front was recognized as a necessary ingredient in sustaining and intensifying commitment to the war effort. Many people left their radios on throughout the day to listen to the music and to stay informed about major developing events.

The necessity of producing planes, tanks, ships, submarines, and other instruments of war provided an empirical test of the productive potential of the country's industrial enterprise. The conversion of the American economy to a war economy was assisted by the existence of excess capacity and high unemployment. All forms of industrial production were placed under the authority of the War Production Board. Assembly lines for making automobiles were diverted to the production of planes, tanks, and military vehicles. The last civilian car for the duration of the war came off the assembly line in early 1942. Production centers throughout the country were devoted to the production of military technology. By the end of the war, the United States had produced nearly 300,000 aircraft, over 70,000 ships, and nearly 90,000 tanks. The capacity of the American industrial enterprise turned out to be the decisive factor in the eventual outcome of the war. A giant had been created, and the American industrial enterprise was to dominate the world economy for years to come.

Manpower shortages were created in the civilian sector as millions of young, able-bodied men volunteered for or were conscripted into military service. Women found employment in jobs that were formerly limited to men. They vacated the household and became riveters, welders, and forklift operators, demonstrating that women have the capability of performing successfully in what previously had been defined as only masculine occupations. Discrimination in employment on the basis of gender temporarily receded into the background.

Job opportunities and new forms of abundance replaced the long-term employment problems and economic hardships of the Great Depression. Displaced farmworkers migrated to urban centers and found employment in factories at wage levels far above that to which they had been accustomed. Southern black sharecropping plummeted toward its ultimate doom. The labor shortage created new opportunities for many of those who had been seriously disadvantaged by the surplus labor and unemployment of the Depression. The labor shortages were especially beneficial to underprivileged groups, such as the physically handicapped, young adults, older workers, and blacks. Workers who had been on the margin of the labor force now found themselves located at the center of the war effort. The new opportunities that were made available at the individual level were accompanied by a clear recognition of danger at the national level and by an awareness that sacrifices would have to be made.

Movies, stage plays, comics, and other forms of popular entertainment also went to war. Hollywood geared up to turn out a large number of patriotic movies to inform, entertain, and inspire. The movies provided dramatic stories that permitted individuals to personalize historical events and to vicariously participate in them. The movies also focused on major happenings on the home front and frequently used humor to provide comic relief from the tragedies of war. The comics also played their part as such superheroes as Batman, Superman, Captain America, and the Green Hornet lent their support to the war effort in their encounters with and triumphs over the evil forces of Germany and Japan.

In collective memories, World War II came to be described by some as "the last good war." Such a designation was not accompanied by images of the enormous casualties that were sustained. The costs to the families, lovers, and friends of the thousands of Americans who were killed or seriously injured in the war were glossed over. The collective emotions of sadness and anger had produced a nationally unprecedented sense of cohesion. Group differences that had divided the nation disappeared or were suspended as nearly all segments of the population became engrossed in the war effort.

The war was looked upon as a good war in the sense of its unifying effects for the country. The reference was to an implied set of criteria for group effectiveness. In contrast to the stalemate in Korea and the unpopular war in Vietnam, the national commitment to winning World War II was clear, definite, and widely accepted. The danger of an external threat had generated a blending of personal goals and national objectives into an inseparable pattern. The war brought out what some saw as the best of human characteristics: a sense of purpose, a commitment to ideals that stood above personal avarice and greed, a sense of belonging, and a sense of national commitment.

Perceptions of the Japanese Warrior

During the war, movies, cartoons, and other forms of war propaganda were designed to incite hatred, anger, and hostility toward Japan. The brutality of the Japanese soldier was prominently emphasized in both news reports and fictionalized accounts. Americans were deeply moved by news accounts of the forced "death march" at Bataan and by other reports of the brutal treatment that prisoners of war received at the hands of the Japanese. Accounts from the Philippines suggested widespread looting and rape of civilians by the Japanese army of occupation. The rules of war and the code of honor that had been associated with wars in Europe seemed to be lacking in the Japanese army. The surprise attack at Pearl Harbor and the subsequent accounts of Japanese atrocities suggested that the Japanese were a brutal, fanatical, and formidable foe.

Early in the war, General Jonathan Wainright surrendered the American bastion at Corregidor when food, military equipment, and other supplies were running out. While resistance to the end may have been heroic, it was also looked upon as senseless. Why sacrifice American lives for a battle that could not be won? Continued resistance, at best, could only postpone for a little longer the inevitable fall of the Philippines to the military forces of Japan. From the American standpoint, very little would have been accomplished through continued resistance. Further, international agreements among the nations of the world called for the humane treatment of prisoners of war.

The Japanese military ideology held otherwise. The Japanese soldiers

---

Box 4
Symbolic Event: The Kamikaze Pilots

The kamikaze corps was composed of Japanese pilots who volunteered for suicide missions that called for diving their planes into American ships and losing their lives in the process. The principle of deliberate self-sacrifice was not new to the Japanese, nor to the ideals of warriors the world over. Extraordinary bravery and self-sacrifice have always provided the raw material for military decorations and awards. Early in the war, a few American pilots had voluntarily dived their planes into Japanese ships, thus sacrificing their lives. But what was new in the later years of the war was the systematic organization of a suicide corps among Japanese pilots.

In organizing the suicide missions, the Japanese military emphasized beliefs in a legendary sacred shield that protected the islands of Japan. In August 1281, a Chinese armada of 3,500 ships with about 100,000 men aboard was moving toward an invasion of Japan. Because of internal wars and conflicts, Japan was in no position to turn back the assault. The Japanese were expecting defeat, captivity, or death, but divine intervention saved them. The invasion was halted by the emergence of a sacred wind. A violent typhoon sank most of the Chinese ships, ended the attack, and preserved the integrity of the islands of Japan. The terrified invaders returned to China, never again to attempt such an invasion. The national mythology of Japan held that its islands continued to be protected by a sacred shield.

Based upon this historical precedent, the term "kamikaze" (sacred wind) was employed to provide inspiration for the Japanese pilots. Implementing the suicide missions resulted in the creation of human gods. Once Japanese pilots volunteered for a suicide mission, they were automatically placed in the realm of the sacred, both in their self-identities and in the responses by others. An aura of extraordinary and awesome proportions came to surround them. They were elevated above the mundane aspects of everyday life and set apart from ordinary human beings. They came to be admired by the Japanese as "thunder gods" who had no earthly desires.

---

looked upon prisoners of war as "cowards," "garbage people," and "defective human beings." Any soldier that allowed himself to be captured deserved harsh treatment. The surrender at Corregidor was seen by the Japanese as symbolic of the lack of will among Americans to resist an enemy of superior moral fiber. Japan's military code placed an obligation on the Japanese soldier to die in battle or to commit suicide rather than to be taken as a prisoner of war. Images of the fanatical commitment of Japanese soldiers were reinforced later in the war by the surprise and horror associated with the organization of a kamikaze corps for conducting suicide missions.

To the American military, the kamikaze pilots were not demons endowed with extraordinary qualities but rather a practical problem that had to be dealt with. American planes were more efficient and had greater maneuverability than the Japanese Zero. Intense antiaircraft barrages from American ships limited the effectiveness of the suicide missions. Further, the pilots employed by Japan were not adequately trained because of the shortage of fuel for planes. Had the suicide missions been organized sooner, the defeat of Japan would probably have been more difficult; however, they represented, at best, acts of desperation.

While the damage from the kamikaze attacks was extensive, the more important message that Americans received pertained to what was likely to happen during the eventual U.S. invasion of the islands of Japan. Some estimates held that nearly a million American lives would be lost in the final assault. Memories were vivid of the heavy casualties sustained by American forces in the conquest of Pacific islands held by the Japanese. Any military assault on the Japanese homeland was expected to be met with tenacious and violent resistance from the entire population, including old men, women, and children. Many Americans believed that the soldiers who had survived the war in Europe would be transferred to the Pacific for the final assault on Japan. The number of gold stars in the windows of American homes would greatly increase.

Well before the defeat of Nazi Germany, the eventual outcome of the war with Japan was no longer in doubt. The United States would win. But it was unclear how long it would take and how many American lives would be lost. Propaganda in Japan was preparing the population to resist for as long as a hundred years if necessary. Japan had recognized the technological and materialistic superiority of the United States, but saw the moral fiber and the spirit of the Japanese people as the decisive factor in the long run.

To Americans, the goal was getting the war over with as soon and as expediently as possible. It was expected that the Japanese would continue to fight even when it was obvious they could not win. Such had been the case in the war against Nazi Germany. The defeat of the German army in the Battle of the Bulge made it evident that Germany would lose the war. Yet German resistance continued even after the Allied forces crossed the Rhine River and pursued their advance toward Berlin. The Germans continued fighting until the Americans and the British met the Russians at the Elbe River. Given the tenacity of Japan in pursuing the war, there was little reason to believe that their resistance to a foreign invasion of their homeland would be any less than that of the Germans.

Ending the War

Plans were already under way for an invasion of Kyushu, the southernmost of the main islands of Japan, when the Americans succeeded in exploding the world's first atomic bomb at a site near Alamagordo, New Mexico. The United States had been working on the Manhattan Project, the development of an atomic bomb, throughout the war. President Roosevelt had been influenced by a letter from Albert Einstein in 1939 suggesting the feasibility of such a weapon based on theoretical scientific knowledge in the field of nuclear physics that had been developed over the first several decades of the twentieth century. It was simply a matter of time before that knowledge would be put to use. Further, there was the possibility that German scientists were working on a similar project. If a nuclear device could be used as a military weapon, Roosevelt felt that it was better for the United States to do it before its adversaries. Following Roosevelt's request, Congress appropriated funds for developing the atomic bomb without actually knowing what it was supporting.

The untimely death of President Roosevelt in April 1945 was traumatic to the nation. Roosevelt's charismatic style had provided the nation with a sense of security and confidence in his leadership. Americans doubted whether Harry Truman as the new president had the political experience and sophistication necessary for dealing effectively with the job at hand. The war was winding down in Europe, but the problem of defeating Japan remained a major challenge. Few presidents had entered the office with so many complex issues to resolve within such a short period of time. For example, the secrecy surrounding the development of the bomb had been of such a magnitude that even the vice president of the United States had not been informed about the progress of the Manhattan Project. Truman found himself required to make one of the most controversial decisions any president of the United States has ever had to make.

What should we do with the atomic bomb now that we had it? Truman's resolution on this issue mirrored the sentiment of the nation in his commitment to end the war as soon as decisively and expediently as possible. Following up on the suggestion that Japan might be willing to end the war, the United States, Great Britain, and the Republic of China issued an ultimatum demanding surrender. The ultimatum also warned that continuation of the war would mean prompt and utter destruction for Japan. At the time, however, there were three important items of information that could not be revealed to Japan for strategic reasons.

These included the fact that the United States had developed an atomic bomb, that Russia had agreed to enter the war against Japan ninety days after the surrender of Germany, and that the United States had already decided to permit the Japanese to keep their emperor. The United States did not want to announce that we had developed an atomic bomb before its effectiveness as a military weapon had been established. The failure to make reference to the emperor in the ultimatum stemmed from not wanting to soften the demand for unconditional surrender. Hesitation in the decision to surrender may have grown out of its incompatibility with values deeply embedded in Japanese culture.

The abruptness with which World War II ended is similar to the abruptness with which it started. Both the beginning and the end dramatized the capacity of modern societies for institutionalized violence. Daily activities around the world were disrupted by the news bulletin on August 6, 1945, that the city of Hiroshima had been destroyed by an atomic bomb, a new weapon of historically unprecedented proportions. The fatalities at Hiroshima far exceeded the number that had been expected. Three days later, a second bomb was dropped on the city of Nagasaki. Approximately 200,000 lives were lost in these aerial assaults using nuclear weapons. The bombing of Hiroshima and Nagasaki provided Americans with an opportunity both to avenge the attack on Pearl Harbor and to end the war.

Qualitative changes in the human condition occurred with the development of the atomic bomb and the demonstration of its destructive potential through its use on human populations. Observing the slow death from radiation sickness among thousands of civilians at Hiroshima and Nagasaki produced some degree of global uneasiness about the possibility that the United States had solved one problem but created additional problems of an even greater magnitude. The survivors at Hiroshima and Nagasaki were faced with serious psychological trauma from seeing their social world instantly vaporized by a weapon about which they had no knowledge. In the months and years afterward, survivors watched with anguish as their friends and family members perished from radiation sickness. For some there was also the horror of giving birth to deformed monstrosities or the shame of being marked by stigmatizing scars from the nuclear explosions.

The end of the war was met with jubilant responses in the United States. The victory celebrations were extensive and enthusiastic. Many single women looked favorably upon the prospect of forming intimate relationships with males of their own age level. They had grown tired of having their social interactions limited primarily to other women, the elderly, and children. The veterans were welcomed home as heroes, and ticker-tape parades were held in their honor. The grateful nation gave a great deal of attention to the successful reentry of veterans into civilian life.

After most wars, veterans were forgotten once they were no longer needed. But the end of World War II was different from the end of other wars. The veterans provided a great deal of social support for each other and received a great deal of support from others within their communities. The benefits accorded to the veterans were extensive. Employers were required to give back to the returning veterans the jobs they had before going off to war. Women who had worked during the war were expected to give up their jobs, go home, get married, and have babies. Educational benefits were made available to veterans through the G.I. Bill of Rights. The government paid the tuition costs of attending a college or a university, paid for books and supplies, and provided the veterans with a generous living allowance. The impact was sufficiently great that it led to a rapid expansion of colleges and universities throughout the country. Under the Veterans Administration, housing was made available to the veterans through guaranteed government loans at a relatively low rate of interest. Thus, in contrast to most wars, the nation was willing to show its gratitude to the returning veterans.

The social psychology of the homecoming had some interesting features for the veterans returning from the South Pacific. For example, the marine unit that was involved at the battle of Iwo Jima had been stationed in the Pacific for more than three years. During this time, the unit saw only about six weeks of combat. The battle for Iwo Jima was intense and the casualties were high, but the Allies were victorious. It was to become one of the most highly commemorated victories of the war. In contrast to the veterans in the assault across Germany, however, many of the veterans in the Pacific had a great deal of time on their hands, during which they fantasized about what life was like in their hometowns and how glorious life would be when they returned. The longer they were away, the greener the grass grew in their hometowns. They glorified family life, imagining getting married if they were single, owning their own home on their own lot, and having a lot of children.

The returning veterans from both the Pacific and Europe assumed that nothing would have changed while they were gone. This turned out not to be the case. They had changed, their hometowns had changed, and the people they knew had changed. They returned to a world that was less familiar than they had imagined. The problems were especially intense for the men who were married before going into the service. Some wives felt that the long years of separation had not been a part of their marriage contract. Fathers who had left when their children were very young or had not yet been born returned to children who did not know them. Their families had become independent and had managed to get along without them while they were gone.

The veterans themselves had changed in personalities and preferences as a result of the war experience. The initial separation in going to war had been painful, and the readjustments after the war were often difficult. It is perhaps for these reasons that the divorce rate was disproportionately high for the veterans returning from the war. The costs of the war went far beyond the immediate cost of participating in the war itself. The personal lives of individuals had been turned upside down by one of the major national traumas of the twentieth century.

Discussion Questions

1. Why was the United States as a nation so unprepared militarily at the time of the Japanese attack on Pearl Harbor?
2. Why did Americans tolerate the violation of the civil liberties guaranteed by the U.S. Constitution with the internment of Japanese Americans during World War II? Was there ever any evidence of subversive activity by Japanese Americans?
3. How would you account for the strong sense of national solidarity after the Japanese attack on Pearl Harbor?
4. What part did movies and other forms of popular culture play in mobilizing support for the war?
5. To what extent did the employment of women in the war effort contribute to the subsequent movement emphasizing equal rights for women?
6. How would you account for the motivations of Japanese pilots to volunteer for suicide missions after the kamikaze corps was organized?
7. What is meant by the reference to World War II as "the last good war"?
8. Why was the divorce rate so high after the war for veterans who had married before they went into military service?

5 • The Fear of Communism

Following the defeat of Germany and Japan, international tensions were of a sufficient magnitude that many Americans did not believe that World War II had really ended. A war with the Soviet Union was believed to be inevitable. For example, General George Patton at the end of the war with Germany observed that we might as well proceed to take on the Russians. In his view, we would have to do this sooner or later, so we should just get it over with. Patton's view of the inevitability of war with the Soviet Union was shared by many Americans. A military defeat of the Soviet Union was seen as necessary for producing a peaceful world.

World War II had an indelible impact on American perceptions of the postwar world. The United States had been thrust into a position of world leadership, and it was apparent that the nation could no longer be guided by the isolationist sentiment that prevailed before the war. The world had become more interdependent. Americans now saw that happenings in remote places could have a direct bearing on their own national security. The calamities of World War II provided the background for conceptualizing and defining the new world order. The generation that directly encountered World War II was the generation that would shape national policies and priorities for many years to come.

Memories of the surprise attack on Pearl Harbor and the country's lack of preparedness for the war became deeply embedded in American consciousness. The slogan "Remember Pearl Harbor" had motivated Americans to mobilize national resources during World War II. After the war, the slogan served to shape national priorities for the next fifty years. Americans came out of World War II preoccupied with national security and resolved never again to be caught unprepared militarily.

Americans saw the dangerous possibilities of the postwar world as resembling those of the 1930s. Historical analogies with the events and conditions leading up to World War II were drawn upon in political dialog for clarifying what must be done in the new world order. Particularly important in these discussions were perceptions of the similarities between the Soviet Union and Nazi Germany. The specific enemy had changed, but the political conditions seemed strikingly similar. Americans were determined to avoid the historical mistakes that were generally believed to have caused World War II.

The United States' monopoly control over the atomic bomb lasted for only four years. In September 1949, samples of unusually high levels of radiation taken by a long-range reconnaissance plane provided overwhelming evidence that the Soviets had exploded a nuclear device similar in magnitude to the one that had been exploded at Alamagordo, New Mexico. The Soviets had developed the bomb much sooner than political and military leaders had expected. As a result, any remaining doubts about the technological capabilities of the Soviet Union vanished instantly. The world had become more dangerous, and it no longer seemed self-evident that the United States would be able to win a future war with the Soviet Union. Many Americans suspected that the Soviets could not have developed the bomb so quickly without receiving secret information from scientists working on the Manhattan Project.

The threat of communism became intolerable as many Americans perceived the tide of international events as favoring the Soviets. Although the United States had developed into an industrial giant, intense feelings of national insecurity persisted. The collective emotions of anger, fear, and uncertainty that had generated a sense of moral community in resisting the threat of Germany and Japan had been extended to the cold war with the Soviet Union. Americans continued to be involved in an epic struggle between the forces of good and evil.

All advances that were made under the banner of communism anywhere in the world were assumed to reflect the unfolding of a master plan that had originated in the Soviet Union. Extraordinary forms of cunning, deceit, and political sophistication were attributed to the inner circle of the Communist Party in Moscow. Such attributions provided a ready-made framework for simplifying the many faces of evil in world politics. The fall of the nationalist government in China to communist forces was seen as promoted by the Soviet Union, as was the expanding membership of the Communist Party of Italy and France and the seizure of power by the Communist Party in Czechoslovakia. The cold war was becoming an extraordinary confrontation with a unified form of evil. Stopping the spread of communism was taking the form of a moral crusade.

The Korean War

In June 1950, the communist forces of North Korea launched a broad-scale attack against the Republic of South Korea. The North Korean army was well trained and armed with weapons from the Soviet Union. Its objective was clearly the unification of Korea as a communist state. Because Americans saw the invasion as part of a master plan to spread communism, they responded with anger and indignation. The efforts of the United States resulted in a condemnation of the invasion by the United Nations and an endorsement of military intervention to preserve the integrity of the Republic of Korea. American troops assigned to the occupation of Japan were reassigned to Korea. Lacking training and preparation for their combat assignment, they sustained heavy losses in setting up a defense perimeter just north of the city of Pusan at the southern tip of the Korean peninsula.

Following a successful buildup of military forces under the command of the United Nations, the North Korean army was driven back across the thirty-eighth parallel, the dividing line between North and South Korea. The tide of the war had shifted, and the American army continued its advance through North Korea. The resistance of the North Korean army was minimal as American forces aimed for control of Korea all the way to the Yalu River. What was expected to be an easy victory, however, soon became a military disaster. More than 100,00 Chinese troops crossed the Manchurian border into Korea, transforming the war into a large-scale military encounter.

The conduct of the war resulted in a major controversy between the field commanders in Korea and the official policies of the U.S. government in Washington. General Douglas MacArthur wanted to conduct bombing raids in Manchuria to cut off the enemy supply lines into Korea. President Truman wanted to contain the war and avoid American involvement in a land-based war in China. Thanks to these limitations, a stalemate developed, and an easy victory for either the Chinese army or the American army was no longer a realistic possibility. The heavy losses in the fighting for the hills along the battle lines of Korea came to resemble the absurdity of the trench warfare of World War I. Neither side could make a major advance against the other without sustaining unacceptable losses.

The continuation of a war that the United States could not reasonably expect to win resulted in low levels of morale for American army personnel. The night patrols, the assaults on enemy-held hills, and the heavy artillery bombardments caused heavy casualties for both sides. Throughout the war, a concern for the possible use of nuclear weapons was paramount. Several military commanders had recommended the use of nuclear weapons to break the stalemate. Earlier in the war, General MacArthur's staff had identified suitable targets in North Korea and in China for the use of nuclear weapons. Even Truman had refused to rule out the possibility of using nuclear weapons in Korea. Our allies in Europe were especially concerned that the conduct of the war in Korea could lead the Soviet Union into an active military

Box 5
Symbolic Event: *The Manchurian Candidate*

The conduct of American soldiers who were prisoners of war in Korea was subject to debate for many years after the war. In public discourse, the term "brainwashing" was frequently used. Both the alarm and the term grew out of the belief that the Chinese had developed new techniques of thought control. "Brainwashing" suggested that American values could be swept aside and replaced by a communist ideology. The hysteria of the times pointed toward the insidious character of communist attempts to manipulate and control the thought processes.

The Manchurian Candidate, initially a novel subsequently made into a movie, provided a dramatic representation of what could be accomplished by using brainwashing techniques. The movie symbolized U.S. paranoia over the demonic and conspiratorial aspects of communist indoctrination during the 1950s. The plot focuses on an American Congressional Medal of Honor winner who is captured by the North Koreans and turned over to Chinese and Russian interrogators. Through the use of forceful indoctrination and brainwashing techniques, his previous values are obliterated and he is turned into a sophistical political assassin. Upon his return to the United States, he is programmed on a prearranged signal to assassinate the president of the United States.

The release of the movie a year before the assassination of President Kennedy may have been a coincidence, but to conspiratorial theorists it was taken as evidence of the probability that Kennedy's killer, Lee Harvey Oswald, had been brainwashed during his stay in Russia. Although demonizing enemies attributes extraordinary capabilities to them from the vantage point of modern social learning theories, the metaphor of brainwashing as sweeping the brain clean and implanting a totally new set of values is more a product of fear and hysteria than a realistic possibility.

involvement and thus precipitate World War III. If either the Soviet Union or the United States encountered a crushing military defeat in a conventional war, it would be forced to use nuclear weapons.

Following a negotiated settlement of the war, Americans were shocked by the news that twenty-four American POWs chose to go to China rather than be repatriated to the United States. The war had been prolonged because of the difficulties in resolving the POW issue. More than 100,000 Chinese soldiers had surrendered during the war as a means of getting out of communist China. The Republic of China wanted them all back, while the United Nations negotiators insisted that repatriation should be a voluntary choice on the part of the individual soldier. The news that several American soldiers selected the option of living in China alarmed the nation.

The tensions generated by the Korean War provided the immediate background for broadening collective definitions of the communist menace. Our capacity to contain the international spread of communism was seen by many Americans as limited by the insidious influences of the communists hidden in our own society. Communism came to be perceived as both an external threat and an internal menace. The erroneous belief that POWs had been brainwashed as captives in Korea was extended in political dialog to argue that American citizens in their everyday lives were susceptible to communist ideologies. The fear of communism that was deeply embedded in American history transformed into mass hysteria. While there was little we could do to prevent Soviet initiatives on the world scene, there was something we could do about the hidden enemies in our midst.

McCarthyism

Fear of hidden communists had its roots in responses to the nineteenth-century efforts of American workers to unionize. Some of the early labor unions drew upon a revolutionary rhetoric, calling for the development of union solidarity, a revolutionary overthrow of the capitalist system, and a control of the factory system by industrial workers. Most members of labor unions found the revolutionary rhetoric unacceptable. Their primary interest was in getting a fair share of the rewards that modern industry had to offer. The labor unions that gained the largest following were those seeking such practical benefits as a shorter workweek, better working conditions, and higher wages. All labor unions, however, were seen by many business leaders and government officials as engaged in an attack on the social system. Unions were widely publicized as under the control of "communists," "bolsheviks," "anarchists," "reds," or other foreign elements whose aim was to overthrow the free enterprise system.

The communist revolution in Russia reinforced these underlying fears. While the communists were not the primary agency in the overthrow of the czarist government, they were successful in gaining control of the government once a revolution had occurred. By developing a small cadre of dedicated revolutionists, they were in a position to take advantage of the confusion of the situation and thus gain control. Americans were dismayed over what had happened in Russia. Communism was no longer an abstract set of ideological principles; it had become a central ingredient in practical politics. Many Americans believed that something similar to what had happened in Russia could also happen here. They believed that by infiltrating labor unions, skilled revolutionists could create a unified labor movement and, through a general strike, gain control of the social system.

Responding to the Red Scare of the 1920s, Attorney General A. Mitchell

Palmer ordered simultaneous raids on scores of cities across the nation. More than 6,000 suspected communists were arrested, frequently manhandled, and thrown in jail. Those arrested were denied legal counsel and held for days or weeks without any explicit charges against them. Newspapers gave extensive coverage to reports from Palmer's office on the gigantic plot against the safety of the country. Although the government found no evidence of plans for an insurrection, the hysteria of the times mounted. Under the wartime Sedition Act, several hundred alien residents were deported. Most were guilty of nothing more than holding radical views on political issues.

The House Un-American Activities Committee was set up in 1945 as a permanent congressional committee to investigate subversion in American life. Special attention was given to the alleged influence of communists in labor unions, the entertainment industry, churches, and universities. Many prominent Americans were called before the committee and questioned extensively about their political attitudes or any connection they may have had with a radical cause. The hearings frequently resembled an inquisition, and guilt was frequently assumed at the outset. Witnesses found themselves harassed by the committee without the protection of due process that would have been available in a court of law. Unwarranted allegations replaced solid evidence, and several people were sent to prison on charges of perjury or for refusing to answer the outrageous questions in the committee's interrogation. The right of individuals to have political convictions without being required to reveal them to the government was violated.

Many individuals who were investigated by the committee became stigmatized, lost their jobs, and had their names placed on a blacklist. Those who lost their jobs encountered closed doors when they sought employment elsewhere. Several hundred names were included on the blacklist on the basis of nothing more than the charge of having a friend or an acquaintance who was a leftist on the political spectrum. Communist leanings were imputed to those who had publicly expressed pro–working-class sentiments during the 1930s, participated in peace demonstrations, or supported whatever the committee defined as a radical cause.

Prominent men and women in the television and movie industries were denied future employment. Employers ran the risk of guilt by association if they hired any of the alleged subversives on the blacklist. Further, the Federal Bureau of Investigation placed those on the blacklist under surveillance. Their activities were monitored, notes were taken on whom they interacted with, and their garbage was examined for discarded mail. Divorces, suicides, illnesses, and heart attacks were common among those who had been stigmatized by the charges leveled against them. A sense of despair resulted from harassment, lost jobs, and ruined reputations.

The McCarran Internal Security Act of 1950 called for the mandatory registration of "communist-front" organizations and for the construction of concentration camps. The camps were authorized for the purpose of interning all suspected subversives if the president or Congress were to declare a national emergency. The legislation also specified that those suspected of disloyalty could be held in detention without trial by jury or a formal hearing. Six camps were established in 1952 and maintained until the early 1960s. The Bureau of Prisons renovated old POW camps and the detention camps that had been used for the internment of Japanese Americans during World War II.

The term "McCarthyism" entered the American vocabulary to describe the fanatical beliefs about the pervasiveness of disloyalty among Americans. In a speech in Wheeling, West Virginia, in February 1950, Senator Joseph McCarthy claimed that communists had infiltrated each of our major institutions and were working to undermine the American way of life. McCarthy asserted that communists were carrying out a blueprint for infiltrating and infecting our schools, churches, labor unions, the news media, the arts, mass entertainment, voluntary associations, and virtually all agencies of government. McCarthy claimed that he had a list of known communists in the State Department and that these hidden communists were responsible for failures in American foreign policy. The fears, anxieties, and frustrations of the cold war were being given free rein in the political arena.

Whether McCarthy actually believed what he was saying is debatable. It is clear that he never actually had a list of "known communists," as he had claimed. The list was a form of histrionics and pure fabrication. The verdict of history is that McCarthy was a little man with big political ambitions. He drew upon collective fears and anxieties in order to build a political constituency as no other man had done in the history of the nation. His appeal, in part, grew out of his image as a lone individual who was taking on the big institutions, such as the State Department and the army, and was having a major impact on them. Admiration for him may very well have provided compensation for the political alienation of Americans who felt helpless and overwhelmed by the complexity of the issues the nation confronted.

Few Americans doubted the seriousness of the communist menace. They remembered vividly that the United States had neglected to take seriously the threats of Nazi Germany and the Empire of Japan. The type of conspiracy theory that had been applied to Japanese Americans during World War II was now being applied to ordinary citizens. The targets of suspicion and distrust included the foreign-born, civil rights advocates, peace groups, and participants in many other types of social movements. All were subjected to critical scrutiny. By a strange system of logic, all those who held views that were to the left of the political center were being lumped into the communist category. The warlike atmosphere of the day called for the creation of a moral community, and nothing less than full compliance with the national goal of stopping communism was regarded as socially acceptable.

The public pronouncements of J. Edgar Hoover, as director of the FBI, added credibility to McCarthy's claims. According to Hoover, the close monitoring of communist activities since the 1920s had indicated increased sophistication in the use of mass agitation, subversion, and infiltration techniques. Both Hoover and McCarthy claimed that hidden communists were to be found lecturing in our universities, preaching from America's pulpits, writing scripts and acting in television and movie productions, and vying as candidates for political office. The difficulty in identifying a communist was reflected in Hoover's comment: "Most communists are ordinary looking people, like your seat mate on the bus or a clerk in one of your neighborhood stores."

McCarthyism as a political ideology resembled the witchcraft theories of an earlier time. Witchcraft theory assumed that there was a cohesive, well-organized, and zealously committed group of individuals who had entered into a conspiracy with the Devil. A demonic order was seen as coexisting alongside the legitimate and normative order of everyday life. Beliefs about the sources of evil had changed, but the system of logic was remarkably similar. Speaking in defense of a person accused of being a communist was considered evidence of disloyalty to the United States. Thus, those who recognized McCarthy as a demagogue were hesitant to speak out against him or to defend those who were outrageously charged with having communist leanings.

Before McCarthyism ran its course, charges were made against each of our major institutions. McCarthy and his supporters claimed that an epic struggle was under way for control over the minds and souls of the masses. Public schools and universities were seen as in a position to politically indoctrinate students with the communist way of thinking. McCarthy's claims were sufficiently credible that universities throughout the country required professors to sign loyalty oaths as a condition of employment. FBI agents routinely checked libraries to identify those professors and graduate students who had checked out books written by Karl Marx or other known communists. Textbooks and library books by American authors, both past and present, were scanned for themes that were seen as sympathetic to the communist cause.

The preoccupation with the communist menace during the 1950s deeply scarred the moral and ethical foundations of American society. The traditional commitment of Americans to maintaining an open and democratic society was compromised. The basic rights of individuals to criticize their government collided with charges of disloyalty, and the demand for conformity had corrosive effects on the integrity and vitality of the system. The self-righteousness of those promoting the anticommunist campaigns had more damaging effects on the American system than any espionage or subversion that may have occurred. The McCarthy episode serves as a grim reminder of the political opportunities that are available to a demagogue within a democratic society.

Many people in the entertainment industry and in the news media found their careers in ruins on the basis of nothing more than the charge that they had communist leanings, that they had associated with someone in the past who was a known communist, or that they could actually be a communist or a communist dupe without even knowing it. While McCarthy's outrageous claims did not result in a single conviction for subversion or espionage, he did win a sizable constituency of admirers by drawing upon latent sentiments and collective fears. Perhaps no other political figure in American life had been more successful as a demagogue in drawing upon the darker side of the national consciousness. By the time the hysteria over the hidden enemies in our midst had subsided by the early 1960s, the nation was on the verge of encountering the terrifying threat of nuclear war.

The Cuban Missile Crisis

Of all the crises of the cold war, none matched the severity and intensity of the Cuban missile crisis. On the evening of October 22, 1962, President John F. Kennedy went on television to make an important announcement to the nation and to the world. The United States had discovered that Soviet missile bases were being constructed in Cuba, only ninety miles off the coast of Florida. With missiles in Cuba armed with nuclear warheads, all regions of the United States would be in easy range. All American cities would be vulnerable to nuclear attack. Kennedy noted that the installation of missiles in Cuba was regarded as an act of aggression that could not be tolerated. He declared that the United States would do whatever was necessary to get the missiles out of Cuba.

Kennedy forcefully announced his plan of action. A strict quarantine would be placed on Cuba. The blockade would maximize the use of American forces to stop further Soviet work on the missile sites. Further, the Strategic Air Command was placed on the highest alert ever. Kennedy announced that the United States would increase its surveillance of Cuba and its readiness for a further response if necessary. Any nuclear missile launched from Cuba to any part of the Western Hemisphere would be regarded as an act of war against the United States. Kennedy stated that this would require a full retaliatory response against the Soviet Union.

For most Americans, this was the most terrifying experience of their lives. The possibility of a nuclear war in the next few days had become real. The worst of nightmares about nuclear war seemed on the verge of being enacted. Even before the Cuban missile crisis, many Americans believed a nuclear war was inevitable. Their perception of when a nuclear war was likely to occur, however, was far enough into the future that they would not have to confront the issue today, although it was not far enough in the future to free themselves of an underlying anxiety about its occurrence. Many Americans believed that neither they, nor their children, nor their grandchildren, would live to the year 2000. Now that the country was on the brink of nuclear war, the time span in the planning of personal lives became greatly shortened.

There had been no previous episode in the history of the world in which the stakes were so high and the fate of the world in so few hands. If the worst possible scenario had been enacted, all traditions, lifestyles, and social relationships would have been irretrievably altered. One's physical safety and personal security could no longer be taken for granted. The decisions made at the centers of power in the United States and the Soviet Union were seen as having potentially drastic consequences for the personal lives of individual men and women throughout the world.

Continuing the activities of everyday life seemed meaningless. For example, students who were working toward a college degree or involved in long-range planning for a career in law or medicine became concerned about what they were doing. Why defer immediate gratification for long-range planning if it was all to end in the futility of nuclear destruction? Why go to class or work on a research paper if there was to be a total destruction of the world as it was known and understood in the next few days? Some people were reminded of the secretaries in Berlin at the end of World War II who were filling out requisitions for the next year's office supplies while the Russian soldiers were marching through the streets. However, because they were not personally able to do anything about the big issues facing the world, most people continued with business as usual. It became difficult to know what one ought to believe or ought to do under such extraordinary circumstances.

The Soviet Union was even more terrified by Kennedy's announcement than the Americans were. Officials in the Kremlin knew several things that Kennedy and his Security Council did not know. For example, Kennedy did not know that some of the missiles in Cuba had already been armed with nuclear warheads. Had the United States launched bombing raids on the missile sites, as some of Kennedy's military advisers recommended, it would have meant World War III. The United States also did not know that the Soviet military unit in Cuba was also armed with tactical nuclear weapons. Had the American military invaded the island to remove the missiles, as some of Kennedy's advisers recommended, the results would have been disastrous.

Contingency plans were directed toward the use of successive military strategies if the Soviets failed to give in to Kennedy's demands for removal of the weapons. His first strategy was the blockade to stop Russian ships from delivering missiles to Cuba. The blockade included hundreds of ships and nearly 1,000 aircraft. It was one of the most formidable armadas ever assembled in the history of the world. If this did not work, there was the possibility of air strikes against the missile sites. Further, more than 100,000 troops had been assembled in the southern United States for a possible invasion of Cuba.

On October 24, the world was glued to its television sets and radios as Soviet ships moved toward the American blockade that had been placed around Cuba. The United States had embarked on a course of action in which the outcome could not reasonably be predicted in advance. Would the Soviet ships attempt to run the blockade? Clearly, the confrontation contained all the ingredients for a dangerous escalation toward war. Kennedy was prepared to do whatever was necessary to stop the Soviet ships. He had no way of knowing what the Soviet response would be.

People around the world drew a sigh of relief when the Soviet ships suddenly stopped dead in the water and turned back. The most intense phase of the Cuban missile crisis had passed. However, work on the missile sites continued, and additional negotiations with the Soviets were necessary.

On October 26, a break came in the crisis. Nikita Khrushchev, the Soviet premier, privately sent a message to Kennedy announcing a set of terms for a resolution of the crisis. The Soviet Union would withdraw its missiles from Cuba (1) if the United States would formally pledge not to invade Cuba and (2) if the United States would remove from Turkey its Jupiter missiles that were aimed at the Soviet Union. The Soviets had installed the missiles in Cuba in response to the American strategy of locating missiles adjacent to their borders.

Kennedy accepted Khrushchev's terms with some qualifications. He would publicly make a pledge that the United States would not invade Cuba, but he did not want to announce to the world that he had agreed to remove U.S. missiles from Turkey. For political reasons, Kennedy did not wish to convey the impression that he was willing to appease or compromise with the Russians. At the same time, however, Kennedy privately assured Khrushchev that the United States would remove the missiles from Turkey. Khrushchev found this agreement acceptable. Thus ended the most dangerous crisis in the history of the world.

The drama of the confrontation between Kennedy and Khrushchev was enacted while the rest of the world watched in terror. Most Americans perceived Kennedy as a man who had demonstrated forceful leadership and saw Khrushchev as a man who had backed down. The missiles were removed from Cuba, and the sense of crisis diminished. Confusion remained, however, over the rapidity with which the entire world had been brought to the brink of nuclear war. The Cuban missile crisis had ended but the cold war was far from over.

Surviving Nuclear War

The acute trauma phase of the Cuban missile crisis quickly subsided in the consciousness of Americans. To dwell on what might have happened would have a pathological quality about it and would be counterproductive to the everyday business of living. Yet the fear of nuclear war persisted in the general population, and policy makers reviewed over and over again the lessons to be learned from the crisis that could be applied to future international confrontations.

The fear of nuclear war in the general population took the form of several questions that could not be answered with confidence. Was World War III inevitable? What was the probability that nuclear war would occur in the next few years? How would a nuclear war start? Would there be an advanced warning or would it begin suddenly and unexpectedly? Would it be possible for humans to survive a nuclear war? These questions attempted to link personal biographies with historical circumstances. While the inherent uncertainty of the historical context precluded clear, definitive answers, these questions were of such importance that some form of response was necessary.

The mushroom cloud over Hiroshima had become a major symbol of the challenges and dangers of the world in which we live. The symbolism of the bomb went far beyond the recognition of it as a weapon. It had become a device for destroying the world. Nothing humans had ever made before had such tremendous power and destructive capability. The crisis was of such a magnitude that the future of the nation and the survival of the species could not be taken as self-evident.

Given the number of nuclear bombs that had been developed by the time of the Cuban missile crisis, all major cities in both the United States and the Soviet Union could be smashed flat within a matter of minutes. Public discourse on the effects of a nuclear war noted that the fireballs and firestorms of nuclear explosions would raise the temperature of the earth to levels matching the surface of the sun. It was believed that the land surface of the earth would be seared and the oxygen in the atmosphere depleted. The heat generated would melt the polar ice caps, which would result in the flooding of the land surface at lower elevations. Immense amounts of gamma radiation would be released over most of the northern hemisphere. Death would result not only from the concussion of the explosion, but also from asphyxiation. Survivors of the initial blast would likely die from acute radiation sickness within a few weeks.

The view was widely held that humans were not yet prepared for having such weapons at their disposal. A nuclear war of the scale that the United States and the Soviet Union were capable of waging could end civilization in minutes, and the greater part of the world's population could be dead within days or weeks. Some believed that a great deal of the earth's animal and plant life would be destroyed as well. Thus, it was not a matter of either side bombing the other "back to the Stone Age," as the contemporary cliché put it; it was a matter of the survival of the human species itself.

During the Cuban missile crisis, there had been a run on supermarkets. Preparing for a nuclear catastrophe was one way people could translate their underlying fear and anxiety into a specific line of action. By storing up provisions for survival, they were preparing for the worst possible scenario. Some people included the purchase of guns in their preparations, believing that they would need some way to defend themselves and their families if there was a breakdown in law and order following a nuclear war. Since there was no realistic way of knowing what the world would be like, survival might very well require being prepared for drastic measures.

The American emphasis on personal mastery and control was reflected in the construction of fallout shelters. Rather than fatalistic resignation in the face of nuclear war, many people expressed a determination to take matters into their own hands. Accordingly, during the late 1950s and early 1960s, some Americans constructed bunkers in their backyards. The bunkers were cellar like constructions covered with several feet of dirt and stocked with food and water in sufficient supply to survive for several days following a nuclear war. When these people were asked what they would do if neighbors attempted to force their way into the fallout shelters, the response was frequently, "We'd just have to shoot them." Personal survival was defined as the major objective in these cases, and self-interest was assigned higher priority than communal interests.

Many major cities throughout the country began planning civil defense strategies. Columbus, Ohio, for example, predicted that the bomb would fall at the intersection of Broad and High Streets (the city center). Assuming a thirty-minute advance notice of an impending nuclear attack, what should the civil defense response be? Should plans be made for evacuating the city or for going underground?

If the city was to be evacuated, what contingency plans must be made?

Were the food supplies in the surrounding countryside adequate to feed the evacuated urban dwellers? What should be done with the poisonous snakes in the zoo? Should they be shot? And what about the prisoners in the Ohio State Penitentiary, which was located in the city? Should the guards just walk away, and if so, what should be done with the inmates? In planning for an evacuation of the city, Columbus officials decided that the streets should all be transformed into one-way streets leading out from the center of the city. A practice evacuation was held, and the result was a massive traffic jam. The planning for civil defense in American cities was seen by many as an exercise in futility.

A variety of viewpoints were expressed about whether there would be survivors following an all-out nuclear war. Some people, turning to the sacred scriptures for insight into the aftermath of nuclear war, maintained that not all would perish. A great flood had once destroyed the world, it was noted, but there were survivors. Noah and his family had been chosen by God to perpetuate the species. This view held that a merciful God would provide humanity with an opportunity for a fresh start.

Other people took a more secular approach and came to less optimistic conclusions. Several scientists elaborated on the concept of a "nuclear winter" and maintained that there would be no survivors. The debris released into the atmosphere from the explosions of a nuclear war would alter the earth's climate by blocking out rays from the sun. The rapid drop in temperature would soon result in a heavy snowfall covering the millions of burned bodies in major metropolitan areas. Drastic environmental changes would occur as temperatures dropped to severely low levels. The plant and animal life upon which humans depend for food would be extinguished.

"The long darkness" or "nuclear winter" argument may be understood as a plausibility argument growing out of conditions of uncertainty. Such concerns stem from the inability to come up with a realistic set of expectations about what would happen during and after a nuclear war. There were no precedents in the human experience for encounters with such severe environmental changes or for such dramatic imperatives for human adaptability within such a short period of time. Yet it was clear that the world would never again be the same. The old world order would be of limited usefulness for any new social world the survivors would be required to create.

Americans could draw upon neither direct experiences nor rational analysis for a reasonable set of predictions about what the world would be like after a nuclear war. For these reasons, Americans turned to such forms of popular culture as the movies, novels, and music for both entertainment and reflections on their underlying anxieties. Prominent in images of nuclear war were such notions as "doomsday," "Armageddon," "the apocalypse," "total destruction," and "a lifeless planet." Such images conveyed the implication that there would be no survivors of an all-out nuclear war. The planet would join the other planets of the universe on which life had never developed or had been extinguished.

The fantasies of popular culture suggested that if only a few survived a nuclear war, the survivors would have a rough time of it. The money in their checking accounts would be useless, food in grocery stores would be contaminated, and there would be no electricity to run appliances. The taken-for-granted supports of everyday life would no longer be available. In the absence of law and order, the ugliest side of human nature would be manifested. Because of the loss of the power of the state, human relationships would become brutal, dangerous, and coercive. Self-interest would prevail, and communal support and mutual caring would vanish. In effect, with the trappings of civilization stripped away, the social environment would become harsh and unresponsive to personal needs and interests. In the absence of any reasonable knowledge of what social life would be like following a nuclear holocaust, imagination was given free rein in developing notions about the forms of human nature that would be tapped and about the types of men and women who would prevail.

The lessons from Hiroshima had suggested that much more was involved in a nuclear war than the deaths initially resulting from the explosion itself. The acute radiation aftereffects at Hiroshima and Nagasaki were grotesque. Symptoms of the "invisible contamination" included severe diarrhea, ulceration of the mouth, bleeding gums, skin cancer, high fever, loss of hair, low white blood cell count, and damage to the central nervous system. There was also evidence that exposure to high levels of radiation would have gruesome effects on future generations: children or grandchildren would be born with genetic abnormalities, and deleterious mutations would occur.

Those who believed the best way to survive a nuclear war was to prevent one took an active political stand against additional preparations. If there were no reasonable circumstances under which a nuclear war could be fought, then why were preparations being made for it? If both the United States and the Soviet Union had an overkill capacity for annihilating all men, women, and children on this planet, then why were additional resources being put into sophisticated weapons of destruction? A large number of books, editorials, sermons, and radical publications expressed anger over the suicidal implications of the escalations toward nuclear war.

While adults were developing coping mechanisms for downplaying their level of stress, the tensions stemming from the threat of nuclear war surfaced for children and adolescents. The civil defense program in the public schools that called for "duck and cover" exercises had unexpected psychological consequences for children. Many children concluded that because of their preparation they might survive a nuclear war but their parents would not. Children were afraid of "being stuck" and not having anyone to take care of them. A few adolescents were fascinated by the idea of nuclear weapons, but most were strongly antinuclear and expressed anger at the older generation for playing with their future and perhaps depriving them of the opportunity to grow up and live out their adult lives. Typical responses of adolescents reflected a mixture of anger with feelings of hopelessness and helplessness. The majority of adolescents were doubtful that either they or their country could survive a nuclear war.

The encounter of adolescents with the fear of nuclear war was subsequently followed by a set of attitudes that were disturbing to many adults. By the middle 1960s, many young adults were openly expressing their anger toward the older generations and placing their faith exclusively in their own generation. This was reflected in the viewpoint that "no one over thirty could be trusted." Resentment about the world that had been created for them by the older generation was translated into attitudes of distrust toward authority and established institutions. Rather than working within the system, young people sought self-fulfillment through impulsive actions. The focus was on here and now, rather than on a future that required making long-range plans and deferring immediate gratification. The pervasiveness of such attitudes was reflected in the behavior of those who dropped out of school, engaged in casual sex, and experimented with mind-altering drugs. In the face of an uncertain future, they took the hedonistic view of "living for today and letting tomorrow take care of itself."

Whether the fear of communism was realistic or unrealistic, it is clear that we were operating between the boundaries of order and chaos, between good and evil, between survival and mass destruction. The quest for military superiority precluded a reduction of the arms race even after the capacity for overkill had been developed on both sides of the Iron Curtain. We may never be able to adequately explain or understand the escalation of the arms race between the United States and the Soviet Union. Whatever else future historians may decide, it is clear that misperceptions, misunderstandings, and mass hysteria were among the ingredients involved. But at the level of human action, what is important is not the truth of the matter, by objective criteria, but what people believe to be true. Humans act on the basis of their beliefs, whether they are valid ones or not.

Discussion Questions

1. What do you see as the connection between the Red Scare of the 1920s and McCarthyism in the 1950s?

2. Why was it necessary for President Truman to fire General MacArthur?
3. What is meant by the term "brainwashing" and how was it illustrated in the movie *The Manchurian Candidate*?
4. What is meant by the term "blacklisting" and how did it ruin the careers of so many Americans?
5. Was an internal communist conspiracy ever a serious threat to the security of the United States? Please justify your answer.
6. What is meant by the term "mutually assured destruction," and was this policy viable for the management of international conflict? Why or why not?
7. What were some of the ways children and adolescents responded to the threat of nuclear war?
8. Had there been an all-out nuclear war, do you think there would have been any survivors? Please justify your answer.

6 • The Vietnam War

The Vietnam War stands beside the Civil War as one of the longest and most enduring traumas in the nation's history. The trauma of Vietnam had no clear and dramatic beginning comparable to the Japanese attack on Pearl Harbor or the Confederate firing on Fort Sumter. There was no single precipitating event, there was no formal declaration of war, and there was no "police action" under the auspices of the United Nations, as there had been in Korea. Instead, the national trauma grew out of an evolving set of conditions that resulted in outcomes that no one intended or really wanted. The cumulative effects of a series of political decisions, each of which seemed reasonable to those who made them, resulted in tragic consequences of epic proportions.

A metaphor for the justification behind U.S. military involvement in Vietnam was provided in a speech delivered by President Dwight D. Eisenhower on April 7, 1954. Eisenhower compared the countries of Southeast Asia to "a row of dominoes." He warned that if Indochina fell to the communists, the rest of the countries of Southeast Asia would "go over very quickly." American political leadership had been called into question by the success of communist revolutions in China and Cuba. In Eisenhower's view, the United States should take a firm stand to prevent the spread of communism to any other country. Eisenhower's domino metaphor served as a guiding principle in shaping our foreign policy and provided a justification for our subsequent military involvement in Vietnam.

On August 2, 1961, President Kennedy announced that he was sending several thousand troops to Vietnam as "advisers." The idea was that American military expertise could be drawn upon to suppress communist insurgency in South Vietnam. Kennedy asserted that the U.S. troops would be armed and authorized to fire on the enemy. Without a formal declaration of war, the United States was becoming involved in a military encounter that would have traumatic consequences for both the Vietnamese and the American people. The growing resistance of the Vietcong resulted in a gradual escalation of the number of American troops sent to Vietnam.

Conduct of the War

From a military standpoint, it appeared that the war in Vietnam would be easy to win. It was assumed that because the enemy did not have helicopters, tanks, planes, armed personnel carriers, and other sophisticated weapons of war, it would soon be defeated. The lessons from history pointed toward the conclusion that a technologically advanced war machine could quickly defeat an unsophisticated and primitive one.

The military paradox of Vietnam was that, although American soldiers had the sophisticated military technology to win World War III, they did not know how to effectively fight a land-based guerrilla war against a peasant people in the rice paddies and jungles of Southeast Asia. Previous wars had been fought primarily by the rules of European warfare, with clear battle lines. The good guys were on one side, the bad guys were on the other, and there was "no-man's land" between them. Under these conditions, military superiority in firepower and manpower could determine the outcome.

The war in Vietnam was different. There were no clearly defined battle lines, and the enemy could not be clearly identified. Vietnamese people who engaged in routine activities during the day became warriors at night. A great deal of the fighting was hit-and-run: the Vietcong would strike a military target, blow up an ammunition dump, ambush an infantry patrol, and then vanish into the jungle or the night. The enemy forces comprised not only military personnel but also old men, women, and children who wore no uniforms.

Demonstrating technological superiority first required finding the enemy, and in Vietnam that was difficult. The Vietcong were dispersed throughout the countryside and were hard to locate. A great deal of the ground action consisted of infantry patrols on search-and-destroy missions. The idea was that the patrols would locate the enemy, draw their fire, withdraw, and then send in the bombers and heavy artillery to finish the job. The idea appeared to be a good one in theory, but failed to work in practice. The Vietcong were the ones to decide on the time and the place for the military encounter. In combat situations, about 80 percent of the initial fire came from the enemy. They would strike ferociously and then disappear. Hundreds of tunnels had been constructed to shield the Vietcong and their supplies.

The U.S. military decided to use chemical defoliants on jungle areas to make it easier to spot the Vietcong and military targets. Approximately 18 million gallons of a herbicide under the code name Agent Orange were dropped on the vegetation in Vietnam. This also turned out to be a strategy that did not work. The destruction of foliage simply made it easier for the Vietcong to spot infantry patrols sooner and at a greater distance. It was only long after the war that official recognition was given to health consequences to American soldiers of prolonged exposure to Agent Orange.

Following the Tonkin Gulf Resolution, the U.S. Air Force carried out intense bombing raids on the cities and military installations of North Vietnam. The idea was that the enemy would become demoralized as a result of this vast devastation. The effects of the bombing raids, however, turned out to be the reverse of what was intended. The bombing raids had a unifying effect on the North Vietnamese people and intensified their determination to continue the war. Pentagon officials believed that if the United States could demonstrate technological superiority, the enemy would recognize that they could not win and would be willing to negotiate a conclusion to the war. Such an assumption turned out to be in error.

The trauma of Vietnam intensified as deep divisions surfaced within the United States over our foreign policy and the frustration of being involved in a war we could not win. Involvement in Vietnam had become a quagmire, and no reasonable exit strategy was available. The frustration of President Lyndon Johnson was reflected in his comments: "I can't get out. I can't finish with what I've got. So, what the hell am I going to do?" Johnson's paralysis over what to do mirrored the collective frustration and confusion of the entire nation.

The war dragged on several times longer than any previous war in American history. Over the years, several fact-finding groups were sent from Washington to Vietnam to assess the situation and to make recommendations on what was needed to win the war. Repeatedly, the expert opinion from our political and military leadership pointed toward the same conclusion: send more troops, send more supplies, and send more sophisticated military equipment. As a result of these recommendations, the military force in Vietnam grew to enormous proportions, yet got no closer to a decisive victory. By 1969, U.S. military personnel in Vietnam had escalated to 541,000 soldiers and marines and nearly 200,000 additional servicemen stationed at air bases within striking distance of military targets in Vietnam. Before the war was over, several million men and women had been on assignment to Vietnam.

As U.S. commitment of personnel and equipment to the war increased, more was needed in the way of accountability. As a gauge of how well we were doing, an emphasis was placed on the body count of the enemy dead. The requirement to produce enemy casualties added to the brutality of the war. Both combatants and noncombatants came to be included in the reported number of enemy killed. In operational terms, anyone killed by an American soldier was by definition "an enemy." The ammunition used, the bombs dropped, and the artillery rounds fired all became measures of the progress the United States was making militarily. A wide gap was developing between the illusions and the realities of the war. In the absence of clearly identified military targets, bombs, artillery, and ammunition were being used indiscriminately. The civilians in Vietnam constituted a disproportionate number of the casualties of war.

Veterans in Vietnam

Several features of the war promoted intense levels of trauma for the men who fought in it. In the absence of clearly defined battle lines, it was difficult to distinguish between Vietnamese civilians and military combatants. The military units composing the enemy forces were to a very large degree invisible. The problem of not being able to identify the enemy was compounded by generalized feelings of alienation and estrangement from the civilian population in Vietnam. Their culture was not understood, and in any given case, the boundaries between friends and enemies were not clearly defined. Some soldiers came to view all Vietnamese as the enemy. In effect, physical proximity to other people was accompanied by an intense sense of psychological distance and apartness.

Adolescents disproportionately fought the Vietnam War. The average age of the American soldier in Vietnam was only 19.1 years, whereas the average age of the soldiers in World War II was 26.5 years. Many had never been away from their homes and families before and lacked adult maturity and judgment. The orderly progression of events in early adulthood had not occurred. A large percentage of them had only a high school education or less, had not yet had time to develop stable relationships with members of the opposite sex, and was unable to emotionally balance and deal with the seeming purposelessness of the war. Some were driven by a hatred of the enemy and by negative perceptions of the Vietnamese people. Killing was experienced by some as excitement that provided an outlet for rage and survivor guilt.

In addition to the selection of the very young for combat assignments, there was also selectivity in terms of race and social class. For example, blacks were significantly overrepresented among those who were drafted into the army, were assigned to Vietnam, served in combat units, and were fatalities in the war. The armed forces placed special emphasis on recruiting racial minorities, in part on the assumption that military service provided a major opportunity for the integration of the underprivileged into the mainstream of American society. But more importantly, the recruitment efforts were directed toward those least prepared to resist the authority of the state in mobilizing manpower for the war machine.

Most previous wars had permitted a sense of camaraderie to develop among "army buddies." The process of confronting a common enemy and sharing the dangers of exposure to enemy fire typically had a cohesive effect on military units. For example, during World War II cooperative actions in the pursuit of a joint enterprise resulted in cohesive bonds among the members of military units. However, in Vietnam individuals sent in as replacements were thrown in with strangers with whom there had been no shared experiences or ongoing relationships. As a result, the replacements were sent on combat assignments without the opportunity to develop a sense of mutual support with those who had been in their units for a longer period of time. The war became a highly individualized experience.

Levels of conflict ran high among men in combat units. Fights frequently broke out, and intense hatred developed between leaders and followers. The new replacements soon encountered practices that were in conflict with their sense of morality and proper conduct in human relationships. Killing is always problematic from the standpoint of basic morality, but when it involves women, children, and innocent civilians, the psychological effects can be devastating. The usual standards for winning and losing among the military became confused. Many veterans became uncomfortable by the pressure from the higher command to increase the number of enemy killed.

The soldiers found themselves in dangerous situations they did not understand. In the absence of any clear set of military objectives, conduct in the field became problematic. The assigned mission frequently lacked a clear set of instructions and did not make sense to the men who were expected to carry it out. For example, heavy casualties occurred in an assault on a hill occupied by the Vietcong; subsequently, however, the hill was abandoned because it lacked strategic significance. Such procedures seemed senseless to the men involved. If the hill had no military value, why were the commanders willing to sacrifice so many men in its conquest? Serious doubts were raised about the competence of officers who sheltered themselves from the risks they exposed others to and who gave improper and malevolent orders. In comparison with other wars, the practice of "fragging" was common in Vietnam. Fragging is the killing of a disliked officer in such a fashion that his death appears to have resulted from enemy action. As one Vietnam veteran stated the matter: "We did not fight the enemy. We fought ourselves. The enemy was within ourselves."

In addition to the conflicts within units, there was also a sense of entrapment in continuing a war that had no end in sight. The war resembled imprisonment with no means of escape. The enemy lay ahead, and there was no avenue of withdrawal or retreat. The combat veterans used the acronym REMFs (Rear Echelon Mother Fuckers) to vent their sense of despair. The

---

Box 6
Symbolic Event: The My Lai Incident

An article that appeared in the *New York Times* in November 1969 described a massacre that had occurred at the village of My Lai. The newspaper reported that under the command of Lieutenant William Calley Jr., all the old men, women, and children in the village of My Lai were rounded up and shot. Subsequent investigation revealed that many of the women were brutally raped before they were killed. According to the eyewitness accounts of the participants in the massacre, an estimated 175 to 200 noncombatants were slaughtered. The news was greeted with shock and disbelief by many Americans. For others, the news came as no surprise. Information had been readily available on American atrocities in Vietnam and the brutal treatment of Vietnamese civilians.

The event became highly symbolic of U.S. involvement in Vietnam and provided a sufficiently close analogy to the atrocities of Nazi Germany that many Americans were seriously disturbed. During the subsequent trial of Lieutenant Calley, he did not deny what had happened at My Lai. He admitted to giving the orders and being immediately responsible for the massacre. However, his defense rested on the claims that he had acted under the stress of war and that in a combat situation he had done "what any good soldier would do," which was to carry out the orders he had received from a higher command. The court martial tribunal found Calley guilty and sentenced him to life imprisonment at hard labor. President Richard Nixon ordered that Calley be placed under house arrest, pending the outcome of his appeal.

The tribunal ruled that even in time of war the individual soldier has a moral responsibility to disobey an order if it is improperly given. Thus, responsibility was placed on individual soldiers, rather than on the broader military system. Many Americans believed that Calley was being used as a scapegoat. Two years later, the secretary of the army reduced Calley's sentence to ten years, and about a year after that, Calley was paroled. All of the perpetrators serving under Calley's command were either acquitted or given an administrative reprimand.

REMFs included the support personnel on cushy assignments in Vietnam, the military command that extended all the way to the Pentagon, and the politicians in Washington who promoted the continuance of a senseless war. It was generally believed that those in positions of political authority could have stopped the war had they chosen to do so. Instead, the REMFs were indifferent and uncaring about the suffering of combat veterans. The victims of war had become pawns in a game that others were playing. The trauma of the combat assignment was reflected in the comment of an experienced combat veteran in the movie *Platoon:* "If you are going to get killed in Vietnam, you are lucky if it happens in the first few weeks. That way, you don't have to suffer so much."

The trauma of Vietnam was increasing in intensity, as Americans in general were becoming aware of the subterfuge and cover-up of military strategies in the conduct of the war. Many suspected that the massacre of noncombatants at My Lai, and at other villages that Americans at home never heard about, had been authorized by the higher military command. The Vietcong employed terrorist tactics, and had U.S. forces not used similar tactics, their capacity for winning the war would be limited. The stalemate of the war and the lack of any clear evidence of military victory were increasingly frustrating; U.S. objectives were becoming increasingly confused. Whatever idealism Americans may have had in the initial pursuit of the war was now being called into question.

As it became apparent that the United States was making little headway toward winning the war, the decision was made by the Nixon administration to deescalate U.S. involvement. Opposition to the war was growing both within the general public and among members of Congress. The president ordered a gradual reduction of the number of American troops in Vietnam. The American withdrawal was accompanied by a futile attempt to turn the actual fighting of the war over to the South Vietnamese, while the United States continued to supply military equipment. As the Americans reduced their commitment to the war, the activity of the Vietcong intensified.

Following a negotiated release of prisoners of war, the last of the American forces were withdrawn from South Vietnam. By this time, the Vietcong had amassed a large military force for an assault on the city of Saigon. Many Americans were shocked by the television coverage of the chaos surrounding the evacuation of Saigon by the Americans and the conquest of the city by the communist forces. While a "settlement" of the war had been negotiated, it was clear that the Americans had lost a major war. The Vietnamese who had aligned themselves with the Americans in the war were now being treated as collaborators or traitors by the communist victors. Loss of the war and the American evacuation of Saigon resulted in despair and resentment by the South Vietnamese who were now defined as traitors.

Following the end of the war, many American families continued to agonize over the 2,266 servicemen who were missing in action. Uncertainty persisted whether all the Americans held as prisoners of war had been released. Whether those missing in action or held as prisoners of war were alive or dead could not be determined. Uncertainty prevented families from going through the usual type of mourning that permits individuals to cope with the crisis of death and to get on with the business of living. The Pentagon in the late 1970s declared all missing servicemen dead, assuming that this declaration was a humane way of achieving closure on the issue. Yet reports continued to come out of Southeast Asia of sightings of Americans who were being held against their will. The inability to achieve definitive closure on the issue resulted in an intense mixture of hope and despair for the families involved. No suitable form of psychological relief from the crisis was available.

Opposition to the War

The Vietnam War was traumatic not only for those who fought in it but also for those who were strongly opposed to it. There was never any formal declaration of war. The official justification for our involvement was that the United States was coming to the aid of a small country that was in the process of being overrun by communist forces. The vast majority of elected officials supported our foreign policy and our increased involvement in Vietnam. Secret government files were kept on the backgrounds and activities of those opposed to the war. Many Americans saw the critics of government policy as subversive and disloyal to the United States.

The initial critique of the war grew out of a lack of confidence in American political leadership. The United States had failed to learn from the French experience in Indochina. Critics believed that American political leaders were unable to distinguish adequately between nationalistic movements and movements that were set in motion by an international communist conspiracy. Out of a concern with the spread of communism, the nation had rejected its own revolutionary past at a time when movements of liberation from the tyranny of colonialism were emerging in third-world countries. The American Declaration of Independence had clearly laid out the conditions under which a revolution is both necessary and justified. The books distributed by the U.S. Information Agency had excluded materials on our own revolutionary past. As a result, the leaders in third-world countries who wanted to know "how to make a revolution" could not readily find such a book from an American source. By rejecting its own revolutionary past, the United States failed to provide an adequate model for many third-world countries to follow. Only the revolutionary rhetoric of Marxism–Leninism remained viable and available. National policy assumed that political stability on a worldwide basis was in the best interest of the United States. Such an assumption led to our support of corrupt and tyrannical governments.

U.S. involvement in Vietnam had become a topic of heated debate by the time of the presidential election of 1964. The conservatives gained control of the Republican convention and nominated Barry Goldwater for the presidency. Goldwater's campaign reflected the view that the United States should vigorously pursue its military objectives in Vietnam. In the nation at large, the battle lines were being drawn between the hawks and the doves. The hawks wanted to step up U.S. military operations in Vietnam, while the doves wanted to reduce U.S. military involvement or get out altogether. Goldwater's campaign emphasized taking a direct and forceful approach to winning the war in Vietnam. Although Goldwater was defeated in the election, the approach he advocated was subsequently adopted by the Johnson administration.

The major opposition to American involvement in Vietnam originated on college campuses among the students of the counterculture generation. The opposition was based largely on a condemnation of the war on moral grounds. Many college students came to believe that the United States was intervening in a civil war, was supporting a corrupt and unpopular government, and was using sophisticated military technology against a peasant population in a third-world country. Large-scale demonstrations against the war surfaced at the University of Michigan, the Berkeley campus of the University of California, the University of Wisconsin, and other colleges and universities throughout the country. "Teach-ins" were held as a way of arousing opposition to U.S. conduct of the war. Marches and demonstrations were staged in major cities and college towns throughout the country, petitions were sent to representatives in Congress, and a series of radical publications emerged to question the legitimacy of public authorities and the militaristic emphasis in American life. The trauma of America's involvement in Vietnam was reflected in the caption on the cover of *Ramparts* magazine in April 1969: "Alienation is when your country is at war and you want the other side to win."

The veterans of World War II were appalled at news reports of young Americans burning their draft cards and burning the American flag. The older generation had not questioned the legitimacy of the requirement to serve in the armed forces during times of war. When college students were no longer deferred from military service, several thousand young Americans expressed their disenchantment by crossing the border into Canada and renouncing their citizenship. The students were not unwilling to make a personal sacrifice for their country, but they perceived it an absurdity to risk making the ultimate sacrifice for a cause they believed unjust. Renouncing their citizenship and going to live permanently in another country is not a step that most Americans are able to take lightly.

Many of the draft-age males who avoided military service were able to do so not because they had moral concerns about the war but because they could take advantage of the system. Very few students at private schools such as Harvard, Yale, or Princeton were conscripted into military service. Accepting the terms of compulsory military service was frequently regarded as stupid. Many who had reservations about the war regarded finding the loopholes as the smart thing to do. The families of privileged youth were influential in obtaining deferments and exemptions. They knew how to draw upon legal technicalities and how to select military alternatives to potential combat assignments. However, requests for exemption on the grounds of being a conscientious objector were frequently denied. Being a conscientious objector to a specific war was not regarded as a legitimate ground for avoiding military service.

The nation had become highly polarized by the time of the Democratic convention in Chicago in 1968. Thousands of protesters from all over the country converged on Chicago to register their opposition to the war. Upon instructions from Mayor Richard J. Daley, the Chicago police were determined to maintain order in the city. On a hot summer night, widespread conflict broke out between the protesters and the police, who used tear gas and clubs in their assaults on the demonstrators. A subsequent presidential commission investigating the violence surrounding the Democratic convention concluded that "the police had rioted." The nation watched the brutal confrontation on television and was appalled at what it saw.

Opposition to the war mounted in intensity as the scope of the war was extended. Following President Lyndon Johnson's announcement that bombing raids would be conducted against North Vietnam, active opposition to the war increased. Some saw the loss of civilian lives from the bombing raids as a further reflection of the immorality of the war. The opposition to the war reached a peak in early May 1970 with President Nixon's announcement of American plans for conducting bombing raids on Cambodia. The concentration of Vietcong forces in Cambodia permitted them to strike American targets and then withdraw rapidly to the safety of a "neutral" country. Those opposed to the war regarded Nixon's announcement as a statement of intent to broaden the war in Southeast Asia rather than to contain it. Demonstrations erupted on college campuses throughout the country.

At Kent State University in Ohio, students protesting the war had burned down a World War II Quonset hut that housed the Reserve Officers Training Corp (ROTC) unit on campus. When the demonstrations spilled over into the town of Kent, the Ohio National Guard was called in to restore and maintain order. The National Guard unit was armed and in response to the tense situation started firing indiscriminately into the students on campus. Four students were killed, and several others were wounded. As the news spread, campuses were disrupted throughout the country. Many colleges and universities were required to suspend normal operations for several days.

The episode at Kent State University became one of the symbolic events of a turbulent decade—and not only because of its immediate impact on college campuses. It also provided a focus for the issues of war and peace, the crisis of authority in modern social life, and the rights of freedom of speech and dissent in an open society. Many of the colleges and universities in the United States were disrupted by student demonstrations and protest. Students were responding not only to the moral issues of the war, but also to the actions of the police and the National Guard on college campuses. Many of those who opposed the war saw the actions of the Ohio National Guard as a form of criminal conduct, the resources of the state being drawn upon to deny individuals their constitutional rights.

The casualties of the war mounted and the purpose of the war became increasingly unclear. In November 1969 approximately 250,000 protesters marched on Washington, DC. It was one of the largest demonstrations in the nation's history. The protesters favored immediate withdrawal of American troops from Vietnam. One of the dramatic features of the demonstration involved veterans who had returned from the war. Several who had been wounded in Vietnam participated in the demonstration by walking on their crutches or riding in wheelchairs. Some who were decorated for valor in Vietnam took off their medals and threw them over the barrier that had been erected to protect the nation's capital. The veterans were symbolically returning their medals to the leaders of the country that had honored them.

Subsequent opposition to the war in Vietnam was based less on the issues raised by demonstrators and protesters than on a recognition that the United States was not winning the war. The escalation of military efforts turned out to be unsuccessful, and since the war could not be won easily by stepping up military operations, many people arrived at the conclusion that we should find a way to get out. Many Americans remembered the moving lines across Europe as the Allies launched their assault on the forces of Nazi Germany. The closer the battle line came to Berlin, the closer the Allies were to winning the war. There were no comparable gauges for assessing progress in Vietnam. The military had drawn upon the body count as a measure of progress, but to the general public it was becoming increasingly evident that the United States was getting no closer to winning the war.

Post-Traumatic Stress Syndrome

The tragedy of the Vietnam War continued for years after the war was over. The veterans returned to an ungrateful nation. The United States had lost the war, and there were deep divisions within the society over whether or not we should have been there in the first place. Americans had grown weary of seeing death and misery each night in the television news broadcasts. Most Americans just wanted to forget about the war. Many of the returning veterans who had actively participated in the war, however, could not forget about it.

The returning warriors were victimized both by their tragic experiences in

Vietnam and by the responses of an unsupportive nation. The trauma of the war continued in recurrent nightmares, in the resurgence of intense feelings of sadness, and in an enduring sense of numbness. Psychologically, the veterans were still fighting the Vietcong and dodging land mines. The veterans were also victimized by returning home to face such negative stereotypes as "ruthless baby-killer," "drug addict," and "having fought in an immoral war." There was a lack of appreciation both by the general public and the American government. The nation wanted to put the trauma of the war behind and get on with the business of restoring normality.

The homecoming for the Vietnam veteran was a highly atomistic event. There were no community ceremonies or rituals, there were no parades or marching bands, there were no cheering crowds, there were no tears of joy, there were no yellow ribbons tied around the trees. The returning veterans were treated casually by others in the community, as if they had been away on vacation. They were expected to behave as if nothing had happened. The nation did not want to be reminded of its disastrous defeat in Vietnam.

The ending of all wars requires some degree of "ritualistic purification" of the returning veteran. The normal guidelines for morality, decency, and humanity become suspended in the war enterprise. Because of what is required in war, the soldier necessarily becomes a changed person. Enduring effects on the individual result from facing death through receiving fire from the enemy, killing someone, seeing someone wounded, or observing gruesome enemy tactics. Such extraordinary experiences fall outside the boundaries of normal life and must be dealt with in some way. At the end of World War II, the victory celebrations helped to "purify" the men who had been required to kill other human beings. There were no such communal forms of purification for the veterans returning from Vietnam.

The veterans returning from Vietnam found themselves disproportionately among the unemployed and the underemployed. Many of them had never been in the labor force prior to military service and did not have a job to return to. The skills developed in the service, particularly among combat veterans, lacked transferability to civilian jobs. To a very large degree, the veterans were ignored by their government and stigmatized by potential employers. A former helicopter pilot was requested to take off his coat so a potential employer could see if there was evidence of needle marks from taking drugs; a nurse who had served in a medical combat unit in Vietnam was assigned to emptying bedpans in a civilian hospital. Thus, self-fulfilling prophecies about the veterans' personal qualifications tended to work against them. There were no special government provisions for helping veterans find a place for themselves in the civilian labor force.

Many of the veterans returned to their hometowns torn and confused about their participation in the war. Uncertainties persisted about what they were doing there and why they did not win. The stress of having participated in the war was expressed in a variety of physical and psychological symptoms. Many veterans developed sleep disturbances, such as difficulty in getting to sleep, waking too early in the morning, or sleeping too much. Sleep was frequently disrupted by recurrent nightmares in which the veterans saw themselves dodging land mines and booby traps, encountering ambushes, watching their buddies die, or witnessing or participating in atrocities. Thus, the war did not end for many of the veterans with their return to civilian life. The problems remained of reconstructing their experiences and their self-identities.

Many of the returning veterans had difficulty in "forgetting" unwanted memories. These included the indelible effects of exploding mortar rounds, which resulted in the tendency in civilian life to overreact to sudden loud noises; recurring visions of comrades cutting ears off enemy corpses as trophies of war; and the pungent odor of decaying corpses in the hot jungles of Vietnam. The memories were also vivid of the blunders of war: comrades were killed by "friendly fire," tanks ran over infantrymen, helicopters accidentally crashed, and marines shot other marines by mistake. These and many other types of accidents are the inevitable consequences of arming large numbers of young men with the lethal and complicated weapons of war.

The returning veterans were faced with difficulties in sharing their war experiences with others. They found themselves in physical proximity to others while psychologically feeling far away. Conversations became strained for both those doing the talking and those doing the listening. Many experiences were too painful to talk about, and family members and former friends did not know how to relate to the returning warriors. Either too much or too little was being read into the messages received from each other. The war experiences had been too disconnected from any shared set of social norms or values to permit effective communication. The veterans became psychologically isolated and thrown back on their own fragile resources at the very time they were in need of social support.

The post-traumatic stress syndrome included persistent feelings of sadness or "emptiness," an inability to derive pleasure from everyday activities, difficulty in concentrating or making decisions, feelings of guilt and worthlessness, eating disorders, thoughts of suicide, and chronic aches and pains that did not respond to treatment. The war veterans were disproportionately represented among alcoholics, hospital patients, the divorced, and prison inmates.

The very conditions that had facilitated psychological adjustment to a combat situation interfered with effective reentry into civilian life. For example, coping with the trauma of war is facilitated by what psychiatrists call the process of psychological numbing. Neutralizing one's emotional responses to the trauma of war serves as a buffer against being incapacitated by the unfolding of events. While soldiers cannot control the occurrence of gruesome events, they can control their responses by developing a sense of emotional neutrality. But in civilian life, the process of psychological numbing lost its usefulness.

Many of the veterans returning from Vietnam had difficulty in forming and sustaining intimate relationships with family members, old friends, and members of the opposite sex. To a very large degree, the difficulties grew out of the loss of a capacity for emotional expressiveness. The basic training in the army and the marine corps required recruits to extinguish expressions of emotion. Emotionality was seen as a feminine characteristic that had no place in the macho world of the military. As one platoon sergeant put it, "Sentiment is a word in the dictionary somewhere between shit and suicide." Later, in combat situations, emotional attachments to other members of the unit were dysfunctional to the adjustment process. Developing attitudes of emotional neutrality became a protective mechanism by which individual soldiers could develop immunity to the potentially devastating effects of war and destruction.

Feeling guilty about being alive was a frequent response of soldiers who survived combat. Some degree of survivor guilt surfaces in questions such as "Why do some men continue to live while others are killed?" and "Why him and not me?" The guilt grows out of the chaos of war. There is a certain amount of randomness to the casualties of war. Stepping on a land mine or being killed in a firefight is, to a large degree, a chance occurrence. Who lives and who dies fails to follow any discernible pattern of divine justice or any set of notions about what is right or wrong in human affairs.

In previous wars, concerns for the symptoms of traumatic stress were directed primarily toward the performance of the soldier in a combat situation. Some saw psychiatric disorders as growing out of a lack of discipline, a weak character, inadequate military socialization, or cowardice. Others regarded disorders of the mind as stemming from the physiological effects of war on the human body. In World War I, the term "shell shock" was employed on the assumption that traumatic stress was caused by high air pressure from exploding shells that affected the brain or caused physical damage to the nervous system. During World War II, the label was changed to "war neurosis" or "combat fatigue." These terms were used to label all psychological disturbances in combat soldiers. Treatment was oriented toward returning soldiers to their units. Very little attention was directed toward the psychological problems of veterans once the war was over.

The war in Vietnam was different. The symptoms of traumatic stress persisted and were widespread for veterans who returned to the United States. The reported number of psychiatric disorders was greater after the war than during it. Prolonged exposure to feelings of entrapment and danger had enduring consequences. While the veterans of all wars are faced with the problem of integrating their war experiences into their overall life designs, the veterans of Vietnam confronted a special set of difficulties. They had confronted events that were outside the usual range of human experiences as well as outside the usual American experiences with war. They found it difficult to set their mind at ease and to find their place within the normal scheme of everyday life.

The Vietnam Veterans Memorial

The nation wanted to forget about the war, as it had forgotten the Korean conflict, but the men and women who served and their families could not. Some degree of closure to the trauma of Vietnam was needed. Such closure in previous wars had been achieved by raising monuments to celebrate the victories that had been won, to idealize the bravery and heroism of those who served, and to promote the themes of personal sacrifice and moral community. The ending of the Vietnam War was different. We had no victories to celebrate. The United States had made a major national commitment to a war that was controversial and morally questionable, to a war we had lost.

Some form of redemption was needed to provide relief for a traumatized nation. While there had been deep divisions over the conduct of the war, there was also empathy for those who had responded to the call for duty and had died. Some form of recognition was needed for the supreme sacrifices that individuals had made on the fields of battle. Some men and women had voluntarily served out of a sense of duty; others had been coerced into servicing the personnel needs of the war machine. Whatever the case, it was clear that hundreds of thousands had innocently carried out the policies of their elected leaders.

With the dedication of the Vietnam Veterans Memorial in 1982, the nation was finally provided with a form of commemoration to facilitate reflections on the meaning of the war. The memorial was designed by Maya Lin to be silent and politically neutral on the controversial issues of the war. The responses of those who came to see the memorial were highly emotional and far from being personally subdued or politically neutral. At an emotional moment in the dedication ceremony, the bitter voice of a veteran cried out, "What were we fighting for?" No attempt was made to give a satisfactory answer to his question.

The memorial is located on a two-acre plot on the edge of the National Mall, artistically in alignment with both the Lincoln Memorial and the Washington Monument. The symbolic structure is a V-shaped granite wall with the engraved names of the 53,000 Americans who died in the war. The wall slopes downward into the ground, symbolizing death, in contrast to the upward thrust of the other memorials in Washington. The memorial is not a celebration of military victories, heroism, a noble cause, or political idealism. Instead, the symbolism is focused on the grimness and the suffering associated with the casualties of war. Listing the names chronologically by the time of death, rather than alphabetically, intensifies the emotional drama of the wall. The wall is low at the beginning and the end but high in the middle, reflecting the number and chronology of the fatalities in Vietnam. Finding a specific name requires personal effort and evokes an awareness of the thousands of Americans who also made the ultimate sacrifice.

Despite the initial criticism of the memorial as "a degrading ditch," "an open urinal," "a gash of shame," or "a wailing wall," it was soon to become a sacred place. No one could have anticipated the emotional impact the wall would have on the millions of visitors who come each year. In the first year alone, 2.5 million Americans made a pilgrimage to the wall. Hundreds of thousands came to look for the name of a loved one, a family member, a friend, or an army buddy. Both those who had actively participated in or supported the war and those who had opposed it came, and they all wept.

Visitors to the Vietnam Veterans Memorial see their own reflections in the black granite wall. The wall not only reveals the names of the casualties of the war, but also provides a mirrored image of what is taking place among those viewing the wall. Such effects do not lend themselves to indifference. The reflections on the wall allow the anger, the hostility, and the ambivalence about the war to surface in a therapeutic fashion. Rather than blocking out memories of the war, the wall brings them temporarily to the surface in a gentle, reflective way. The commemoration thus provides a mechanism for Americans to reflect on the sacrifices that were made through the nation's involvement in a chaotic and meaningless war. It also permits the Vietnam generation to reflect on what they were doing during the war and the part they personally had to play.

More than thirty years after the fall of Saigon, there were still deep divisions within the nation over the Vietnam War. For example, in the presidential campaign of 2004, charges and countercharges were made about the military service of the candidates during the war. Although John Kerry was decorated for valor, unsubstantiated claims were made about whether he deserved the medals that he was awarded. While George W. Bush was able to avoid combat by serving in the National Guard, questions were raised about his missing records and whether he had actually completed his military commitment. The passing of a generation may be required before national closure can be obtained on the Vietnam controversy.

Discussion Questions

1. What were some of the major ways the Vietnam War became a national trauma?
2. Why was our military capability of winning World War III not applicable to the war in Vietnam?
3. Was the war trauma any more severe for soldiers in Vietnam than for soldiers in any other war? Why or why not?
4. What are some of the implications of the trial of Lieutenant Calley for the conduct of soldiers in subsequent wars?
5. Why were Americans so deeply divided over the Vietnam War?
6. What is meant by the term "post-traumatic stress syndrome," and how is it applicable to Vietnam veterans?
7. What accounts for the intense emotional response of Americans visiting the Vietnam Veterans Memorial?
8. Discuss the relevance of service in Vietnam (or avoiding service in Vietnam) for the presidential election of 2004. Did this concern have an effect on the outcome of the election? How so?

7 • Political Assassinations of the 1960s

The 1960s was one of the most turbulent decades in American history. The cultural wars were heating up with the introduction of the birth control pill and the availability of legal abortions. The youth of the nation were engaged in rebellion and the promotion of alternative lifestyles. The future did not look very bright, given the trauma of the Cuban missile crisis and the threat of nuclear war. The conflict over the Vietnam War intensified and the civil rights movement encountered a great deal of violent opposition.

It was within this context that the assassination of some of America's youngest and brightest political leaders had severe traumatic effects on the nation. Americans were in a state of shock with the news on November 22, 1963, that President John F. Kennedy had been shot. The orderliness and predictability of social life were shattered, a tragedy of epic proportions was unfolding, and there was a great deal of uncertainty about what would happen next. Throughout the nation, individuals expressed their feelings of shock, disbelief, and horror. Some were stunned to the point of silence, while others wept without embarrassment in expressing their sense of grief.

The initial shock was followed by a sense of national vulnerability. Some felt that the assassination was a forerunner of similar disturbing events to follow. Memories of the Cuban missile crisis and the threat of nuclear war were still vivid. People worried whether the assassination was a self-contained event or an indicator of additional tragedies to come.

Within hours, it was established that the shots had come from the sixth floor of the Texas School Book Depository and that the suspect was Lee Harvey Oswald. News accounts were then directed toward his background. Oswald was identified as a misfit and troublemaker who had twice been court-martialed as a marine. It was noted that he had formerly renounced his U.S. citizenship and traveled to Russia, only to later return to the United States with a wife and a baby daughter. His violent action was understood as growing out of a generalized sense of rage and disaffection. Yet there remained some uncertainty about his ties to the Soviet Union and his earlier expression of pro-Castro sentiments.

The sadness on the part of Americans was accompanied by expressions of grief worldwide. In Tokyo, Japan, Buddhist priests offered prayers before a portrait of Kennedy; Nairobi, Kenya, issued a proclamation of pain; news bulletins were displayed on the streets of Seoul, Korea; flags were flown at half-staff in London, England; and mourners marched in commemorative torch parades in Berlin, Germany, and in Bern, Switzerland. President Kennedy had captured the hopes and aspirations not only of Americans but also of the peoples of the world. Berliners recalled the help provided by Americans during the Berlin Airlift and remembered Kennedy's speech on a visit to Berlin in which he proclaimed "Ich bin ein Berliner." People around the world felt they had lost a personal friend and experienced some degree of insecurity with the loss of a world leader.

On Sunday morning, November 24, church bells tolled across the country as millions of Americans went to their places of worship to pray. After the emotional drain of the weekend, the day promised to be one of quiet reflections on the tragic events; however, it turned out otherwise. In Dallas, the television cameras were covering the transfer of Oswald from the city prison to the county jail. The nation was shocked and horrified to witness on live television the shooting of Oswald by Jack Ruby. Thus, a trial for determining Oswald's guilt or innocence was precluded.

The lack of clarity surrounding Ruby's motives was to plague the nation for years to come. Was Ruby acting on behalf of someone else? How did Ruby get through the security guard around Oswald? Were the Dallas police negligent in allowing this to happen? The perceived vulnerability of the nation to further unexpected and tragic events continued to build. The stability of the social order seemed to be breaking down.

The nation was engrossed in television coverage of the funeral ceremony at St. Matthew's Cathedral and the subsequent funeral procession to Arlington Cemetery. The funeral march was embellished by an honor guard, muffled drums, a horse-drawn caisson bearing the casket, and a riderless horse with empty boots reversed in the stirrups. The dignity of the ceremony and the symbolism of the funeral march were accompanied by intense feelings of sadness.

Many heads of state came to Washington to pay their respects and to share in the tragedy. The funeral procession, which was three miles long, included such world figures as General Charles de Gaulle of France, Emperor Haile Selassie of Ethiopia, and the presidents of the Philippines and South Korea. Emissaries represented nearly all the major noncommunist countries of the world. In some respects, the tragedy of Kennedy's death resulted in one of the most impressive summit meetings in history.

The president's burial in Arlington Cemetery, rather than in the Kennedy family plot in Massachusetts, indicated that he now belonged to the nation and to the world. Since the days of the Civil War, Arlington Cemetery has been a sacred place for ordinary people as well as the famous who made the ultimate sacrifice for their country. The ceremony at the graveside included a twenty-one-gun salute and a flyover of fifty jets to represent the fifty states. After the playing of taps and the folding of the American flag, an emotionally drained nation started thinking about returning to business as usual. In the years that followed, millions of Americans made pilgrimages to Kennedy's grave. Along with the Tomb of the Unknown Soldier and the Lincoln Memorial, Kennedy's grave was to become one of the most sacred places in the consciousness of the nation.

Following Kennedy's death, the sense of grief and mourning was shared by the rich and the powerful as well as the poor and disadvantaged. Kennedy had come to symbolize the hopes and aspirations of the nation in the creation of an agenda that he would no longer be able to implement. His death was out of place, seen as a senseless event that should never have occurred by the standards of what is normal and natural, within the social realm. Kennedy's untimely death precluded the fulfillment of what many saw as his historical destiny.

The Sanctification of Kennedy

The youthfulness of Kennedy added to the intensity of the trauma. He was only forty-three years of age when he was elected president, the youngest man ever elected to that office. He brought to the presidency an aura of youthfulness, vigor, energy, and idealism. The first president born in the twentieth century, he was admired by the youth of the nation and regarded as a spokesman for the new generation. His election elevated politics to a noble enterprise, and Kennedy's style was oriented toward enhancing optimism, idealism, and commitment. To have it all ended at a relatively young age precluded him from fulfilling his political promise. Both his family and the nation were deprived of what he had to offer.

Following his death, the images and memories of Kennedy became selective and more vivid as they took on sacred qualities. As is generally the case when people die, it became taboo to say negative things about Kennedy. Criticism of the man and his tenure in office was no longer socially acceptable. There were no references to the narrow margin by which he had been elected president, nor to the fiasco of the Bay of Pigs invasion, nor to the concerns of many Americans with our growing involvement in Vietnam. In the process of becoming sanctified, Kennedy was removed from the mundane world of practical politics.

Box 7
Symbolic Event: The Kennedy Curse

In the months and years following the president's assassination, Americans identified closely with the tragedies of the Kennedy family. The president's older brother, Joseph Jr., the pilot of an explosive-laden bomber, had been killed during World War II. His sister, Kathleen, had been widowed during the war and subsequently died in a plane crash. The loss of a valued family member, whether from an accidental death or as a casualty of war, is universally a tragic event for the survivors. The tragedies of the death of his children were especially intense for Joseph Kennedy Sr. because of the career aspirations he had held for them. The nation sympathized with the Kennedy family, recognizing that their glories and triumphs had been accompanied by the unfolding of extraordinarily tragic events.

Out of a sense of despair, Robert F. Kennedy once remarked that one would have to go back to the ancient Greek tragedy to find a family that had experienced such mind-boggling calamities. Robert F. Kennedy had been a major confidant and adviser as attorney general in his brother's administration. After his election to the U.S. Senate, Robert Kennedy waged a dynamic campaign during the Democratic presidential primary in 1968. During Kennedy's victory celebration at a hotel in Los Angeles, Sirhan Sirhan waited to carry out a planned assassination. The shock of Senator Kennedy's murder was intensified by the fact that the assassination of Martin Luther King Jr. had occurred just two months previously.

The notion of "the Kennedy curse" was not only embedded in family history, but also believed by many Americans. The scope of the tragedies seemed to defy rational explanations and go far beyond just chance occurrences. The nation was alarmed at the news in 1999 that John F. Kennedy Jr. was missing in a small plane that failed to show up when expected in Hyannis Port. His wife and his wife's sister perished with him in the crash of the plane in the ocean near Martha's Vineyard. The tragedies of the Kennedy family seemed to be without end.

Many people remembered Kennedy's idealism, as expressed in his speech at Rice University in which he announced the national objective of landing a man on the moon before the decade was over. Others remembered his role in negotiating with the Soviet Union a ban on nuclear testing in the atmosphere. He was seen as providing strong, effective leadership in seeking a resolution of the Cuban missile crisis. Still others recalled his style of oratory, which inspired a sense of social consciousness and clearly indicated a personal commitment to making the world a better place. The themes of his speeches drew heavily on "civil religion" by effectively blending references to God and other sacred symbols with patriotic values in attempts to create a sense of moral community.

In popular literature and music, references were made to Abraham Lincoln in the sanctification of Kennedy as the ideal man and the ideal president. Each had been assassinated under conditions of crisis and social tension. In Lincoln's case, the Civil War had recently ended, and his assassination was linked with the thousands of soldiers who had sacrificed their lives on the field of battle. The enormous task of rebuilding a divided nation remained unfinished. The trauma of Lincoln's assassination added to the trauma of the war itself. By elevating Lincoln to the status of a martyr, his assassination provided the world with a sanctified model of what a great leader ought to do in the quest for social justice and human rights.

The experience of Americans with the assassination crisis precluded thinking about either Kennedy or the presidency exclusively in rational, political, or bureaucratic terms. Instead, the positive images many Americans had held of Kennedy before the assassination were elaborated and embellished. Americans came to experience his existence as a unique gift. Emphasis was placed on his intelligence, his good looks, his youth, his wealth, his family background, and his dedication to the American people. In effect, extraordinary qualities were imputed to him.

While Americans are frequently ambivalent about their political leaders, they also tend to surround the office of the presidency with an aura of charisma. The White House is a sacred shrine to Americans, and its occupant symbolically represents the nation. The hopes and aspirations of the nation become vested in the office of the presidency. At the apex of authority, the president is seen as shaping the political agenda of the nation. It is within the president's power to recommend and designate priorities in the allocation of national resources. It is the president's responsibility to serve as the custodian of collective interests in the decision-making process. During times of crisis, the charisma of the officeholder and the charisma of the office provide the raw materials for the creation of a special gift.

Through charismatic identification, Kennedy was looked upon both as "one of us" and as "the best of us." He had a special appeal to the socially disadvantaged and the underprivileged. In contrast to Dwight Eisenhower, who had been seen as a part of the establishment, Kennedy was seen as a leader from the periphery—a man of wealth and influence who had identified with the underprivileged and defined their problems as his problems. During his presidential campaign in West Virginia, he had visited the coalfields and poverty-stricken towns to listen to the people and to propose solutions to their problems. The people of West Virginia responded to his charm, wit, and insight by giving him a decisive victory in the presidential primary. A state whose population was 95 percent non-Catholic clearly demonstrated that a Catholic could be elected as president of the United States.

Who Killed Kennedy?

In the days and weeks following the funeral, attention shifted away from Kennedy's idealism and his political agenda to the circumstances of his assassination. Did Oswald act alone or were there also shots fired from the grassy knoll overlooking the motorcade? Was Oswald just the trigger man for some organized conspiracy? Was Lyndon Johnson implicated in some way? Was there political intrigue on the part of some organized group that condoned the use of violence to achieve its ends? These are questions Americans raised upon hearing the initial news from Dallas. The same questions were raised over and over again for many years afterward.

The immediate task of Lyndon Johnson was to move beyond the tragedy of the assassination and to get on with the business of government. Johnson's success in doing this, however, was limited. The assassination did occur in his home state of Texas, and it was known that his relationship with the Kennedys was something less than friendly. Some suspected that Kennedy intended to drop Johnson as his running mate in the next election. While there was never any evidence that Johnson had anything to do with the assassination, there remained the suspicion that if he were not involved he may have engaged in a cover-up of what he did know.

By presidential order, Johnson created the Warren Commission to investigate the circumstances and causes of Kennedy's death. It did not appear that separate investigations by the Federal Bureau of Investigation (FBI), the state of Texas, congressional committees, or other agencies would be able to resolve adequately the many issues of responsibility that were likely to be involved. Suspicions still prevailed that Oswald may have been a sacrificial victim for either a domestic or a foreign conspiracy. The intent was to establish a blue-ribbon panel of distinguished Americans who would conduct the investigation in a prompt, systematic, authoritative, and dignified manner. Johnson assumed that the investigative report of such a distinguished panel would bring closure to the case and resolve any remaining doubts. Given the emotionality surrounding Kennedy's death, along with the fear and distrust of the Soviet Union, the consequences of any official evidence of communist involvement would have been disastrous. Dangerous capabilities were at the forefront of public perceptions. Hopefully, no evidence of a communist plot would be uncovered.

Those who accepted the lone-gunman theory tended to emphasize either social or psychological explanations of the motives of the assassin. Those who saw Oswald as a social misfit argued that he had been cheated in the marines, felt he was being persecuted, disliked Kennedy's policies, was discontented with the American way of life, and took the president's life for personal vengeance. Such attributions of motives reflected the idea that some individuals have a rough time finding a satisfactory place for themselves in the modern world. They feel that they have received a raw deal from life and tend to strike back by becoming violent. Oswald's horrendous act of violence was thus seen as growing out of the accumulated frustrations of being required to play roles for which his capabilities and interests were limited.

While the report of the Warren Commission provided an official closure to the case, the issue of who killed Kennedy failed to go away. The motivations for the assassination remained sufficiently obscure to generate widespread discussion for many years. The simple notion that a single individual, acting alone, had killed the president was insufficient for many people who were emotionally involved with the event.

Hundreds of books and magazine articles were written, and are still being written, to offer alternative explanations to the official government investigation. Although twenty-six volumes of testimony and exhibits accompanied the Warren report, claims were made that the commission had arrived at its conclusions hastily and had failed to take into account all the relevant information that was available. The basic conclusion of the Warren Commission report that Oswald had killed the president was seen as inadequate, incomplete, and possibly a cover-up.

The arguments for alternatives to the Warren report were often based on the assumption that it is important to set the story straight for the historical record. Accordingly, plausibility arguments were structured in such a fashion as to have the appearance of being believable. Filling in the gaps in the news media coverage and in the Warren report became a widespread preoccupation. The number of bullets fired, the time interval of the firings, the direction that bullets came from, and the number of people involved received close scrutiny. There were also questions raised about the adequacy of the forensic conduct of the autopsy. The speeches of Kennedy were combed for clues on his agenda for the nation and the policies he planned to implement. The question of who killed Kennedy was being transformed into the question of who would have liked to see Kennedy dead.

One of the conspiracy theories held that a combination of J. Edgar Hoover, director of the FBI, and the Mafia were implicated. Allegedly, Hoover had known that a Mafia contract had been issued on the life of President Kennedy and had done nothing about it. The security forces that were assigned to protect the president in Dallas had been surprisingly lax. It was generally known that there was animosity between Hoover and the Kennedys. Hoover had used the resources of the FBI to amass personal files on top political leaders and was in a position to use these files as a form of blackmail. Kennedy resented the capacity of the director of the FBI to intimidate the president of the United States and was seriously considering what could be done about it. While there was no evidence of Hoover's direct involvement in the assassination plot, it was believed that he deliberately had decided not to act on the information available to him.

Conspiracy theorists argued that the military, business corporations, and secret agencies within the government had vested interests in continuing the cold war. The profitability of many corporations was highly dependent on defense contracts, and some of the employees of the Central Intelligence Agency (CIA) would stand to lose if Kennedy's plans for reducing the tensions of the cold war were implemented. Evidence was presented to support plausibility arguments that Kennedy's assassination was plotted by either the CIA or by corporate America. Such arguments were constructed primarily around "motives" for the assassination rather than a concrete demonstration that a plot had occurred.

Conspiracy theorists frequently invited the public to serve as a "jury" to weigh the evidence being presented. In the courtroom metaphor, conspiracy theorists were playing the role of prosecutor. However, the analogy breaks down in an important respect. There was no judge to invoke "the rule of irrelevance." In courtroom proceedings, judges occupy a central place through their authority to decide what is admissible as evidence, to determine what information does or does not have bearing on the specific case. In the absence of judicial restraint, conspiracy theorists set no limits on the claims that they made. Some maintained that Kennedy's body was secretly altered during the flight to Washington to disguise the wounds made by a second gunman. Others claimed that Kennedy's body was not in the coffin buried at Arlington, that Kennedy was still alive, although brain dead and kept in protective custody by the Kennedy family.

The extraordinary responses of Americans to the images of Kennedy were commensurate with the extraordinary responses to his death. The collective sadness over the slaying of the president had temporarily bound the nation together in a moral community. It was both an intensely integrative experience and an intensely disorganizing experience. Keeping alive the Kennedy memory is meaningful to some and met with cynical indifference by others. Cynics find the recurring attention to Kennedy disgusting: The man is dead, and nothing can be done about that. Whatever happened in Dallas on that fateful day may never be known or knowable, and it really does not matter. The time has come to close the case. Others regard Kennedy as the model of a man to emulate. They continue to be intrigued with the mystery of his death and to ponder the question of how the world would have been different had he lived.

The Assassination of Martin Luther King Jr.

On April 4, 1968, the nation was shocked by the news that Martin Luther King Jr. had been shot by a sniper while he stood talking on the balcony of a motel in Memphis, Tennessee. He died shortly afterward in St. Joseph's Hospital from a wound in the neck. He was only thirty-nine years old at the time of his death. King had been in Memphis to lend his support to a strike by sanitation workers. As the symbolic leader of the civil rights movement, he had delivered hundreds of speeches and sermons in the quest for social justice. He had succeeded in transforming the politics of social change into a religious responsibility. The trauma of his assassination brought into sharp focus the epic struggle of the quest for racial equality. He had mobilized a large constituency to address the question of how to bring about an end to the blatant forms of racial discrimination in American society. King had taken a direct-action approach by staging large demonstrations and working within the courts and legislatures to bring about changes that had long been needed.

On the eve of his assassination, King delivered his speech, "I Have Seen the Promised Land." This speech, like several previous ones, contained clear references to a premonition of his own death. He said, "The nation is sick. Trouble is in the land. Confusion is all around." While noting the desirability of living a long life, he observed, "I am not concerned about that now. . . . I have been to the mountain top" and "I have seen the promised land." After saying, "I may not get there with you," he noted that as a people, "we will get to the promised land." Moral and spiritual convictions were combined with a strong belief that history would eventually correct the injustices implicit in the maltreatment of American citizens of African descent.

At the disturbing news of King's death Americans reflected on issues of social justice that had been ignored or glossed over in everyday life. In effect, the civil rights movement held up a mirror in which Americans were able to see themselves, and many did not like what they saw. They saw the ugliness of racial discrimination, and they saw police violence directed toward peaceful demonstrators. What they saw was shocking and appalling. The moral foundation of society was turned upon itself.

The nation was shocked and saddened by the death of an American who had received the Nobel Peace Prize for his contribution to human rights and social justice. The assassination of King occurred only a little more than four years after the assassination of President John F. Kennedy. The moral conscience of the nation was disturbed as Americans made comparisons between Kennedy and King. Both were seen as martyrs with strong convictions, with idealistic visions for the future of the country, and with personal commitments to the cause of social justice.

James Earl Ray was later captured and convicted of King's murder. As with the Warren Commission report on Kennedy's assassination, serious doubts continued to surface for years afterward about the credibility of the official closure of the case. It was noted, for example, that the personal profile of Ray failed to follow the psychological profile of the political assassin and that he had no personal convictions that had bearing on the civil rights movement. Serious questions were raised about whoever else may have been implicated.

Over the years, the suspicion developed that the FBI may have been involved in the assassination. The size of the FBI file on King was larger than the file for any other single individual. J. Edgar Hoover's preoccupation with the communist menace had led to his belief that the social disruptions surrounding the civil rights movement were communist inspired. While no convincing link with communism was ever made, the belief persisted that the struggle over civil rights was a stigma that the United States could not afford because it reduced the government's effectiveness in winning the neutral countries of the world to our side in the cold war. Any challenge to the status quo came to be broadly defined as unpatriotic and thus a threat to American national security. The climate of the cold war did not favor examining the contradictions that were inherent in the American system.

Intense feelings of sadness and anger surfaced within the black community. King's assassination was seen as bearing a close resemblance to the violent, repressive measures that were deeply embedded in patterns of racial discrimination and exclusion. The anger became sufficiently intense that widespread rioting and looting occurred in metropolitan areas throughout the country. Urban areas became volatile powder kegs as pent-up frustrations were expressed through violent and aggressive outlets. The oppressed were no longer able to endure what they perceived as an unjust system.

The assassination of King marked the end of the civil rights movement. Under his leadership, the strategies of nonviolent resistance had resulted in the Civil Rights Act of 1964, ending the most glaring forms of racial discrimination in the public sphere. The enactment of legislation guaranteed blacks their civil liberties and directed all agencies of government to put an end to discriminatory practices. King had demonstrated that the development of a strong, cohesive organization for the protection of minority rights can make a difference. King's symbolic leadership in an epic struggle provided a major reference point for Americans to reflect on issues of social justice and political action.

A Fragmented Society

The militancy of the civil rights movement forced Americans to recognize that the United States had been a highly fragmented society. Decades of oppression, exploitation, and physical abuse had produced routine feelings of fear and anger among African Americans. The unwillingness of blacks to further endure the humiliations that had been imposed upon them produced an acute crisis for those committed to upholding the status quo. The nation became traumatized by having to confront its own internal contradictions.

Segregated schools, buses, lunch counters, swimming pools, rest rooms, and drinking fountains restricted the freedom of movement of black Americans. Discrimination in voter registration, housing, college admissions, and employment relegated blacks to an inferior status. All of these practices reflected deep-seated racism in American life and contradicted the ideology held by those in positions of power and influence that "America is a land of equal opportunity for all."

In mobilizing a constituency, King drew heavily upon two major documents in the heritage of the nation: the Constitution and the Declaration of Independence. These were central ingredients in shaping the national identity of Americans. King described these documents as "promissory notes" that guaranteed "the inalienable rights to life, liberty, and the pursuit of happiness" for all. King declared, however, that America had defaulted on her promissory note to her citizens of color. The words of Jefferson that "we take these truths to be self-evident, that all men are created equal" were taken seriously by King, who regarded them as justifying a call to action.

It was the Montgomery bus boycott that thrust King into a position of national prominence. On December 1, 1955, a black woman named Rosa Parks was ordered by a bus driver in Montgomery, Alabama, to relinquish her seat to a white man. Rosa Parks had spent a hard day at work and was tired. She refused to give up her seat. The bus driver's attempts to intimidate her were unsuccessful and she was arrested. The arrest evoked the anger of African Americans over the preferential treatment of whites and the requirement that blacks sit only in the back seats of buses. Few practices evoked such bitter resentments among blacks as the humiliation of legally sanctioned segregation in public transportation.

The arrest, imprisonment, and conviction of Rosa Parks resulted in meetings of the Montgomery Improvement Association to plan a line of action within the black community. Rather than a compliant acceptance of racial injustice, the association made the decision to seek remedial action through a bus boycott. The local chapter of the National Association for the Advancement of Colored People (NAACP) selected King to provide leadership for the organized protest.

King was only twenty-six years old at the time and was more a privileged than a deprived member of the African American community. He was selected on the basis of his moral commitments, his education, his intelligence, and his speaking ability. As is often the case, leadership of movements among the oppressed comes from the privileged members of society who identify with the plight of the underprivileged.

King's oratory had an electrifying quality about it, not only because of the relevance of what he had to say but also because of his mode of delivery. Following a style of delivery that was prominent among black clergy, he used extensive repetition of central themes and a wide range of voice inflections to maximize the effect. While those opposed to King and the civil rights movement saw him as a dangerous demagogue, his speeches symbolized the hopes and aspirations of his constituents.

The black bus riders' defiance of the Jim Crow laws in Montgomery provoked whites into using terrorist and repressive measures. King was arrested on a trumped-up speeding violation, and a bomb was exploded on the porch of his Montgomery home. The leaders of the bus boycott were charged with being parties to a conspiracy to prevent the operation of a business without "just or legal cause." Attempts were made to terminate car-pooling as an alternative to riding buses. Participants in the boycott were subjected to harassment, and some lost their jobs. The boycott ended with a decision by the U.S. Supreme Court that Alabama's state law requiring racial segregation on buses was unconstitutional. Federal injunctions were issued to state officials as well as to city and bus company officials in Montgomery.

The conflict between local governments and federal authority was a central ingredient in the struggle for civil rights. A major confrontation occurred in Little Rock when the governor of Arkansas attempted to block nine black students from attending an all-white high school. In response to the defiance of federal authority, President Dwight D. Eisenhower federalized the Arkansas National Guard to enforce the U.S. Supreme Court order for school integration. When James Meredith attempted to enroll at the University of Mississippi, it was necessary for him to be escorted to campus by U.S. marshals. Governor George Wallace stood in the doorway to block the entrance of black students to the University of Alabama. President Kennedy had to federalize the Alabama National Guard to enforce the mandate for school integration. The racial caste system in the South was crumbling. Local areas were using stopgap measures to prop up a repressive and unjust system.

Local law enforcement agencies attempted to use the coercive powers of the state to suppress the civil rights movement. The issues became sufficiently dramatic, however, that the entire nation watched the confrontations with a sense of alarm and dismay. Americans watched on television as police used dogs, fire hoses, and other violent means against peaceful demonstrators. The millions of television viewers constituted a type of judiciary whose attention became focused on issues of racism and social justice. Few Americans were able to remain indifferent to what they were observing. The moral conscience of society was turned upon itself.

The civil rights movement succeeded because it was able to involve the entire nation with issues of social justice. The success of King in building a biracial coalition was evident in the number of people who participated in the civil rights march on Washington in 1963. On August 28, King addressed a crowd of more than 200,000 demonstrators who had come to Washington. Speaking in front of the Lincoln Memorial, King laid out his vision for America. In his "I Have a Dream" speech, he emphasized the themes of civil religion. Christian values and spirituality became blended with the ideals of the Declaration of Independence, the Constitution, and the Emancipation Proclamation. He noted that the new militancy of the black community was linked with the destiny of the nation. "Storming the battlements of injustice" was seen as a necessary task for all Americans. He argued that the freedom of black Americans was inextricably linked to freedom for all Americans. He observed that his personal dream was "deeply rooted in the American dream" and that the values he promoted were the values central to the national identity of Americans. He noted, "Injustice anywhere is a threat to justice everywhere."

The credibility of King's arguments was enhanced by his ability to recognize the uncertainty of the outcomes of political protest in any given case. His central theme was that conditions of racism were intolerable. To achieve a sense of personal dignity and pride, African Americans had an obligation to take decisive steps to create a sense of moral community. While organized protest might very well evoke a violent response from the oppressors, it was a risk that was necessary to take. It was clear to his followers that he was asking nothing more of them than he was willing to risk for himself. Imprisonment, death threats, the bombing of his home, and being stabbed were among the forms of intimidation and physical injury that King had personally endured. His refusal to give in to fear and despair inspired his followers and won a sympathetic response from neutral observers throughout the nation.

During the last years of his life, King concluded that the problems of racism were inseparable from the problems of poverty and the violence associated with the war in Vietnam. All were interrelated and, in King's view, equally wrong. The blockage of opportunities for social participation and restrictions on freedom of movement were among the class-related aspects of minority status. Racial minorities were disproportionately caught up in lifestyles of deprivation and poverty. King abhorred the institutional violence associated with the Vietnam War and saw minorities and the poor as disproportionately bearing the brunt of the tragedies involved. In his view, equating patriotism with militarism and war was both unwarranted and a dangerous tradition.

The success of public demonstrations in securing passage of civil rights legislation had suggested that pressure from the grassroots level might be necessary for effectively addressing the problems of poverty and militarism in American life. These were problems that seriously affected all Americans at the lower socioeconomic levels, including whites as well as blacks. Some form of redress was seen as necessary for attenuating the exploitation of some segments of the population for the benefit of others. King had made plans for a "poor people's march" on Washington shortly before his assassination. King hoped the march would develop a recognition of the integrity of the individual personality and increase the opportunities for full participation in a moral community for all Americans, thus enriching the American quality of life.

Strategies of Nonviolent Resistance

The success of the civil rights movement to a very large degree stemmed from the tactics and strategies that King advocated and refined in his efforts to bring about social change. Drawing upon the writings of Henry David Thoreau in the United States and the example set by Mahatma Gandhi in India, King's contribution may be summarized as the notion of nonviolent resistance. Thoreau demonstrated civil disobedience in his writings and in his refusal to pay taxes into a government that supported the institution of slavery. Gandhi incorporated ideas from Thoreau in advocating nonviolent methods for resisting British colonial rule in India.

King advocated deliberately violating laws and practices that were unjust and in violation of basic human rights. The injustices of the system could be demonstrated through disturbing the tranquility of everyday life. Through an appeal to a higher level of morality, the movement underscored and highlighted the underlying defects of the social system. The goal of King's approach was full and equal participation of all citizens in the life of the nation.

The events surrounding the Montgomery bus boycott generated a great deal of attention in India, the Soviet Union, and other nations of the world. The country that had been foremost in promoting a policy of human rights in the United Nations was now required to confront its own contradictions. Following an invitation from Prime Minister Jawaharlal Nehru in 1959, King spent a month in India talking to top government officials and others about the success of the techniques of passive resistance in toppling the British regime. What King found to be remarkable was the manner by which India had won her independence in 1947 without bloodshed and without evoking the hostility of the British. Mahatma Gandhi had succeeded in transforming political conflicts into moral and spiritual issues in order to achieve his objectives.

In his appeal to the oppressed, King emphasized the importance of spiritual values and a demonstration of moral superiority. Warning African Americans not to become distrustful of all white people, he stated, "The battlement of injustice must be carried forth by a bi-racial army." Rather than developing a hatred of the oppressors, blacks should regard whites with compassion. King offered his followers hope as an alternative to despair and self-pride as an alternative to the negative imagery provided by racial stereotypes. The central ingredients of the national identity shared by all citizens, black and white, were the ones that would prevail in the long run. A sense of self-authenticity could be achieved through the discipline of placing one's life on the line for a cause believed to be just.

Open confrontation took a particularly violent turn in the voter registration campaign at Selma, Alabama, in 1965. In Selma, 99 percent of the registered voters were white, although blacks constituted more than half of the population. Literacy tests were used to systematically deny blacks the right to vote, regardless of level of education. Even blacks with a college education were judged to be illiterate by voter registrars. In contrast, the literacy tests were not used in determining the eligibility of whites for voting. When an organized group of blacks marched to the courthouse in Selma to demand the right to vote, they were blocked by law enforcement officials. The demonstrators met with police violence and were forcefully dispersed as television cameras recorded the event for the entire world to see. Evidence of police brutality and an institutional system of oppression became apparent.

In response to the failure in Selma, civil rights organizers decided to conduct a fifty-mile march from Selma to Montgomery to call national attention to the discriminatory voting laws of Alabama. The nation watched with shock as the peaceful demonstrators were met with violent resistance from the sheriff's department and state police at the bridge leading out of Selma. Although the demonstrators were forcefully turned back and dispersed, plans for the march continued. Out of a sense of indignation over the conduct of the police, hundreds of sympathizers descended on Selma to participate in a continuation of the march. In response to pressures from Washington to provide police protection for the demonstrators, local officials maintained that public safety or protection could not be provided for criminals and agitators. President Kennedy then federalized the National Guard of Alabama to provide protection for the demonstrators in their march to Montgomery. The subsequent passage of the Voting Rights Act in August 1965 put an end to the discriminatory practices that had denied blacks the right to participate in the electoral process.

In the campaign to overturn segregation laws in public transportation, "freedom rides" through the South were organized. The laws prohibiting integration of public transportation were deliberately violated by whites riding in the back of buses and by blacks occupying the front seats. Angry crowds gathered and violence erupted when the freedom buses stopped along the way. The nation became indignant as it watched mob action being directed toward peaceful demonstrators while the police looked on passively. The violence of local citizens, however, was regarded by white segregationists as a reasonable and appropriate response to what they defined as criminal conduct.

The tactics of lunch counter sit-ins, swimming pool wade-ins, freedom rides, and voter registration campaigns were initiated to call public attention to discriminatory practices. Since all these actions involved an attack on the existing social order, they became newsworthy events. The television news coverage of these events provided an authenticity to the issues that could not have been attained through other means of communication. Hearing or reading about an event does not have the emotional impact that is provided by the visual materials presented on television. The brutal beatings and the use of tear gas, fire hoses, and police dogs were institutional forms of terror that could not go unnoticed. People were psychologically required to pay attention and to serve as a public judiciary for making decisions on the issues in question. Reflective attitudes were generated, and the holders of power found it necessary to examine their own moral conscience.

The participants in organized social protests cannot alone solve the problems of social injustice. They must win sympathy and support for their cause through an appeal to the mass judiciary of newspaper readers and television viewers who sit in judgment on the issues in question. The participants in the civil rights movement ran the risk of being labeled deviants, criminals, or troublemakers. It was also possible that they could win admiration by becoming champions of a heroic cause and by making personal sacrifices for the improvement of social conditions. Success or failure in the use of nonviolent resistance rested outside the hands of the participants themselves. The final outcomes resided with public opinion and with the responses of social control agencies.

As the level of protest escalated in the civil rights movement, the decision at the higher levels of power was whether to use coercive measures to reduce the level of turmoil or to recognize the need for a more just system. While segregationists favored using coercive measures to suppress dissent, most Americans recognized the legitimacy of the claim that remedial actions were necessary. When Lyndon Johnson presented his arguments for civil rights legislation to Congress, he ended his address with the words of the title of a famous civil rights song, "We Shall Overcome," thus drawing upon the vocabulary of the civil rights movement. National opinion clearly supported ending segregation in the public spheres of life, but fell short in favoring full equality in the nonpublic spheres. The most blatant forms of discrimination had ended by the time of King's assassination, while deep-seated attitudes of racism continued to be held.

With the subsequent designation of King's birthday as a national holiday, formal recognition was given to the importance of social justice in the life of the nation. On the anniversary of his birth, the news media tap into collective memories by selectively reproducing his speeches and showing photographs of civil rights demonstrations and marches. In reflecting on the issue of race, a good deal of attention is directed toward King's question, "Where do we go from here?" An unfinished task is that of working out a satisfactory resolution to the racial and ethnic diversity of the nation in view of deep-seated resistance, among both minorities and the more privileged sectors of society, to a policy of full assimilation.

In King's speech before the Lincoln Memorial, he observed, "I have a dream that my four children will one day live in a nation where they will not be judged by the color of their skin but by the content of their character." This implied a hope that the dignity and integrity of individual personalities would be recognized without regard for race, ethnicity, or other social characteristics that are often used to separate people from each other. King's vision was based on the notion that we are all interrelated. The freedoms and opportunities of individuals are intertwined with the forces that bind the nation into a sense of moral community.

Discussion Questions

1. What accounts for the intensity of the emotional responses throughout the country to the assassination of President Kennedy?
2. Describe the process by which the death of Kennedy contributed to his sanctification.
3. Why was there such a widespread rejection of the Warren Commission report that a lone gunman was responsible for the death of President Kennedy?
4. What is the basis for beliefs in "the Kennedy curse"? What is a curse?
5. How did the television coverage of the civil rights movement contribute to its success?
6. Why were the strategies of nonviolent resistance so effective in advancing the quest for social justice?
7. Did the Civil Rights Act of 1964 put an end to racial discrimination in the United States? Please justify your answer.
8. Why was the birthday of Martin Luther King Jr. designated as a national holiday?

8 • The Watergate Affair

High crimes and misdemeanors, the obstruction of justice, and the abuse of power were among the Articles of Impeachment against President Nixon that were passed by the House Judiciary Committee in 1974. A vote on these articles by the full House of Representatives was precluded by Nixon's resignation. Most Americans followed the episodes surrounding the Watergate scandal as though they were watching a detective fiction story or a morality play unfold. Through his resignation, Richard Nixon had precluded attaining a place for himself among the legacies of such men as Franklin D. Roosevelt, Harry S. Truman, Dwight D. Eisenhower, and John F. Kennedy. The tale that unfolded seemed fictional, incredible, and unbelievable.

Criminality is usually associated with street crimes in the thinking of most Americans. They could not readily comprehend the notion that the president of the United States was a "criminal." Elements of both belief and disbelief blended in public perceptions. After all, Nixon's presidential election campaign of 1972 had drawn upon the latent fears of Americans about potential criminal victimization through burglary, robbery, and other street crimes. The notion that the man who had waged a "law-and-order" campaign might himself be a criminal was shocking.

The Watergate affair was characterized by a gradual development and a slow beginning. Newspaper reports in June 1972 indicated that burglars had been caught breaking into the Democratic Party headquarters located in the Watergate apartment–office complex in Washington, DC. There was nothing unusually noteworthy about this. On a daily basis, newspapers are filled with such stories about minor offenses. Why anyone would want to break into the Democratic headquarters and what the burglars expected to accomplish were initially questions of only minor concern.

The term "Watergate," however, eventually entered into the American vocabulary as a synonym for scandal and political corruption among government officials. While Watergate, in and of itself, was only a limited affair, it subsequently became symbolic of a broader series of illegal activities. Before the scandal ran its course, such terms as "dirty tricks," "political espionage," "illegal wiretaps," "smoking guns," "stonewalling," "hanging tough," "cover-up," and "hit list" worked their way into everyday vocabularies. It was not the Watergate affair that produced a national trauma, but the scope of the criminal conduct among the staff and associates of the president of the United States.

The Democrats attempted to make the break-in an issue in the 1972 presidential election campaign, but were unsuccessful. Democratic presidential candidate George McGovern claimed that tapping phone conversations in the Watergate break-in was a form of political espionage that undermined the democratic process and should not be tolerated. Such a claim, however, was not taken seriously by the voters. It appeared to be a desperate strategy on the part of a man who was far behind in the polls. On Election Day, McGovern carried only the state of Massachusetts and the District of Columbia.

The plot thickened during the subsequent trial and conviction of the five men who had been caught in the burglary. These men exhibited skills for engaging in criminal activities, such as unlawful entry and wiretapping, that had not been learned casually or accidentally; they were as refined and elaborate as those of the agents who engaged in the covert activities of our national security system. What were the motives of these men? Why did they break into the Watergate? Who were they working for? Whose orders were being followed? In effect, suspicions developed that the Watergate break-in represented only a small part of a much larger scandal. Much more had to be involved.

The staff at the *Washington Post* recognized that there was an important story that needed to be told. Accordingly, two reporters, Bob Woodward and Carl Bernstein, were assigned to investigate the episode on a full-time basis. Their phone calls and interviews with government employees revealed evidence of a vast cover-up of illegal activities at the center of power, evidence suggesting that the Watergate burglary was not an isolated event. It turned out to be only a small part of the illegal activities that had surrounded Nixon's reelection campaign.

Woodward and Bernstein encountered a great deal of resistance in their attempts to interview government employees. A tense atmosphere prevailed in Washington, and many government employees were afraid to reveal what they knew. Jobs were at stake and individual employees ran the risk of personal humiliation. A break in the case came with the release of information by a single informant, to whom the reporters gave the code name "Deep Throat." Their informant occupied a central position in the White House branch of the government. As a person of integrity, the informant was uneasy about what was going on and held the personal conviction that the nation had a right to know. In May 2005, after maintaining his silence for more than thirty years, a high-ranking FBI official during the Nixon administration revealed that he was Deep Throat. W. Mark Felt's identity was later confirmed by Woodward and Bernstein.

High Crimes and Misdemeanors

In addition to treason and bribery, the U.S. Constitution designates high crimes and misdemeanors as grounds for impeachment. While the Constitution was deliberately silent on the specific offenses that constitute high crimes and misdemeanors, it is clear that the abuse of power and obstruction of justice would be included. The House of Representatives has the power to vote impeachment, while the Senate has the authority for trial and conviction. Thus in response to criminal conduct by top government officials, Congress serves as a federal judiciary.

In addition to the criminality of the Watergate episode, the Campaign to Re-Elect the President (CRP) had engaged in subversive activities during the election campaign of 1972. Recognizing that serious problems were developing, many records and written documents were shredded by the CRP staff to minimize the risk of anyone establishing a link between the Watergate burglary and the political campaign.

Investigations by news journalists and an independent federal judiciary revealed that political espionage had been used during the Democratic primaries to discredit and humiliate Senator Edmund Muskie of Maine, who was seen as a formidable candidate in the upcoming election. Reports of the investigations revealed that corporations making large contributions to Nixon's reelection campaign were given preferential treatment in awarding defense contracts. Additionally, CRP had spent large amounts of cash without any formal accounting procedures. The methods of obtaining and keeping secret files on members of Congress and on individuals designated as enemies of the White House had been illegal and undermined the democratic process.

In the thinking of Richard Nixon and his associates, the metaphor of "war" was applied to the political campaign. The domestic enemies in the war consisted of all those opposed to Nixon's leadership or his policies. In the White House, an elaborate plan was devised for dealing with those whose names made the "enemies list." Men from the CIA and Nixon's immediate circle of advisers elaborated strategies for conducting covert operations, labeled "dirty tricks." The plans included infiltrating the headquarters of each of the Democratic contenders, tapping their phones, stealing their stationery, forging signatures, and making photocopies of their written documents. Further plans included the use of the Internal Revenue Service (IRS) for harassment and leaking information to the press that would discredit specific individuals, including unwarranted allegations about drunk driving and sexual misconduct.

The domestic foes included not only leaders of the political opposition, but also employees of the government who leaked information to the press about questionable government operations. Foremost among these was Daniel Ellsberg, who leaked the Pentagon Papers to the *New York Times*. The Pentagon Papers revealed that many forms of deception and misrepresentation had been employed by both military and political officials to cover up blunders during the Vietnam War. President Nixon was outraged. He saw loyalty to his administration as a primary responsibility of all government employees. Anything that would reflect negatively upon government policies was seen as subversive. Accordingly, a unit designated as the "plumbers" was created to prevent the leak of information to the press about government operations. Special efforts were made to embarrass and discredit Ellsberg; for example, the plumbers broke into his psychiatrist's office to uncover information about him that would be personally damaging.

Several critical events unfolded to establish links between the White House and the Watergate burglary. The first was an announcement from Judge John J. Sirica that he had received a letter from James McCord, one of the men convicted of the Watergate break-in. McCord's letter indicated that the defendants had been paid to maintain their silence, that they had committed perjury, and that numerous participants in the episode had not yet been identified. Before the case ran its course, McCord and several others expressed concern about becoming scapegoats in efforts to conceal the involvement of top government officials. Serious crimes had been detected, and now someone would have to pay the price by becoming the sacrificial lamb.

Successful leaders frequently are able to remain aloof from the unsavory work that is required in politics. The dirty work may be delegated to subordinates who are less visible and thus able to work in an underhanded way without being detected. While denying any White House involvement in the Watergate affair, the president attempted to use the CIA to circumvent an investigation by the FBI that was initiated by the federal judiciary. In effect, he was using one agency of the government to prevent another agency from doing its job. Such an attempt to obstruct justice suggested desperate efforts at concealment and cover-up. Eventually, it was Nixon's persistence in concealment and cover-up that resulted in the charge of obstruction of justice in the articles of impeachment that were drafted by the House Judiciary Committee.

After the evidence became clear that members of the White House staff were involved in attempts to cover up the Watergate affair, the Senate initiated its own investigation. Public opinion polls were indicating a rapid erosion of public trust in Nixon's leadership. A member of the White House staff, John Dean, was granted immunity to tell the Senate Watergate Committee in televised hearings what he knew about the cover-up. In a lengthy prepared statement, Dean testified that both the president and his aides had participated in attempts to stonewall the Watergate investigation.

Some of the Republicans on the Senate Watergate Committee took extreme measures to discredit Dean's testimony. Each question and each answer was closely monitored within an adversarial context. Dean was a ready-made target as the first high-ranking official to reveal his own illegal activities and those of other members of the White House staff. There was a great deal of uneasiness both within the government and within the general public. The substantive issues of Nixon's complicity were far from being settled.

As Dean's testimony unfolded, the nation responded with astonishment. Both those who had voted for Nixon and those who voted against him felt betrayed. Divided opinion was reflected in the debates that took place throughout the country. Stalwart supporters of Nixon could not believe the accusations that were made against him. Americans have the freedom to criticize the president of the United States in any way they wish, but the discourse was seen by some as sinking to new levels.

Determining "what the president knew and when he knew it" was foremost in the minds of many people. Dean's allegations stood in sharp contrast to Nixon's persistent denials. The president had previously announced publicly that an investigation from his office indicated that no member of the White House staff was involved. Whom should one believe, Dean or Nixon? An answer came through the testimony of Alexander Butterfield, a former White House aide. Butterfield revealed that a sophisticated recording system had been installed in the White House early in 1971 for recording all conversations and phone calls. Certainly, the recording of all conversations in the White House would indicate whether the president was involved. The tapes potentially contained the "smoking gun" for implicating the president.

Both the special prosecutor, Archibald Cox, and the Senate Watergate Committee issued a subpoena for the White House tapes. It was the first time a subpoena had been issued to the president of the United States since the administration of Thomas Jefferson. Nixon refused to comply on the ground of executive privilege. He maintained that the tapes were confidential and the exclusive property of the president. When Cox insisted, Nixon ordered Attorney General Elliot Richardson to fire him. Richardson's refusal resulted in what came to be called the "Saturday-night massacre." Nixon removed from office both Richardson and his deputy, William Ruckelshaus, who also had refused to fire Cox. Solicitor General Robert Bork carried out Nixon's order by firing Cox and sealing the records in the special prosecutor's office.

Public outrage at this abuse of power resulted in further demands that Nixon release the tapes and that a new Watergate prosecutor be appointed.

As the pressure for the release of the tapes mounted, the impasse was resolved by placing the case before the U.S. Supreme Court. As a last-ditch effort, Nixon was convinced that the court would rule in favor of the principle of executive privilege. The Court did not. In a unanimous decision, the Court ruled that Nixon must turn over the tapes as requested by the special Watergate prosecutor and by the Senate committee. Nixon responded by agreeing to release a transcript of the tapes, with only irrelevancies deleted, but not the tapes themselves. The proposal of releasing only an edited transcript was rejected by the judiciary. Nothing short of a release of the tapes themselves would be acceptable. Even the president of the United States must comply with an order issued by the Supreme Court.

When the tapes were finally released, eighteen minutes of a conversation, taped shortly after the Watergate burglary, had been erased. However, the tapes clearly indicated that the president had knowledge of the attempted cover-up from the very beginning and had participated in it. The nation was shocked by the vulgarity of the conversations among those in the inner circle at the White House and by what they were talking about. Clearly those at the center of power saw themselves as standing above the law as they planned clandestine operations against individuals and against other agencies of the government. The evidence was now clear that Nixon had participated in an obstruction of justice and thus had violated his oath of office.

In the midst of the heightened ethical scrutiny of political conduct in Washington, Spiro Agnew resigned as vice president of the United States on October 10, 1973. Unrelated to Watergate, an investigation by the FBI indicated that Agnew had been implicated in criminal activity during the course of his political career. The evidence seemed clear that Agnew had violated public positions of trust by accepting kickbacks from contractors and bribes from corporations while he was governor of Maryland. Further, there was evidence that he had failed to report and pay income tax on the funds he had received. With his resignation as vice president, he pleaded no contest to tax evasion and received a three-year suspended prison term.

Nixon's popularity plummeted with the growing revelations of the pervasive political corruption in his administration. John Mitchell, the former attorney general who served as chair of the CRP, was revealed as a man who lacked scruples and was subsequently convicted of perjury and sent to prison. Before the Watergate affair was over, twenty-five of Nixon's aides and confidants, including three former cabinet members, were charged and convicted of criminal conduct.

Those having a serious interest in American politics quickly saw a threat to the American system of government. The crimes of the Nixon administration had been exposed, and if they were ignored, all future presidents could consider themselves free to arbitrarily abuse the power that was inherent in the office. A failure to act when action was necessary would set a precedent for transforming the American system of government. Either the president would have to resign or he would have to be impeached and legally removed from office.

The move to impeach a president is a serious undertaking. Prior to the impeachment proceedings against Nixon, only one other attempt had been made to impeach a president in the history of the nation. In 1868, impeachment proceedings were brought against President Andrew Johnson. Historians now agree that the charges brought against Johnson were politically motivated and based on shameful and unwarranted allegations. Andrew Johnson was seen by his political opponents as overly conciliatory in his attitudes toward the South and in his plans for reconstruction following the carnage of the Civil War. Several members of the House Judiciary Committee were now fearful that history was about to repeat itself. They believed that the charges brought against Nixon lacked credibility. Many believed that the enemies of Richard Nixon were out to get him. Others were convinced that impeachment would be justified and that the charges against Nixon were credible.

Following the release of the tapes, support for the president eroded rapidly, even among many whom previously had been loyal to him. Calls for his resignation were issued by newspapers, by Republican leaders in the Senate, and by influential people throughout the country. The trauma to the nation was of sufficient severity that prolonging the agony seemed unnecessary. From the erosion of public support and the mounting evidence of guilt, all members of the House Judiciary Committee were now in favor of impeachment. Earlier indecision evaporated as the high drama recorded in the White House tapes was revealed. Very few people in Congress, in the federal judiciary, or in the public at large desired to have Nixon remain in office. Consensus had now been reached that Nixon would either resign or be impeached and convicted of the crimes he had committed. The reasonable options available to the president were diminishing very rapidly.

Full impeachment proceedings in the House and subsequent trial and conviction in the Senate would be a long, drawn-out affair that very few, if anyone, really wanted. The time had come for political action and only a small number of stalwarts were willing to further support the president. The two-thirds vote in the Senate that was needed for his conviction now seemed a certainty. Yet Nixon tenaciously held on to the office. After all, he had been duly elected as president of the United States, and in his view, his actions were fully in the best interests of the nation.

There was concern about what Nixon might actually do out of a sense of desperation. As president, he was the commander in chief of the armed forces and had final control of nuclear weapons. Out of concern about Nixon's growing depression and despair, there was uncertainty about his potential use of presidential power, either domestically or with the Russians. Defense Secretary James Schlesinger issued a directive to military commanders that no direct order from the White House should be carried out without his countersignature. The dangers inherent in the situation seemed to warrant such precautions.

The personal despair and anguish of Nixon were preventing him from attending to the affairs of state. With some degree of uneasiness, the president's assistant, Alexander Haig, had for some time been doing most of the routine work that was needed for the continuity of the office. Some of those close to the president were also concerned that he might commit suicide. Personal appeals were cautiously made to Nixon for him to resign with dignity. It was no longer in his own best interest or in the best interest of the nation for him to continue.

On August 8, 1974, the nation encountered one of the most emotional moments in its history when the thirty-seventh president of the United States went on television and announced to the world, "I shall resign the presidency effective at noon tomorrow." The drama of his resignation has often been described as having the ingredients of a Greek tragedy. The agony of recent events was rapidly coming to a close. The following day, the nation watched as Nixon gave his farewell to the White House staff and boarded a military helicopter for his move into exile. With mixed emotions, the nation sighed with relief.

Gerald Ford, as the new president, issued a pardon one month later for any of the crimes Nixon may have committed while in office. Prior to Ford's pardon, plans were being made on Capitol Hill for the trial and conviction of Nixon. Now the case was officially closed; Nixon could not be convicted and sent to prison. However, serious questions about the secrecy surrounding government operations continued to surface and resurface in the concerns of many Americans. The majority of Americans disapproved of the pardon and believed that the same rules of conduct that are applied to others should also be applied to the president of the United States. Many were relieved by the closure of the Watergate affair, while others were convinced that an easy way out had been provided for a criminal president.

The Morality of Power

The Watergate affair confirmed the worst suspicions of Americans about the immorality of public officials. Politics has always been regarded as a "dirty business" by many Americans. Yet, drawing upon the images of such presidents as George Washington, Abraham Lincoln, and Harry S. Truman, Americans also expect their presidents to be people of integrity and to stand above the dirty work that is involved in the political process. The Nixon scandal was traumatic to the nation. Extraordinary forms of political deviance get a lot of attention in the daily press, but when the extraordinary deviance implicates the president of the United States, the effects are electrifying.

Historically, Americans have agreed with Lord Acton's dictum that "power corrupts, and absolute power corrupts absolutely." It was for this reason that the framers of the Constitution built checks and balances into the system and deliberately limited the powers of the presidency. Certain forms of authority were delegated to the Congress, other forms of authority were delegated to the executive branch of government, and yet other forms of authority were delegated to the judiciary. Limiting the powers of the president was a way of preventing absolute power from corrupting absolutely. The rules binding the conduct of public officials are well known to any man or woman who achieves a top position of authority in our society.

Public response to the Watergate affair became divided along the lines of perceptions of the man and perceptions of the office. Was the conduct of Nixon an aberration that reflected the moral character of the man, or were "high crimes and misdemeanors" symptomatic of the way the political system works?

Some thought the issue of morality was primarily a system problem. They believed that no man who had come so far so fast in American politics could have done so without acquiring a blunted sense of moral responsibility. The ideology of America as the land of opportunity lends itself to schemers and manipulators who evaluate the quality of their character on the basis of the outcomes they achieve. They consider bending the rules acceptable if it achieves the results that are intended. Insofar as morality was seen as a system problem, Nixon was regarded as "one of us," but perhaps "not the best of us" because he got caught.

Some who emphasized the problems with the system saw Nixon as a product of the cold war mentality. He was foremost among those promoting the fear and hatred of communism, foremost among those who were hostile toward antiwar activists, and foremost among those who believed that domestic enemies had infiltrated our government and were working to undermine the American way of life. Nixon drew upon the darker side of the American consciousness and was willing to circumvent the democratic process if it was seen as a threat to national security. Nixon's career had largely been built around the image of forcefully standing up to the communists. Patriotic sentiments became linked with support of cold war initiatives. Nixon's efforts at concealment and cover-up were simply a spin-off from the widespread use of misrepresentation and deception during the course of the Vietnam War.

Sociologists have argued that if deviancy did not exist, there are circumstances in which it would have to be created. It is through specific cases that moral boundaries are drawn and the rules binding conduct are confirmed. What constitutes political sophistication and what constitutes criminal conduct frequently cannot be determined until the courts have spoken. Penalties and sanctions must be imposed in specific cases to establish the rules and guiding principles that are binding on the conduct of public officials.

The Watergate affair may very well have been necessary for establishing limits to the abuse of power. Certainly other presidents have abused the power of their office in a variety of ways. Some Americans remembered the attempts of Franklin Roosevelt to pack the Supreme Court, the Teapot Dome scandal during Warren Harding's administration, and John Kennedy's role in the Bay of Pigs fiasco and possible implication in a plot to assassinate Fidel Castro of Cuba. There was no historical precedent, however, similar in scope to the blatant abuses of power during the Nixon administration. Accordingly, many believed that there was nothing wrong with the system, that it worked well, and that the problem was simply Nixon's immorality.

What manner of man would engage in such nefarious practices while holding the position of president of the United States? The answer was sought in the character flaws of Nixon. The term "tricky Dick" was widely used by Nixon critics who perceived him as a devious character. He was seen as a little man with big political ambitions and a lack of moral scruples.

It was noted that Nixon's early career was boosted substantially by the tenacity with which he sought to expose "hidden communists." His paranoia about the communist menace was subsequently extended to the belief that other people, including political opponents, antiwar activists, the press, and liberal intellectuals, were out to get him. The only way he could win in this type of situation, he apparently believed, was "to give them the sword." Nixon saw politics as resembling war in that it is permissible to incapacitate or neutralize the opposition. Personal strength and political efficacy are determined by whose will prevails in the face of opposition and conflict.

For Nixon, the prize of the political game was personal power and what he personally saw as being in the best interests of the country. Regardless of the scandals of Watergate and his forced resignation, Nixon apparently believed that history would look favorably upon his administration. In his view, it is political accomplishments that really matter, rather than the means employed in attaining them. Those who stand in opposition to "national interests" have to be dealt with in a heavy-handed way. Civil liberties and due process must be suspended if they interfere with "national security" concerns.

The autobiographical writings of former presidents, in some way or another, address the differential between the experience "of power" and the experience "with power." Lyndon Johnson, for example, had a reputation for arm-twisting; however, he was not able to set the national agenda he wished to promote. The emerging issues that require the attention of presidents are frequently not of their own choosing. Further, the personal power of presidents is limited by the many constituencies that they have to confront and deal with. Harry Truman wrote about the loneliness of the office that grows out of the monumental decisions that the president alone must make and accept responsibility for. Presiding over a nation thus involves much more than the personal desires and wishes of the person who holds the office.

In the special case of Richard Nixon, he regarded his election as a personal mandate. The sense of power that accompanied the office was translated into a sense of personal invulnerability. He felt free to do whatever illegal acts he wanted to do as long as they were concealed from the public. To avoid the loneliness described by Truman, he surrounded himself with like-minded individuals. His primary criterion for the selection of subordinates was total loyalty and dedication to his leadership. He drew upon the ideology of "national interests" and "national security" to justify the use of unethical procedures.

Some Americans believed that the forced resignation of Nixon confirmed the integrity of the political process. All the major branches of government played a key role in the removal of Nixon from office. Some officials of integrity chose to resign rather than carry out Nixon's orders, which were improperly given. Even the Nixon supporters within his own party came to feel betrayed and decided that nothing short of Nixon's resignation was acceptable. The abuse of power became an insult to the men and women of integrity who had devoted their lives to public service.

The Legacy of Watergate

The primary legacy of Watergate was to confirm the importance of constitutional authority. The American system governs by laws rather than the whims and actions of individual men and women. Individual presidents may come and go, but the integrity of the system remains. All future presidents will be aware of the risks involved in an obstruction of justice and the abuse of political power. Whether the precedent actually serves as a deterrent to misconduct is a debatable point. However, it is clear that the machinery for dealing with misconduct in office is firmly in place. The Constitution had not been changed, but the meaning it has for the conduct of public affairs has been clarified. Nixon's resignation confirmed that under a constitutional government, even the most powerful man in American politics could be convinced to give in to political pressure and quit.

We now know of the intensity of the trauma that is involved in an effort to impeach the president of the United States. The matter was not taken lightly in Nixon's case, and constitutional scholars agree that the issue of impeachment should not be taken lightly in the future. Political disagreements with a president are not grounds for impeachment, but a serious violation of the oath of office is. Some degree of leeway in personal style must necessarily be given to political leaders, but at the same time it is clear that the resources of the office are not to be used primarily to serve personal ends.

The impeachment proceedings subsequently brought against President Bill Clinton in 1998 raised several basic issues about our governmental process. Is consensual sexual misconduct an adequate basis for removing a president from office? Numerous biographies of former presidents, especially John F. Kennedy, Franklin D. Roosevelt, and Warren G. Harding, have presented suggestive evidence of extensive extramarital sexual activity. But in these cases, their sexual conduct was not made available for public scrutiny while they were in office. European observers shook their heads in astonishment that Americans were engaged in impeachment proceedings against a president for lying about his sexual conduct. It is very likely that most people would attempt to avoid the full truth about their sexual infidelity.

In Clinton's impeachment, the wisdom of our founding fathers in maintaining a separation of power again prevailed. Most of us would agree that lying about sexual misconduct does not constitute adequate evidence of the impeachable offenses defined by the Constitution as "high crimes and misdemeanors." The partisan basis for bringing impeachment proceedings against Clinton seemed to represent an overextension of legislative power and responsibility. The offenses for which Clinton was charged did not grow out of affairs of state, but out of a failure on his part to control his sexual impulses and to keep his personal and private life separate from his political and public life.

In Nixon's case, it was not the overt behavior of the man in office that generated the initial cry of moral indignation. Instead, it was the public disclosure of his failure to do anything about the crimes that had been committed by his friends and subordinates. The most successful crimes are those that are never detected and thus are never brought forward for public scrutiny and reaction. Getting caught represents ineptness and carelessness in the area of crime itself. Ineptness in the Watergate affair was reflected in the activities of the former CIA agents who were supposed to be experts in covert activities. Nixon's

Box 8
Symbolic Event: The Impeachment of President Clinton

The question of what constitutes an impeachable offense became an issue during the administration of President Bill Clinton. The Republican-dominated Congress had appointed an independent counsel to investigate the Clintons' financial background. It was through his capacity as a federal investigator that the authority given to Kenneth Starr was extended, and he became preoccupied with the sexual scandal involving the president and Monica Lewinsky.

It is reasonable to assume that a twenty-two-year-old White House intern who was having sex with the president would talk about it. This was indeed the case. Monica Lewinsky talked to more than a dozen people about her affair with the president. One of her confidants, Linda Tripp, tape recorded a conversation with Lewinsky and subsequently made it available to Kenneth Starr. Lewinsky's sharing of secret information about her personal life subsequently had unintended consequences when it was disclosed to the entire nation through the news media.

Paula Jones had brought a suit against Bill Clinton for sexual harassment during his tenure as governor of Arkansas. The Supreme Court ruled against Clinton in his bid for immunity from civil suits during his tenure in office. This permitted Jones's suit against Clinton to be pursued. It also permitted the Starr inquiry to subpoena both the president and Lewinsky for depositions on their sexual misconduct. Both in his deposition and on public television, Bill Clinton asserted, "I did not have a sexual relationship with that woman, Miss Lewinsky."

Clinton was not aware at the time of his statement that Monica Lewinsky had saved a semen-stained dress that would subsequently prove through DNA analysis that the president had indeed had a sexual relationship with her. On the basis of little more than lying about his sexual behavior, impeachment proceedings were brought against President Clinton on charges of perjury and obstruction of justice. Political enemies of the president were determined to have him removed from office.

With a vote along party lines, an easy conviction was obtained in the Republican-dominated House of Representatives. By the provisions of the U.S. Constitution, the chief justice of the Supreme Court presides over the Senate in trial proceedings on impeachment charges, and a two-thirds vote is required for removal from office. It turned out to be a political trial, rather than a legal trial. Senate Republicans did not have the required sixty-two votes for removal and the charges were dropped. The checks and balances in our governmental system had prevailed, but serious questions were raised about the damage to the Constitution from these proceedings.

ineptness was reflected in the fact that he had bugged himself in the elaborate recording system that had been installed in the White House. Apparently, Nixon regarded "the president" as invulnerable and believed that the power inherent in the office was his personal power to use as he wished.

Had there not been ineptness on the part of the Watergate burglars and had there not been an attempt to conceal White House involvement, the high crimes and misdemeanors of Richard Nixon might never have been revealed. The atmosphere in Washington during the Nixon administration was sufficiently tense that government employees who knew what was happening preferred to remain silent, rather than to risk their jobs or personal humiliation. Certainly, Woodward and Bernstein, the *Washington Post* reporters, encountered a great deal of resistance from many of the government employees they attempted to interview.

The investigative reporting of Woodward and Bernstein confirmed the importance of freedom of the press and elevated the stature of the news media in American life. Through efforts to inform the nation about consequential events, the news media play an increasingly important role in the political process. Political leaders have a high degree of visibility, and all aspects of their personal and public lives have become fair game for public scrutiny. The Watergate affair sent important messages to future generations about the parameters of acceptable behavior for the occupant of a political office.

Those convicted of street crimes, such as burglary or armed robbery, tend to receive stiff prison sentences. Those who hold high positions of status and power tend to receive relatively light sentences for their crimes. The conspirators in the Watergate affair spent only a short time in prison, and the prisons where they served their time were more like country clubs than maximum-security institutions. A cynical view held that justice did not prevail. The combination of the seriousness of the crimes they committed with the relatively light sentences they received confirmed the view that we do not live in a just world. The social consequences of an armed robbery are small in comparison to those crimes that undermine the basic values and ideals of the democratic process.

Rather than express guilt and remorse, the conspirators attempted to justify themselves. For example, G. Gordon Liddy, a conspirator in the Watergate break-in, clearly stated that he had no regrets about what he had done but only regretted that he had been caught. At no time did President Nixon express regrets about his conduct in office or apologize to the nation. Instead, he spent a great deal of time over the next twenty years extolling the accomplishments of his presidency, his political competence, and the value of the political advice he had to give to the nation.

Part of the legacy of Watergate was a confirmation of the cynical view that "crime pays." Americans apparently had an interest in knowing more about the Watergate affair than had been reported in the news media or in judicial and legislative reports. The "high crimes and misdemeanors" mentioned in the House documents prepared for impeachment proceedings against Nixon were never fully investigated because of Nixon's resignation and his subsequent pardon. In effect, Nixon became only, in legalistic terms, an "unindicted co-conspirator." Several of the men who were convicted of criminal conduct in the Watergate affair subsequently benefited financially from the royalties of their books. These included G. Gordon Liddy and E. Howard Hunt who were directly involved in the break-in and H.R. Halderman, John Ehrlichman, John Dean, and Charles Colson of the White House staff. Nixon also profited greatly from the sales of his memoirs and other books he wrote to vindicate his tenure in office.

The role of secrecy in government temporarily became an issue following Watergate. Many people believed that there was too much concealment and cover-up of what was going on in Washington. Americans were shocked by the scope of the covert activities that had become a standard part of government operations. Particular dismay was expressed over the lack of accountability by the FBI and the CIA. However, in reflections on secrecy, a distinction needs to be made between the backstage routines that are necessary in the government process and those covert activities that are designed as domestic espionage. Americans were indignant that techniques that were refined in our espionage operations against enemies overseas might be employed to embarrass, humiliate, and incapacitate U.S. citizens who were considered "enemies" by the party in power.

The "war" metaphor is misleading as a guiding principle in the conduct of a political campaign. Indeed, the primary objective of a national political party is to win an election and to supply the nation with the personnel to run the government. However, attempts to morally discredit men and women of integrity and to prevent them from waging a political campaign go beyond the pale of common decency. The purpose of an American political party is to put together a coalition that is broadly supported by public opinion for setting the agenda of the nation. The democratic process calls for debates to test the validity of ideas and to permit the electorate to assess the relative qualifications of candidates. These ideals are undermined when the goal is defined as winning the election by whatever means are necessary. Clearly, the use of personnel from national security agencies to circumvent the electoral process should not be tolerated.

There is a widespread belief that the presidency tends to promote the personal growth and development of the person who holds the office. Americans remembered Harry Truman as a man who had grown with the office and made monumental decisions that went far beyond the capabilities expected of him when he was inaugurated as president. The case of Richard Nixon, however, suggested no evidence of such growth and development as a result of holding the office.

The unfolding of the Watergate episode intensified the suspicion and distrust of government. Growing out of the deep divisions within the society, cynics maintained that misrepresentation and deception are widespread in the political process and that news conferences and political speeches are not to be taken at face value. Those looking behind verbal statements for the hidden motive often assume that government officials serve the special interests of business corporations rather than the interests of the total society. Within a context of distrust, many Americans justifiably reacted with disgust to Nixon's claim that everything he had done was for the benefit of the country.

The lessons of Watergate resemble stories that have been told and retold in various forms over the past 2,000 years or more. Unrestrained ambition can result in a crisis of authority and the destruction of the individual. Violations of the oath of office and a disregard for basic rules of social conduct are likely to have serious consequences. Yet after Nixon's resignation as president, he continued to be active in the public domain. His writings were designed to achieve historical redemption, and he continued to offer advice to subsequent presidents, especially to Ronald Reagan and George Bush Sr. The man who resigned to avoid impeachment partially succeeded in cultivating his image as a senior statesman.

At the funeral of Richard Nixon on April 27, 1994, few references were made to the disgrace of his conduct in office. The eulogies emphasized his great political leadership and accomplishments—how Nixon had opened relationships with China, how he had pursued détente with the Soviet Union, and how the Vietnam War had ended during his tenure in office. Reverend Billy Graham described him as "one of the most misunderstood men" and "one of the greatest men of the century." Former president Ronald Reagan observed that "his foreign policy accomplishments will secure his exalted place in history." Former president George H.W. Bush noted, "The difficulties he encountered in office may have diminished his presidency, but what should be remembered are his many outstanding achievements, both foreign and domestic."

National responses to the televised funeral were ambivalent. Some Americans regarded Nixon's personal conduct as no worse than that of other presidents, while others had a sickened reaction to the praise directed toward Nixon and his leadership. As a nation, Americans have not yet recovered the trust they had in their presidents prior to Nixon. Following Watergate, close scrutiny has been given to the character and personal qualities of top political leaders. The legacies of both Richard Nixon and Bill Clinton placed personal morality and the moral dimension of political leadership at center stage in subsequent presidential campaigns.

Discussion Questions

1. What prevents the president of the United States from using the resources of the government for the advancement of personal ambitions and interests?
2. Why did the Watergate conspirators receive more favorable treatment in prison than ordinary criminals?
3. Was it in the best interests of the nation for President Ford to pardon Nixon for any crimes he may have committed while in office?
4. What are the lessons of Watergate for the exercise of power by a future president of the United States?
5. Why is the separation of powers such an important component of the American system of government?
6. Does sexual infidelity by a president of the United States constitute an adequate basis for impeachment? Why or why not?
7. How would you account for the fact that the U.S. Constitution (with only twenty-seven amendments) has endured for more than 200 years?

9 • Technological Accidents

Advances in sophisticated technology are foremost among the spectacular achievements of the twentieth century. We have split the atom, landed people on the moon, traveled beyond the speed of sound, and eradicated smallpox worldwide. Such spectacular achievements in technology have provided us with new images of ourselves and of the world in which we live. The central message seems to be that there are many more possibilities for the human condition than previous generations could have recognized.

Our technological emphasis is oriented toward an active mastery of the world, and according to some it is the capacity for developing technology that sets humans apart from others in the animal kingdom. While developing sophisticated systems of technology may be the crowning human accomplishment, it also provides grounds for uneasiness. Solutions to identifiable problems frequently have consequences that are unexpected and unintended. We become aware of the unintended consequences of technology when airplanes crash, when ships sink, when dams break, when bridges collapse, and when nuclear reactors explode.

The elaboration of technology has grown out of the prevailing assumption that there is a technological solution to any identifiable problem. Once a goal has been specified, resources can be mobilized to determine the feasibility of a variety of potential means for achieving the outcome in question. Overall objectives are broken down into a series of highly specific tasks, and the solution to one problem permits moving on to the next. Thus, sequential and cumulative problem solving serves as a guide to all major technological enterprises.

Technological systems become vulnerable to disruptions primarily because of the complex interdependency of their component parts. For a system to function efficiently, its constituent parts must be calibrated into an interrelated pattern that is stable and predictable. A malfunction in one specific part of a system may have ripple effects on the rest of the system. For example, in November 1965, a small malfunction in the power transmission system at Niagara Falls set off a chain reaction that triggered an electrical blackout throughout the northeastern United States. In New York City, an estimated 800,000 people were trapped in subways, many people were stuck in elevators, the streetlights went out, and major traffic jams developed when the traffic lights failed to work. Systems become overloaded when the demands that are made push the system beyond the limits it can tolerate. A repeat of the electrical blackout occurred in August 2003 when a malfunction in Cleveland again had ripple effects over a large geographical area.

A casual inventory of technological disasters during the course of the twentieth century includes a variety of mishaps and failures. These include the sinking of the *Titanic* in 1912, after it had been publicized as an unsinkable, state-of-the-art ship. The *Hindenburg* crashed at Lakehurst, New Jersey, in 1937 following widespread optimism about the efficiency of dirigibles as a means of international travel. The nuclear mishap at Three Mile Island in 1979 cooled optimism about nuclear power as a means of meeting the growing energy needs of the nation. The explosion of the space shuttle *Challenger* in 1986 occurred at a time when the excitement about human explorations of outer space was pervasive. Such episodes generated traumatic responses throughout the nation because of the dangers they suggested for the world in which we live. Unscheduled, unplanned, and unintended events cause shock waves that humans have to deal with in a manner and at a time that are not of their own choosing.

Space Program Tragedies

Spectacular achievements in the uses of technology inspire a great deal of the idealism of the modern world. This idealism was well expressed in the speech delivered by President John F. Kennedy at Rice University in 1962 in which he announced the importance of space exploration as a national priority. Kennedy laid out the specific objective of sending a man to the moon and bringing him back again "before this decade is over." In announcing an acceleration of expenditures on the space program, Kennedy noted that "it is one of the great adventures of all times" and that "space can be explored and mastered."

The subsequent technological display of landing people on the moon did indeed serve as a way of announcing to the world the American capability for technological development. The moon landing was presented by the news media as emblematic of the cultural supremacy of the United States. The spectacular episode confirmed the wisdom and courage of its political leaders, the intelligence of its scientific and technological personnel, and the superiority of the American political system. The moon landing, seen by millions on television, was one of the proudest moments in the history of the nation.

Comparisons were made between the trip to the moon and the voyage of Columbus and the expedition of Lewis and Clark. Each involved travel into uncharted territory, a sense of adventure, and a courageous undertaking. The trip to the moon, however, involved risks that went beyond any earthbound activity. There was the possibility that our sophisticated technology might fail to work in a new and unknown environment. There was also a concern about what the astronauts might bring back from the moon; it was not actually known whether there were biogenic agents on the moon to which we had no immunity. After the splashdown, the astronauts were placed in isolation for extensive examination to determine the presence of any novel form of contamination.

The astronaut emerged as a new type of hero in a world in which heroes were becoming increasingly scarce. Space flights captured the imagination of the American public, and such names as John Glenn and Neil Armstrong became familiar to most Americans. Astronauts were seen as intelligent, honest, competent, physically fit, cool, and courageous. They were recognized as exceptionally gifted individuals who epitomized cultural values and ideals. As the title of a book that was subsequently made into a movie suggested, the astronaut was an American hero with "the right stuff."

The initial astronauts were selected from a cadre of test pilots. The competition was stiff, and those selected became the envy of others. Acceptance of danger was a necessary ingredient for their flight assignments. The rockets they would take into outer space were, in effect, launched by the explosion of a "controlled bomb." The possibility of death was part of the folklore of test pilots and astronauts. Commitment to flying was at the risk of the loss of one's life.

Many problems developed in the elaboration of the sophisticated technology for space travel. Most Americans were aware of the spectacular accomplishments in space, but not of the blunders and mishaps, nor of the intense conflicts among the personnel at the National Aeronautics and Space Administration (NASA). The scientific and technical personnel were under intense pressure from management to solve complicated problems under deadlines from Washington. As a result, there was a great deal of risk-taking in many flights that had been launched prematurely. Even the initial moon flight came close to a disaster. At the mission control center in Houston, Texas, it took about four hours longer than expected to calibrate the liftoff from the moon for a rendezvous with the orbiting spacecraft that would return the astronauts to earth. Any further delay would likely have had catastrophic results because there was only ten seconds' worth of fuel left in the craft that had lifted off the moon.

Following the initial moon landing, public interest in the space program weakened. The United States had clearly demonstrated to the world that American space technology was superior to that of the Russians. About 600 million people around the world watched television coverage of Neil Armstrong and Buzz Aldrin walking on the moon. Few people followed with interest subsequent moon flights. The mystery of the possibility of traveling to the moon and exploring its surface had been solved. The moon turned out to be a relatively uninteresting place for most people. The turbulence of the times seemed to require a focus of attention on more immediate and urgent problems, such as the war in Vietnam, the civil rights movement, and the civil disorders in metropolitan areas.

Now that the United States was ahead of the Russians, the continuance of prior levels of funding for space research was no longer assured. Some people believed that the engineering feats performed in outer space had only a limited use here on earth and were not worthy of the claims that were being made on a stressed federal budget. NASA also came under attack for its criteria in the selection of astronauts. It was argued that test pilots were not actually needed, because the maneuverability of the spacecraft was largely under the guidance of computers from the mission control center. There were doubts about whether astronauts were even necessary aboard a spacecraft. Social pressure was put on NASA to recruit women, minorities, and civilians for the cadre of astronauts.

To reverse the declining interest of Americans in space research, a special flight of the space shuttle *Challenger* was planned for early 1986. The notion that space travel could be made available to ordinary people was being promoted. In the flight design, the seven crew members were to include two members of minority groups and two women. A high level of excitement was generated through national competition in selecting a public school teacher for the space flight. The success of previous flights had generated enough confidence to include civilians along with military personnel in *Challenger*'s crew. Several astronauts disagreed with the decision, believing that only test pilots had the expertise that might be required for dealing with emergencies in outer space.

On the day of the *Challenger* flight, hundreds of friends and relatives of the astronauts gathered at hotels near the Kennedy space center in Florida. Millions of students in schools throughout the country were glued to television sets to watch the astronauts enter the space shuttle for their historic adventure. Christa McAuliffe, the schoolteacher from New Hampshire who had won the competition, was prepared to conduct experiments for classrooms that would be broadcast from outer space. Teaching from outer space was expected to provide a powerful role model and revitalize basic American values and ideals.

One of the most traumatic moments for a generation of Americans was on the verge of unfolding. The launch of the *Challenger* seemed to go smoothly enough, but only seventy-three seconds after liftoff a huge explosion occurred. Initially, there was uncertainty about what was actually happening, but soon it became evident that a major disaster had occurred. There was no chance of survival for any of the seven crew members aboard. The nation was in a state of shock as the television coverage played and replayed the tragic event.

Millions of schoolchildren throughout the nation were traumatized by their experience. They had encountered the reality of death, some for the first time, and were required to deal with it. Seeing a major role model obliterated on live television was shocking. Several students quickly changed their minds about wanting to become an astronaut when they grew up. Teachers set aside time in the classroom for students to express their concerns. Clinical psychologists and psychiatrists gave advice to parents on how to deal with nightmares and other stress responses in children. At McAuliffe's high school in Concord, New Hampshire, psychological counseling was made available for any student who wanted or needed it. Many adults saw a resemblance between the sadness of the event and the sadness they had experienced with the death of President Kennedy.

An investigation into the *Challenger* explosion revealed that the accident was caused by the failure of an "O"-ring, a synthetic rubber ring designed to ensure that the separate sections of the booster rocket held together. Problems with the "O"-ring had been noted in technical reports, but these reports remained hidden in administrative files. Engineers at the space center were well aware of recurrent technical problems with the space shuttle. The failure to coordinate the expertise of the many specialists in the space program was regarded by some as evidence of incompetence on the part of the agency that had successfully landed people on the moon.

Some blamed the political pressure to launch the flight prior to President Ronald Reagan's State of the Union message. Reagan apparently wanted to mention the success of the *Challenger* flight to embellish his address to the nation. As a result of the pressure to launch the flight prematurely, the weather conditions at Cape Canaveral were not properly taken into account. There had been icicles on the launch pad that morning, and no previous shuttle flight had been launched at such a low temperature.

Several retrospective judgments were expressed in response to the tragedy. Technicians in the space program felt that there was a need to resist politically motivated timetables for the deployment of exotic, high-risk technologies. Racing with the Russians, or meeting the timetable set by politicians, requires a willingness to sacrifice lives and to take risks that are unwarranted. Some held the view that because of the risks in the use of exotic technologies, each mission should be regarded as an experimental launch and no civilians should be aboard unless they have important scientific missions to perform.

Traumatic events provide the raw materials for a great deal of cultural elaboration, in part because disruptive events document the limited abilities of those in trusted positions of power and authority. With a disruptive event, the social system fails to work the way that it should. Something has gone wrong and repair work is necessary. For this reason, experts, technicians, and authority figures become objects of attention and subjected to close scrutiny when technological accidents disrupt a social system. The conferral of authority involves presumptions about both qualifications and trustworthiness. As symbols of group effectiveness, authority figures become accountable when failures and mishaps occur.

There are multiple realities to all collective experiences. The research of John Portmann suggests that many people derive some measure of pleasure from the suffering of others. While tragedy produces intense feelings of sadness for some, the same event may have pleasurable and integrative effects for others. The unity generated by sharing a tragedy may serve as a buffer against the loneliness and dullness of everyday life. The tragic events reported in newspapers become conversation openers among strangers in our urbanized society. In cases of technological accidents, barroom humor may provide a sense of relief from the risks and dangers that are inherent in our modern technological society.

Following the *Challenger* explosion, hundreds of improvements were made in the space shuttle, and it seemed that all was going well. But on February 1, 2003, the space shuttle *Columbia* disintegrated upon reentry into the earth's atmosphere. The entire seven-member crew was killed, and the nation was again in a state of shock. The *Columbia* had journeyed more than 6 million miles in space and was only minutes away from the completion of its scheduled mission. Another engineering failure had occurred, and the space program was suspended. In his address to the nation, President George W. Bush observed that each crew member "knew that great endeavors are inseparable from great risks" and assured the nation that the space program would continue.

Travel Accidents

Travel several times the speed of sound in a rocket launched into outer space is beyond the direct experience of all but a few Americans. Yet, using less complex technologies than those of space travel, the speed and efficiency of travel over the surface of the earth are very much a part of experiences in the

Box 9
Symbolic Event: Tragedy and Pleasure

The pleasure people derive from a tragic event remains primarily at the latent level. The open expression of happiness in response to suffering of others is gruesome and unthinkable. But when people gather in small groups to reflect on tragic events, there is a certain amount of pleasure derived from the shared experience. Some sense of unity grows out of sharing sadness and being jointly involved in reflection on the implications of tragic events for personal lives and for the human condition. Through sharing crises and tragedy, lonely and isolated individuals become temporarily integrated into a local community.

An obvious form of pleasure growing out of newsworthy events is derived from the ugly jokes that surface following a tragedy. Students of popular culture noted that a large number of sick jokes surfaced a few weeks after the explosion of the space shuttle *Challenger*. Many of them were focused on the schoolteacher, Christa McAuliffe, who was scheduled to conduct a class from outer space. The tragedy was drawn upon in barrooms across the country, in the skits of standup comedians, and in late night talk shows. Jokes about the disaster reflected underlying disenchantment with public education, the mass media, and national expenditures on the space program. The following jokes are representative:

What color were Christa McAuliffe's eyes?
Blue. One blew this way and one blew that way.

What was the last thing Christa McAuliffe said to her husband?
You feed the dog and I'll feed the fish.

How do we know that Christa McAuliffe was a good teacher?
She only blew up once in front of her class.

What do you call seven astronauts at the bottom of the ocean?
A good beginning.

Although the jokes seemed to express belligerent cruelty, they served the function of releasing some of the tension stemming from the tragedy. Telling *Challenger* jokes was a way of sidestepping awareness of one's own mortality and the fragility of the technological environments upon which we increasingly depend. Humor provided a symbolic way of expressing ambivalent attitudes toward the many forms of technology in the lives of individuals—technologies designed to make life easier, but over which individuals sensed a lack of personal control.

modern world. The lifetime travel of the average person before the twentieth century was limited to a radius of a few miles from the place of birth. As public transportation became cheaper, faster, and safer, long-distance travel for business and pleasure became possible. Indeed, the development of so-phisticated systems of both land-based and airborne travel contributed greatly to the economic, political, and social integration of the nation. Being able to cross continents and oceans in a few hours has greatly altered the human condition. The popularity of long-distance travel is evident in the fact that several of the largest airlines now carry more than 200 million passengers each year.

Despite the popularity of airplanes and automobiles, people travel in them without knowing much about the technical principles by which they operate. There are mysterious and magic-like qualities to the technologies that have become a central part of the modern landscape. The devices used for rapid transit involve ingredients of both excitement and danger. Some degree of uneasiness grows out of dependency on technologies that are little under-stood by those who use and benefit from them. The risks embedded in sys-tems of transportation have recurrently surfaced in collective consciousness with the unfolding of extraordinary tragedies and disasters.

Shortly before midnight on April 14, 1912, one of the most tragic epi-sodes in travel history occurred with the sinking of the *Titanic* in the North Atlantic. The *Titanic* was designed as a luxury ship that would beat out all competition in transatlantic travel. The ship was 11 stories tall, 883 feet long, and 91 feet wide, and it weighed 46,000 tons. It was designed to be the largest, the most luxurious, and the most powerful ship ever built. Nothing was spared in providing luxury accommodations. The passenger list for the magnificent "floating luxury hotel" included many rich and famous Ameri-cans on their way home from travel in Europe.

By designing the ship with sixteen watertight compartments, its builders and promoters intended to make the ship "unsinkable." If water ever entered any of the compartments, an automatic switch would close doors to adjacent compartments, keeping the ship afloat. However, there were flaws in the design of the compartments. The ship would remain afloat only if no more than two of the compartments were flooded at the same time. After all, how often does an automobile have more than two flats at the same time? Further problems in design stemmed from the fact that all the compartments were located above the waterline on the assumption that any accident would stem from a frontal collision.

About forty-eight hours after being launched on its maiden voyage, the claims for the ship were put to an empirical test. The *Titanic* struck an iceberg that ripped the underside of the ship, shearing a series of gashes and flooding six of the compartments. The ship was traveling about twenty-two nautical miles an hour in an attempt to set a new record for a transat-lantic crossing.

Within minutes after striking the iceberg, it was clear that the ship would sink and that a serious state of emergency existed. The ship carried only sixteen lifeboats, which had been regarded as unnecessary for an "unsinkable" ship. Following a basic rule of the sea, the decision was made to limit the lifeboats to women and children. Husbands were separated from their wives; fathers were separated from their children. Shortly after the lifeboats were launched, the ship tilted almost vertically and plunged nose down into 13,000 feet of icy water. More than 1,500 passengers went down with the ship. What had started out as an exciting and memorable trip ended as an extraordinary tragedy. Since most of the passengers were Americans the nation was shocked.

The loss of lives among the rich and famous is an especially newsworthy event. The names of both the survivors and the fatalities, along with selective biographical sketches, were listed in newspapers across the country. Accounts of the tragedy provided the raw materials for many documentaries, novels, movies, and other forms of popular culture. Eighty years after the event, the story of the sinking of the *Titanic* continued to capture the imagination of Americans. It was not just the tragedy of the deaths of the rich and the famous that produced the trauma for the nation. Instead, the trauma was embedded in perceptions of the qualifications of experts and the dangers inherent in long-distance travel.

Despite the vague dangers associated with long-distance travel, the increased efficiency and comfort of travel added to the excitement of the times. The solo flight of Charles Lindbergh across the Atlantic in 1927 created a new national hero from the vicarious thrills of adventure and travel. The world was becoming more interdependent, and people were excited at the prospect of having direct experiences with events and places that were far removed from the mundane character of everyday life.

The new technologies in transportation, however, were accompanied by several extraordinary tragedies. In 1937, the world watched with interest as Amelia Earhart embarked on an around-the-world flight. Her flight ended with the disappearance of her plane over the South Pacific. What happened in the course of her flight remains a mystery and continues to provoke a great deal of speculation. The Amelia Earhart episode holds a prominent place in the collective memories of the nation about the triumphs and tragedies of the transportation technologies.

New and innovative forms of commercial travel across the Atlantic continued to capture the imagination of Americans in a century of rapid technological advancement. In 1936, regular flights were scheduled on lighter-than-air dirigibles flying from Europe to the United States. On its first flight to the United States from Germany, the dirigible *Hindenburg* carried fifty-one passengers and fifty-six crew members. The dirigible also carried a gas volume of 7.3 million cubic feet, which gave it a gross lifting capacity of 418,000 pounds. On its initial voyage, the craft elegantly soared upward at Friedrichschafen, Germany, and was pointed westward for a 4,000–mile journey. In its ten transatlantic crossings during the first year, the craft carried more than 1,000 people. The passenger list included many dignitaries from Europe and America.

On May 6, 1937, a crowd of thousands, amazed at the novel sight, gathered in Times Square to cheer as the *Hindenburg* flew over New York City. Minutes later, the dirigible crashed and burned as it approached its landing site at Lakehurst, New Jersey. The lighter-than-air gases that kept the craft afloat were highly flammable and explosive. Sparks from the engine, or perhaps even static electricity, were believed to have ignited the hydrogen gas aboard. Doubts about the desirability of gas-powered crafts for long-distance travel became widespread.

Such tragedies as the sinking of the *Titanic* and the explosion of the *Hindenburg* call into question the technical competence of the many specialists and experts upon whom we increasingly depend. As individuals we do not possess the knowledge that is necessary for assessing the claim that a given ship is "unsinkable" or that a trip across the Atlantic in a dirigible is "safe." The choices we make in our personal lives are dependent to a very large degree on trust. We expect the designers and producers of sophisticated systems of technology to be competent, and we expect those who promote those technologies to be committed to communal values and to hold an ethic of social responsibility. Without making such assumptions, the social world would become disorderly and individuals would have difficulty achieving their goals.

Today, commercial airlines promote the notion that traveling by air is one of the safest forms of travel over long distances. The available statistics seem to bear out this claim. For passengers on commercial flights, there is now an average of less than two fatalities for each 100 million miles flown. While comparable data are not available for other means of travel, national statistics do indicate that there are approximately 40,000 deaths each year from automobile accidents compared to 200 from commercial flights. However, among those who had doubts about the safety of commercial air travel, reinforcements were received from the terrorist attack on September 11, 2001. There were four plane crashes on that day, and there were no survivors.

Although personal control over the safety of a flight is lacking for passengers, most people accept the claim that flying on commercial airlines is a safe and efficient way to travel. At the same time, millions of Americans have a fear of flying, including those who fly on commercial planes as well as those who do not. In part, the fear of flying grows out of a recognition that humans evolved as land-based creatures and that flying through the air at high speeds is not something humans do naturally. The use of technology to enhance human capabilities involves a great deal of risk and danger.

While commercial airlines generally do provide safe and efficient forms of travel, there are occasions when serious accidents do occur. Planes sometimes lose their wings or propellers, run out of fuel, collide with each other, and crash into rivers, bridges, or mountains. There is no way we can have highly sophisticated technologies for rapid transit that are completely free of risk. Newspapers give a great deal of coverage to airplane crashes but very little to automobile fatalities, highlighting the sense of vulnerability and potential trauma that is connected with commercial aviation.

Today the fear of flying goes beyond a concern for pilot error or mechanical failure. Notions about the vulnerability of commercial flights to acts of terrorism are confirmed as passengers are exposed to close scrutiny at security checkpoints in airports. During the Gulf War, concerns with security intensified and passengers sensed the tense atmosphere that prevailed. With only limited resources, terrorists have the ability to commandeer a plane, take the crew and passengers hostage, and change the destination of the flight, all as a means of obtaining major political concessions. The apparent helplessness of passengers adds to the feeling of personal vulnerability.

On December 21, 1988, a Pan Am flight bringing Americans home from Europe crashed over the town of Lockerbie in Scotland. All 258 aboard the plane and 18 people on the ground were killed. The crash was caused by a bomb that had been placed on the plane by terrorists as a form of revenge for the downing of an Iranian airliner by an American ship. The security check at Frankfort had failed to detect the small plastic bomb, which had been placed aboard the plane in a suitcase. The newly developed bombs that are small, highly explosive, and nonmetallic are not likely to be detected, despite the precautions that are taken by airports in their security checks. A plastic bomb no larger than a pack of cigarettes can have an explosive capacity that is sufficient to bring down a commercial airliner.

Despite mechanical failures, collisions, crashes, and acts of terrorism, commercial air travel continues to be a primary source of travel for business and pleasure. The crowded airports confirm the public appeal of commercial flights as a form of travel. The acceptance of some degree of risk and uncertainty is necessary for an adaptive response to the conditions that prevail in our time and place. Those who refrain from flying out of a sense of fear are responding to a basic need for order, predictability, and security in their personal lives. But if humans have a basic need for safety and security, they also have a basic need for excitement and adventure. The fear of flying has a

hemming-in effect, preventing individuals from having some of the plea-
sures and experiences that are valued by others in modern social life.

Three Mile Island

Attitudes of ambivalence toward sophisticated technologies were reflected
in the heated debates and controversy in the United States over the use of
nuclear power plants. The optimistic view of using nuclear energy for the
betterment of the human condition collided with pessimistic views about the
dire consequences of producing a highly radioactive environment. Commercial and political ideologies clashed with underlying anxieties and fears among
individuals about the risks of exposure to nuclear contamination.

Following World War II, the general sentiment of the nation favored finding new and innovative uses for nuclear energy. Some nuclear experts were
optimistic about the prospects of harnessing the recently discovered source
of energy for generating electricity. Just as Elias Howe's sewing machine
replaced the needle and Cyrus McCormick's reaper replaced the sickle, nuclear
power could replace fossil fuels in meeting the energy needs of the nation.

In President Dwight Eisenhower's speech in 1953 on "atoms for peace,"
he set the agenda for the further development of nuclear technology for civilian and commercial purposes. Emphasizing peaceful uses of nuclear power,
his speech had the effect of muting the negative imagery surrounding
Hiroshima and Nagasaki. Nuclear power was being packaged around the
link between technology and human progress. Nuclear power was promoted
as clean, safe, efficient, and essential. Some optimists believed that the generation of electricity would become so efficient in the future that it would not
be necessary to monitor its use or charge for it.

Initially, there was widespread public support for the development of
nuclear power plants. The population was increasing rapidly, leading to a
growing consumer demand for electricity. But while there was an emphasis
on atoms for peace, there was also an escalation of research on nuclear weapons. The effects of testing nuclear devices in the atmosphere became a major
public concern. Increased levels of radiation from testing nuclear weapons
showed up in the polar ice caps, in the grasslands of Wisconsin, and in the
cow's milk consumed by babies. Insidious health hazards had shown up in
dramatic and unexpected ways. It was partially from such concerns that the
United States and the Soviet Union in 1963 negotiated a ban on nuclear testing in the atmosphere.

Opposition to nuclear power plants increased with the growing concern
for the environment. Fears were expressed about the accidental leakage of
radioactive materials into the atmosphere. The tide of public opinion was

moving in a negative direction by the time of the nuclear accident at Three Mile Island near Harrisburg, Pennsylvania, in March 1979. A leak of radioactive steam from a nuclear generator set off an intense national controversy over the risks and benefits of nuclear power plants. The emerging controversy over the use of nuclear power not only tapped concerns about the technical problems in generating electricity, but also strengthened general attitudes about the dangers and hazards created by modern industry and technology.

The media coverage of the Three Mile Island accident was dramatic, and for several days the episode remained the lead item in the news. Anxieties were raised about the potential hazards of increased radioactivity in the surrounding area and about the possibility of a nuclear explosion. A mishap of potentially catastrophic proportions was building up in the nuclear reactor. The valves for regulating the flow of water through pipes for cooling the nuclear reactor failed to work properly. Following the failure of a series of backup systems, a hydrogen bubble developed in the containment building, and there was the risk of a major explosion. From the heat that continued to build in the reactor, there was the risk of a nuclear meltdown. Deep public fears grew out of the uncertainty over what was happening and what was going to happen next.

Despite pronouncements by the Metropolitan Edison Company, the local utility company, that everything was under control, the governor of Pennsylvania advised pregnant women and those with preschool children to evacuate the area if they lived within a five-mile radius of the damaged reactor. After Hiroshima it was widely known that exposure to radiation was associated with birth defects and cancer in young children. Confusion mounted as the police went from door to door instructing people to remain inside, to close all windows, and to turn off their air conditioners. During the first few days after the accident, more than 150,000 people living within a fifteen-mile radius of the damaged reactor either evacuated the area or had a member of their family evacuated. Many of the thousands who left the area did so with the feeling that they might never see their homes again. Many who remained did so with a sense of uneasiness. Work obligations and other daily responsibilities kept them from leaving. One of the bars near Three Mile Island tapped into attitudes of resignation and fatalism by holding an "end-of-the-world party."

Initially, guidelines from government committees on the location of nuclear reactors emphasized the importance of keeping them as far from densely populated areas as possible. The intent was to minimize the dangers of exposing a large number of people to any serious release of radioactivity from an accident with a nuclear reactor. The initial precautions, however, were subsequently set aside as an increasing number of electric utility companies developed nuclear power plants. There were few remote sites available in areas where the commercial needs for electricity were greatest. Remote sites would increase the costs of power transmission and would be less convenient for those who manage and operate the plants. The Three Mile Island plant was located on a long, narrow strip in the Susquehanna River, only eleven miles from the center of the Harrisburg metropolitan area.

According to some estimates, the nuclear reactor at Three Mile Island came within thirty to forty-five seconds of a complete meltdown before it was brought under control. The problems of the aftermath were of a type and a magnitude that neither the utility company nor government regulatory agencies were prepared to handle. Some means had to be found for disposing of the thousands of gallons of radioactive water in the containment building. Scientists have never developed any satisfactory way of disposing of large amounts of radioactive waste materials. Moving radioactive waste materials from one location to another does not fully solve the problem.

Despite assurances from the utility company and government officials that the crisis was over, many people remained doubtful. Millions of Americans watched on television as radiation detectors were used to check people and food supplies for possible contamination. To alleviate anxieties, President Jimmy Carter visited the damaged power plant, and officials reported that his exposure to radiation was less than that which occurs any day of the year in high elevations, such as in Denver, Colorado, or at the altitudes flown by jet airplanes.

Ample evidence was available to suggest that several mishaps had already occurred at nuclear power plants in other parts of the country. Some of the troubles grew out of flaws in design and shoddy construction. Others grew out of ineptitude in working with sophisticated systems of technology that were not well understood by anyone. Additional problems stemmed from having a large number of valves and pipes that could become defective and wear out at unexpected times. It was revealed that the Diablo Canyon nuclear power plant near San Luis Obispo, California, was located near an earthquake fault. Another nuclear power plant was located within the flight pattern of a landing strip at a metropolitan airport. Images of what might happen if a jet plane crashed into a nuclear power plant were terrifying. Some people thought of Murphy's law, which held that "what can go wrong will go wrong, and at the least opportune time."

While Three Mile Island became the major symbol in the controversy over nuclear power, a more serious accident had occurred previously at the Fermi demonstration reactor located on Lake Erie, south of Detroit. In October 1966, a nuclear meltdown occurred in the core assembly during an experiment for achieving the power goal that had been set by the company. The heat built up faster than expected, and the automatic safety devices for the cooling system failed to work. Following several terrifying months and a series of complicated decisions, the fuel assemblies were removed with great difficulty, cut into pieces, and cooled for months in huge pools of water. It took more than three years to remove the radioactive materials from the plant and seal them in steel drums for storage. Throughout, there was serious risk to the health and safety of several hundred thousand people. As the title of a study about the accident put it, "We almost lost Detroit."

Following the Three Mile Island episode, concerns were registered in public demonstrations throughout the country, and a hastily organized rally in Washington, DC, drew a crowd of about 100,000. At the antinuclear rallies, anger was directed toward both utility companies and regulatory agencies. Electrical utilities were seen as being compulsive in their pursuit of profits and negligent in their disregard for the health and safety of people living in surrounding communities. Government regulations were seen as ineffective because the regulatory agencies were committed to promoting the use of nuclear energy. The controversy over nuclear power commanded the attention of the nation and tapped into attitudes about the costs and benefits of modern technology and industry.

Even before the Three Mile Island episode, many Americans had already become doubtful about claims for the safety of nuclear power plants. Anxieties had been intensified by a movie, The China Syndrome, starring Jane Fonda as an investigative reporter for a television news program. The movie conveyed the idea that nuclear power plants were unsafe, that attempts had been made to cover up defects in the design and construction of a nuclear power plant, and that employees who attempted to talk to news reporters or to investigative committees met with violent and mysterious deaths. In effect, the movie's message was that a technological failure of catastrophic proportions was on the verge of happening. The metaphor of "the China syndrome" expressed the notion that a nuclear meltdown would start a chain reaction that would continue until it burned a hole through the entire earth.

Folklore metaphors and analogies were drawn upon to express fears and concerns about the development of nuclear technologies. The nuclear power plant was seen as a time bomb waiting to explode, a Frankenstein monster that would turn on its creator, and a powerful genie that, once released from the bottle, could not be put back in again. Humans were seen as playing God with the fundamental forces of the universe. Such descriptions were ways of placing unknown dangers within a framework that could be understood. The concern was that technology would become uncontrollable. Radiation is invisible and people may be exposed to lethal doses without knowing it; the many harmful effects of radiation may not show up until later. Such fears frequently tapped into perceptions of danger and feelings of fatalism.

At the time of the Three Mile Island episode, many Americans still believed that the development of nuclear power plants was a good idea. However, those living within several miles of a nuclear power plant frequently expressed the view that they would prefer to have the plant located someplace else. The minority opposed to nuclear power plants held their opinions with a high level of intensity. They were willing to back up their attitudes with action. Nuclear power plants throughout the country were surrounded by picket lines and active protest against the use of nuclear power. Those who reported being in favor of nuclear power plants did not hold their attitudes with a high level of conviction; even experts could not agree on the feasibility, safety, and efficiency of nuclear power plants.

Some of the worst fears about nuclear power plants were confirmed by the nuclear accident at Chernobyl in the Soviet Union in April 1986. An explosion occurred within seconds after the beginning of a test of the backup electrical system. A rapid acceleration of the reactor generated intense levels of heat and an explosion resulted. A roof weighing a thousand tons was blown off the reactor, and radioactive isotopes were sent half a mile into the atmosphere. An intense fire started and burned for several days. Thirty workers at the plant were killed by the explosion, and several of the firefighters later died from exposure to radioactivity while putting out the fire. Initial attempts by the government to cover up the accident resulted in delayed evacuation of the area and hence prolonged exposure of thousands of people to radioactive contamination. After admitting the scope of the disaster, more than 52,000 people were evacuated from the hazardous areas between 1992 and 1999.

Clouds carrying radioactive isotopes from Chernobyl had spread over a 1,200–mile radius. The Ukraine, Belarus, and Russia, three republics of the former Soviet Union, received about 90 percent of the total fallout, which covered 84,000 square miles. The health of more than 6 million people living in these provinces was seriously affected. The disaster led to a dramatic rise in the cases of thyroid cancer, leukemia, and birth defects.

The accident at Chernobyl confirmed the view of antinuclear activists that there is no ideal location for a nuclear power plant. Clouds carried from Chernobyl increased radiation levels in the countries of western Europe. Thousands of tons of vegetables were condemned as unsafe to eat as far away as Italy, and children in Eastern Europe were advised not to drink milk. Reindeer herds as far away as Lapland were decimated by the effects of the contamination. The costs in human life and suffering were of a serious magnitude.

By the time of the Chernobyl incident, public opinion in the United States had solidified around the basic position of the antinuclear activists. A national survey in 1986 revealed that 70 percent of Americans were now opposed to nuclear power plants. Earlier claims for nuclear power plants as safe and efficient were rejected. From an economic standpoint, it was becoming increasingly evident that nuclear power plants were not cost-effective. Risks to the personal safety of workers, to the health of people living in the surrounding area, and to the environment were seen as risks not worth taking. Public sentiment coalesced around the notion of "no more nuclear power plants."

Calamities to Come

For thousands of years, religious prophecies have been directed toward a cataclysmic destruction of the world. According to the sacred texts, the apocalypse would result from the wrath of an angry god who would seek retribution for human sinfulness and moral decay. Today, our visions of the apocalypse have become more secular in character. Visions of the end are more typically directed toward accelerated technological changes that will result in disastrous consequences for the physical environment. The most serious human sins are not the violations of conventional forms of morality, but the technological accomplishments associated with the doctrine of progress.

While predictions about the future have been notoriously off base in the past, it is reasonable to direct attention to some of the major predictions that segments of the population are making about the calamities that are to come. While some traumas take the form of "a bolt out of the blue," other traumas gradually evolve over long periods of time, build in intensity, and result in serious unwanted consequences. Environmental and health concerns are foremost in the anxieties that underlie the apocalyptic visions of the future.

The majority of Americans believe that environmental dangers to the average person's health and safety have increased in recent years. If the environmentalists are correct, the worst technological accidents are yet to come. A new vocabulary has emerged to describe some of the consequences of our technologically oriented lifestyles: "acid rain," "endangered species," "radioactive waste materials," "environmental degradation," "destruction of the ozone layer," and "the greenhouse effect." Underlying these new terms are concerns about whether social life as it is presently known and understood can be extended into the future and about the type of world we will be leaving to future generations.

Throughout most of the past, waste materials produced by human activity were primarily organic in character and thus biodegradable within a relatively short period of time. The waste materials of modern civilization are of a different order. The metallic, chemical, and radioactive qualities of our current waste materials are much more toxic and have much more enduring effects. Several decades have passed since the launching of the nuclear age, but we still lack an adequate solution to the problem of disposing of radioactive waste materials. It is only in recent years that we have even located and inventoried the hazardous waste dumps of the past. Apparently many industries disposed of chemical waste materials in a socially irresponsible manner.

Concerns with the greenhouse effect are focused on the consequences of human activities for the atmosphere surrounding the earth's surface. The fossil fuels used in the pursuit of everyday activities have increased the level of certain gases, such as carbon dioxide, nitrous oxide, and methane in the atmosphere. Because these gases serve as an atmospheric shield, the heat radiated at the earth's surface cannot escape back into space. The effect is a potential warming trend on a worldwide scale. Global warming could have the effect of melting the polar ice caps, which in turn would raise the sea level along coastal areas and flood a great deal of Florida, Louisiana, and other lowlands throughout the world. The suitability of many areas of the world for agriculture would be altered, and many dramatic changes could occur in climate and weather conditions.

Through the use of medical technology, vaccines and antibiotics were developed for the treatment of communicable diseases. The use of these drugs has permitted a large part of the population to survive many of the debilitating illnesses of the past. Nevertheless, some see serious catastrophes lurking in the background. Microorganisms are now evolving that are immune to antibiotics. Further, new forms of disease are disseminated much more rapidly as a result of international travel. Diseases originating anywhere in the world may be transmitted to the United States at the end of a transcontinental flight.

We know from the AIDS epidemic that viruses may develop for which we have no immunity. The concern about a major calamity grows out of the possibility that a lethal virus will surface for which we will not be able to develop an immunity fast enough. We are now aware that the Europeans' conquest of Native Americans was facilitated not so much by the Europeans' superior weapons as by the diseases they brought with them for which there was no native immunity. We also know that about 30 million people around the world lost their lives in the influenza epidemic of 1918–1919. While health concerns are foremost among the overriding anxieties of Americans, we have no reasonable basis for assessing whether these are realistic or neurotic responses to a future that is unpredictable.

The modern preoccupation with technology derives from the recognition that humans shape their destinies—within limits—by acting on the information they have at their disposal, however incomplete or inadequate that information may be. These limits may be more restricted than we currently imagine. If we have little doubt about our capacity to build a better world, it is only because we have not adequately confronted the complexities of our lifestyles and the complexities of the world in which we live.

Discussion Questions

1. What is the basis for ambivalence toward technology in American society?
2. What are some of the major reasons that space travel is inherently dangerous? Is it possible for it to be otherwise? Why or why not?
3. What accounts for the use of humor in response to such tragedies as the explosion of the *Challenger* and the disintegration of *Columbia?*
4. Why do Americans continue to maintain such a high level of interest in the sinking of the *Titanic?*
5. What accounts for the strong opposition to the development of nuclear power plants to meet the growing energy needs of the country?
6. Does the concern with global warming reflect unfounded hysteria or does it represent awareness of a potentially serious problem? Please defend your position.
7. What accounts for the popularity of disaster movies (e.g., *Dr. Strangelove, The Towering Inferno, The Day after Tomorrow,* etc.) in the American experience?
8. To what extent do societal accomplishments in technology translate into an increased sense of personal mastery and control at the individual level?
9. What are some of the reasons that solutions to specific technological problems have unintended consequences?

10 • Domestic Terrorism, USA

The shock effects of unprovoked acts of violence are both consequences and products of turbulence within a social system. A society is always characterized by inherent contradictions and by attitudes of cynical indifference toward problems that need attention. Individuals striving to realize their hopes and aspirations run into blocks that prevent their attainment. The perceived need for social change may collide with the forces upholding the status quo. Rage and anger over episodes of social injustice may seem intolerable and impel individuals to engage in acts of violence. The many sources of conflict and turbulence within a social system provide ingredients for the emergence of terrorism and violence.

A special exhibit at the International Spy Museum in Washington, DC, in 2004 focused on the history of terrorism in the United States from the American Revolution to the present. At the start of the exhibit, terrorism was defined as the "unlawful use of force or violence against persons or property to intimidate or coerce a government, the civilian population, or any segment thereof in furtherance of political or social objectives." The exhibit drew upon visual representations to depict the many expressions of terrorism in American history. Images from a turbulent past provided potential insights into contemporary forms of terrorism.

Extraordinary turbulence was evident in the United States before, during, and after the Civil War. For example, historians have noted that before the Civil War there were more than 200 slave uprisings involving ten or more people. While slave revolts could not topple the institution of slavery, the violence did succeed in instilling high levels of fear in slave owners and their families. The immediate proximity of slaves permitted food poisoning and other indirect acts of retribution for abuse and brutality.

Terrorism was also expressed in the deep social and political divisions between the abolitionists and the defenders of the institution of slavery. On October 16, 1859, a raid led by John Brown captured the federal arsenal at Harpers Ferry, Virginia. The raid was intended to provoke a general uprising among African Americans and to provide the insurgents with weapons to support a war against slavery.

A military unit under the command of Colonel Robert E. Lee surrounded the arsenal and nearly all the insurgents were killed or captured. A severely wounded John Brown was hastily tried and convicted as a traitor. Before he was hanged, Brown declared that his actions were in accordance with God's commandments.

The distinguishing feature of terrorism is the illegitimate use of force or violence to promote a social or political cause. The cause is often endowed with sacred qualities, and there is frequently a strong sense of dedication and commitment to using force and violence as attention-getting devices. The explosive character of violence is expressed in killing others to dramatize a societal need for remedial action. Since terrorism is designed to instill fear in the general population, the specific victims are intended to be randomly and indiscriminately selected. The victims of random acts of violence are often innocent spectators. Such events as the bombing of an abortion clinic, the burning of black churches, and random and indiscriminate shootings at McDonalds are dramatic and unusual happenings that reflect troubles in the social realm.

The primary terrorist organizations in the United States in recent years include racial hate groups, neo-Nazis, militia groups, left-wing radicals, and extremist religious groups. Their commonality stems from advocating and preparing for the use of violent methods to express their anger and sense of discontent. There is no single ideological cause or set of special concerns that unifies these hostile and threatening groups. Their objectives are as diversified as the pluralism of the society with which they express their disenchantment. While the specific motives of perpetrators and the forms of violence are highly variable, each episode of violence intensifies the sense of vulnerability and fear of living in modern society. The effectiveness of terrorism is dependent to a very large degree on its arbitrary character and its lack of predictability.

The psychological impact of terrorism derives from the difficulty people have in living with a sense of danger and uncertainty. Humans apparently have a need for living in a predictable and understandable world. Our assumptions about living in an orderly society are invalidated when we read in the newspapers about such episodes as the murder of Sharon Tate and her friends by the members of the Charles Manson cult or the random shooting of students as they walked across campus at the University of Texas.

Although most of the violence in our society occurs within intimate relationships, the violence that does occur in public places becomes particularly disturbing. The sudden, unexpected death from an act of terrorism reminds us that it is possible for our darkest fears to be validated here and now at any public place and at the least expected time. Reading a newspaper about the fatalities stemming from terrorism suggests that death is always lurking as an unwelcome intruder and is not limited to some unspecified time in the future.

Only a small number of Americans are killed each year by terrorists in contrast to the large number that die from automobile accidents and from homicide. Yet it is not the number of fatalities but the manner in which the deaths occur that is of primary concern in collective consciousness. Accidental death can be understood as a by-product of the normal, everyday activities in which people are engaged. In contrast, death from an act of terrorism is seen as a senseless event by those who believe in a just world. It represents an event that violates everyday notions about what is normal, natural, and inevitable in human affairs.

Traumatic events impinge directly into the life-worlds of individuals without the cushioning effects of intermediate layers of social organization. There are no filtering or cushioning effects for such dramatic events as the school shootings at Columbine, the mass suicides of a religious cult, the anthrax scare, or the bombing of the federal building in Oklahoma City. The effects of such events upon the nation are direct and immediate. Through awareness of these events, individuals become increasingly atomized, feeling unprotected from the dangers of the modern world. While individuals are bound together by the common authority of the state, their safety and security may be undermined at any time by forces outside of themselves and over which they have no control. Memberships in families, friendship circles, and local communities do not protect or insulate individuals from the dangers of social living.

Terrorists could not achieve their objectives without the news coverage of the mass media. The publicity given to destructive acts of violence may require people to pay attention to whatever is troubling to both the perpetrators and the victims. From the publicity given to events and to victims, the nation responds with sadness and sympathy. But whatever the social or political cause domestic terrorists wish to promote, their intended message is usually lost in the process of empathy for the victims. In most cases, the responses are disproportionately focused on the drastic impact of the unprovoked acts of violence on innocent victims and their families.

The modern state has a monopoly over the legitimate uses of violence. The use of coercive force is necessary for law enforcement and for maintaining tranquility in the social realm. But in a democratic society, the use of coercive force in upholding the law is limited. The rights guaranteed to all citizens by the U.S. Constitution preclude unreasonable search and seizure, the torture of prisoners, and cruel and unusual punishment. In a totalitarian society, by way of contrast, state terrorism becomes the primary instrument for maintaining social control over the population.

The many forms of terrorism include the vigilante groups that go beyond the rule of law in using violence to instill terror in a subgroup of the population. For decades, the vigilante forms of terrorism used by the Ku Klux Klan and White Citizens Councils, although illegal, had been tolerated and approved by law enforcement agencies. The endorsement and participation of the police themselves accompanied the insidious practices of cross burning and lynching. In such cases, law enforcement personnel encouraged terrorism rather than stopping it.

Terrorists act out of a state of discontent with their society and with one or more of its institutions. Values central to their self-identity may be eroded by historical trends that are not working in their favor. Rather than following a pattern of fatalistic resignation to the unalterable conditions of their existence, terrorists take an activist approach toward transforming their society or a segment thereof.

Estrangement from Society: The Unabomber, Columbine, and the Bombing of Abortion Clinics

In contrast to those who derive a sense of pride from living in the United States, there are those who have developed a sense of estrangement from society and the culture it currently manifests. These are Americans whose personal identities are threatened by the direction in which history is moving and who feel that our basic institutions have failed to perform their essential functions. The larger society is perceived as unresponsive to personal needs and interests. Estrangement from society finds expression in hostile attitudes toward the government and in the cultural wars over the increased freedom of choice in intimate social relationships.

Some respond to estrangement from society by seeking living conditions that facilitate social isolation, solitude, and the opportunity to pursue personal interests without interference. This is reflected, for example, in the preference of about 20 percent of Americans for living alone, rather than with a spouse, a partner, a friend, or anyone else. Such a lifestyle maximizes freedom of movement and does not require the individual to calibrate personal activities with those of anyone else.

While such conditions of isolation and privacy are among the rights of individuals in a democratic society, they also permit secrecy and planning for clandestine operations. Privacy and isolation permit a cover-up of activities that would be regarded as immoral or reprehensible if they were known. For example, from a cabin in an isolated region in Montana, Theodore

Kaczynski engaged in acts of terrorism over an eighteen-year interval before he was apprehended as the "unabomber."

Kaczynski used the U.S. Postal Service to deliver bombs to intended victims. His sophistication was reflected in developing an explosive that would be detonated when the package delivered by a mail carrier was opened. His actions were those of an alienated individual who had no affiliation with any terrorist organization. The targets of his bombs were scientists who were among the nation's elites and located in different parts of the country. The Federal Bureau of Investigation (FBI) spent eighteen years working on the unabomber case without a clue to his identity. It was only after his brother turned him in as a suspect that the FBI was able to locate and apprehend Ted Kaczynski.

Kaczynski was exceptionally intelligent, had been educated at Harvard, and was totally disillusioned with modern society. In his trial, he expressed a desire that his lawyers not pursue a mental illness defense. Instead, he wanted his acts of terrorism to focus the nation's attention on a manuscript he had written that developed theses on the deleterious effects of modern technology. After pleading guilty to thirteen counts of bombing and murder, he received several consecutive life sentences. His manifesto was subsequently placed in a chat room on the Internet, but no one wanted to take seriously what he had to say. Rather than listening to the message of Kaczynski, many Americans became a little more nervous about opening a letter or a package from an unknown sender or without a return address. Throughout the country, the presence of an unidentified package became a sufficient reason to evacuate a public building.

We usually think of schools and churches as among the safe and secure places in our society. Yet one of the most shocking episodes of public violence occurred on April 20, 1999, at Columbine High School near Littleton, Colorado. Two teenage students, Eric Harris and Dylan Klebold, carried out a planned shooting spree that killed twelve other students and a teacher before they committed suicide.

Harris and Klebold had also planted bombs around campus, including two in the cafeteria. Had the detonators on their bombs worked as they intended, the calamity would have been even more severe. They had planned to detonate the bombs in the cafeteria when about 500 students would be there on their lunch break. An analysis of their journals indicated that their plans also included a massacre in the neighborhood and then hijacking an airplane that they would crash into a building in New York City. The actual scope of the damage from their planned attack was far more limited than they had initially intended.

While there had been previous school shootings, the Columbine massacre was the most dramatic in U.S. history. The violent episode evoked several explanations of what is wrong with our school system, the turbulence of youth and adolescence, and the prominent place of the gun culture in American life. Some sought to link the school shootings with the violence in video games and movies. While not specific to Harris and Klebold, others noted the victimization of classmates by school bullies. Yet others noted how the change in the American family had increased the neglect of children by their parents. None of these explanations seemed to be adequate.

Although images of children as innocent and angelic had been challenged in recent years by movies portraying children as monsters or as devil babies, it was a shock to discover that in real life children could also be terrorists. The motives of the perpetrators remain shrouded in mystery. In response to the episode, greater security measures were introduced into schools in order to reduce the probability that such an episode would happen again. Many schools instituted anti-bullying measures and bans on the use of threatening behavior. Policies of zero tolerance of bringing weapons to school were initiated and wireless video surveillance systems were installed.

The school shootings at Columbine became an important symbolic event in the life of the nation. In elaborating on the symbolism of the tragedy, Michael Moore's documentary video titled *Bowling for Columbine* concentrated on the gun culture that has been elaborated in our society. The documentary observes that the high homicide rate in the United States may be due to the scope of gun ownership and the availability of guns in the home. Most households with firearms have them stored in unlocked locations that are readily accessible to all household members. Their ready availability becomes manifested in the aggregate data on homicide, suicide, and accidental death. While gun ownership is a constitutional right, many Americans have guns in their home from a fear of criminal victimization and a perceived need to defend themselves from potential unknown intruders.

Studies subsequently funded by the U.S. Department of Education revealed the many ways that the gun culture has an impact on children and adolescents. Almost a hundred children are expelled in the United States each week for bringing a gun to school. Why so many children take guns to school and why they kill remains a complex and, as yet, not well understood issue. While the motives remain unclear, it is evident that children frequently bring guns to school with the intention of using them. Recurrent episodes of shooting and killing classmates and teachers demonstrate a clear need for the early training of youth in conflict management. Such training may reduce the tragic loss of young lives, the trauma for classmates, and the soul-searching of many adults.

As the Columbine episode worked its way into collective memory, an alternative to the themes of alienation and disenchantment was developed. The personality of both Harris and Klebold may very well have been characterized by an exaggerated sense of self-importance and self-esteem. They were not victims of bullies and the occasional ugliness of peer group pressures. Instead, they were highly respected by their classmates and held positions of leadership in their school. An examination of their diaries suggests that planning for the shooting spree may have grown out of an exaggerated sense of importance and an interest in demonstrating their superiority over other people. Scheduling the school shootings on the birthday of Adolf Hitler may have reflected an interest in demonstrating their superiority by getting rid of what they saw as "inferior people."

Whether the referent is schools, churches, scientific laboratories, the government, or the family, no basic social institution has been completely free from acts of terrorism in recent years. One of the most widespread and turbulent forms of terrorism has been the bombing of abortion clinics and the murder of abortion providers.

Abortion is perceived as a master symbol of moral decay by religious extremists who strongly opposed the Supreme Court decision in *Roe v. Wade*. While women now have a legal right to terminate an unwanted pregnancy, some extremists regard the exercise of this right as a form of murder. The bombings, burnings, and other violent assaults on abortion clinics are regarded by their perpetrators as a form of violence "favored by God," and if it involves the murder of abortion providers it is regarded as justifiable homicide.

Thousands of disruptive and violent acts have been directed toward abortion clinics over the past thirty years. Legal and constitutional rights to abortion have been violently opposed by such acts of aggression as harassment, posting pictures of medical records on the Internet, and sending letters through the mail containing substances resembling anthrax spores. Somehow there seems to be a contradiction between endorsing the "right to life" slogan while manifesting a willingness to murder abortion providers.

Antiabortion activists convicted of murder have included members of an underground organization designated "The Army of God." The terrorist activities of this organization included posting a "Nuremberg File" on the Internet that included the names of doctors and staff that have worked at abortion clinics. The stated goal of the Web site was "to record the name of every person working in the baby slaughter business across the United States of America." Drawing on an analogy with the Nuremberg trials of Nazi Germany, the list was designed to punish "these people for slaughtering God's children." Such terrorist procedures were based on beliefs about the infallible correctness of the group members' own position and a commitment to imposing their own morality on others by means of violence.

Vigilante Terrorism

In contrast to the sporadic acts of public violence described above, vigilante terrorism is pervasive and persistent in generating fear in a subgroup of the population. This is a form of terrorism that operates outside the legal framework of courts, legislative assemblies, and law enforcement agencies. Instead, vigilantes take the basic functions of government into their own hands. Their activities become clandestine through using such tactics as secret membership, secret meetings, and the wearing of hoods in public places. Since the Civil War, the dominant form of terrorism in the United States has consisted of vigilante violence directed toward African Americans.

Instead of being able to enjoy the freedom promised by the Emancipation Proclamation, blacks were subject to an extreme form of maltreatment with the emergence of the Ku Klux Klan and other vigilante organizations. Hooded night riders burned crosses and destroyed the homes and property of African Americans. The encounter with terror on the part of former slaves was accompanied by fear among whites that the emancipated slaves would retaliate against their masters who had previously abused them. The turbulence of the times promoted an atmosphere of reciprocal fear and distrust.

The ideological justifications for slavery persisted and provided support for the continued maltreatment of African Americans. The freed slaves were vulnerable and became scapegoats for Southerners' pent-up anger and hostility over losing the Civil War. Former Confederate officers and enlisted men created and joined vigilante organizations in order to support the notion that they were not among those who had surrendered at the end of the war. As members of the KKK, they were able to wear hoods to conceal their identities as they engaged in acts of violence and aggression in order to instill fear in African Americans.

The violence employed by the KKK and White Citizens Councils was tolerated and approved by local community leaders and law enforcement agencies. Blacks could be victimized for any minor infraction of the unwritten rules concerning their subordinate status. The effectiveness of terror as a form of social control depended to a very large degree on its arbitrary character and its lack of predictability. Acceptance of marginal status required recognizing that color lines were not to be crossed and that the many forms of humiliation, brutality, and injustice were to be endured in silence.

The vigilante forms of terrorism not only inflicted immediate physical damage but also sent symbolic messages to the black community. News reports of racial crimes increased African Americans' perceptions of risk and danger as well as imposing serious restrictions on their freedom of movement. The damage involved feelings of vulnerability, anger, depression, physi-

---

Box 10
Symbolic Event: Picture Postcards of Lynchings

In 2000 the nation was shocked by an unusual exhibit that opened at the Roth Horowitz Gallery in New York City. The exhibit consisted of a collection of picture postcards depicting lynchings in the United States. Between 1882 and 1968, an estimated 4,742 blacks met brutal and violent deaths at the hands of lynch mobs. The lynchings were the culmination of the extreme measures vigilantes were willing to take to instill terror in the black population. Many of the postcards in the exhibit were worn from their circulation through flea markets and antique shops.

Images on these postcards indicated that the vigilante violence often had the full support of leading citizens in the cities and towns where the lynchings occurred. Rather than reflecting indignation, the activities of spectators in the picture postcards displayed a festive, carnival-like atmosphere. In contrast, most viewers of these depictions in a gallery exhibit experience some degree of pain, anger, and collective guilt. Some pictures portrayed the burned bodies of black men who had been brutally mutilated and, in some cases, castrated, before being lynched. The message on the back of one of the postcards read: "This is the barbecue we had last night." Others contained references to the protection of "the White Womanhood of the South."

Administrators at Emory University had reservations about a public display of the postcards that had been donated to them. There was uncertainty about the degree to which the depictions would have the unintended consequence of reinforcing the racism deeply embedded in American culture. These reservations diminished with the long lines that formed to see the exhibit when it was displayed in New York, Pittsburgh, Atlanta, and other places. Some viewers compared the emotional impact of the exhibit to that of the Holocaust Museum in Washington, DC.

Once the postcards were collected and put together in a gallery exhibit, the function of the depictions shifted from expressing approval of the practice of lynching to requiring a modern generation to confront the ugliness of its social heritage. While such practices today clearly fall within the framework of criminal conduct, lynchings and other extreme forms of racial brutality still occur sporadically.

---

cal ailments, and other symptoms of stress disorder. The message being sent was that racial and ethnic minorities were regarded as inferior and undesirable. On balance, racial crimes did more damage to perceptions of society as moral community than all other crimes combined. Such violations had unmistakable effects in aggravating community conflicts and tensions.

Historically, lynching was one of the major forms of terror directed toward black males. Self-appointed defenders of racial purity and the status quo inflicted terrible violence on black citizens. The burning of blacks' homes, beatings, stabbings, and other forms of brutality, torture, and property destruction were long used as a means of maintaining the caste system in race relations. Extreme measures were used by both law enforcement officials and by members of the white majority who were committed to "keeping blacks in their place."

Racial terrorism continues to be expressed in the thousands of racially based hate crimes that still occur each year in the United States. About 30 percent of these crimes involve such property offenses against blacks as robbery, vandalism, theft, or setting fires to homes, stores, or places of worship. The remaining 70 percent involved violence against a person, such as assault, rape, and murder. Intense levels of racial prejudice and stereotyping frequently serve to promote and justify the immorality of such acts of aggression. The deep-seated racism in our society may lead perpetrators to believe that they have permission to engage in acts of violence against blacks and Asians.

The openness of the terrorism involving a lynching and a viewing audience stands in contrast to the clandestine character of the burning of crosses and the bombing of black churches. The burning and bombing of black churches escalated with resistance to the civil rights movement. The black church was the primary institution for offering a sense of catharsis for the agony and despair that African Americans experienced in a hostile and unfriendly environment. In this way, churches provided stable anchoring points as the soul of the black community. Many black churches worked collectively to address racial discrimination, segregated schools, and the special concerns of their members. It was perhaps because of the symbolic meaning of churches in black communities that they became primary objects of racially motivated violence.

The firebombing of the Sixteenth Street Baptist Church in Birmingham, Alabama, in 1963 became symbolic of racial terrorism in America. The destruction of this church had an especially profound effect both on the black community and on the entire nation. This attack evoked strong empathy for the four children killed as well as for the several people injured. The sense of security provided by black churches could never again be taken for granted. Unfortunately, this act of terror was not an isolated event. Episodes of burning African American churches persisted into the 1990s. For example, between January 1995 and July 1996, more than seventy black and multiracial churches were burned. Recurrent episodes of racial terrorism are still an ugly reality of our society.

Further expressions of racial terrorism include the large number of armed militias that have been organized in recent years. These groups combine racial hatred with selected religious ideologies and hostility toward the federal government. The basic beliefs of many of these groups are designated as "Christian Identity," which holds that only "those of the white race are God's chosen people." All others are regarded as impure and defective. The armed militias have assembled arsenals of weapons to draw upon for implementing their objectives when the appropriate time arises.

Insurgency Terrorism: Ruby Ridge and Waco

In contrast to the vigilante form of terrorism whose objective is to instill fear in a subgroup of the population, insurgency terrorism involves engaging in acts of violence and aggression against the established social order. This form of terrorism consists of a psychological withdrawal from society, elaborating an ideological position, and defining the existing forms of government as immoral, oppressive, and tyrannical.

Some instances of insurgency terrorism involve extremist religious groups that insulate themselves from the surrounding society, create large arsenals of weapons for defending themselves, and prepare for Armageddon. Their religious ideologies emphasize absolute truth claims, complete obedience to a charismatic leader, and a willingness to die for a holy cause if necessary. In cases of mass suicide, self-destruction arises not from a state of despair, but as a means of making a transition to a higher state of being.

The nation was shocked on November 18, 1978, when the news media reported to the nation on the mass suicides by an American cult that had migrated to Guyana. The People's Temple, under the leadership of the Reverend Jim Jones, was investigated by Congressman Leo Ryan from California who went to Guyana to evaluate the claim that members of his constituency were being held against their will. When he returned to the airport for his departure, all members of his party were shot. Upon nothing more than a request from their charismatic leader, more than 900 people then committed suicide by drinking a cyanide-laced grape punch. The Guyana case remains the largest and most disturbing episode of mass suicide in the past century. The dividing line between suicide and homicide is a thin one in the emotional intensity of public responses. It is for this reason that mass suicides implicitly involve an attack on society itself.

The fear of cults generated by the episode at Guyana was expressed in several ways. The greatest fear for many middle-class parents was that a son or daughter would join a religious cult. Such religious organizations provided a strong sense of moral community, a clear sense of purpose in life, and a buffer against the many forms of alienation experienced by young adults. Many parents held a conspiratorial view of brainwashing as a device for conversion and producing an extremist commitment.

The widespread fear of cults may have influenced the responses of federal marshals at Ruby Ridge, Idaho, and Waco, Texas, in 1992 and 1993. The criminal justice system and particularly law enforcement officials are faced with the problem of how to deal with religious extremists who are heavily armed and willing to die for what they perceive as their sacred cause. Yet specific individuals cannot be exempted from the laws and regulations that were designed to be applied universally in an orderly society.

Randy and Vicki Weaver had become increasingly disillusioned with modern society and wished to escape from what they perceived to be a sinful world. It was their quest for a simple life that led them to locate their home in an isolated region of northern Idaho only a few miles from the Canadian border. The rustic cabin built by the Weavers at Ruby Ridge had neither electricity nor a telephone. They were Christian Identity believers, held that the end of the world was near, and wanted to be left alone as they waited for Armageddon.

After collecting a large supply of weapons, Randy Weaver got into trouble with the law for selling two sawed-off shotguns to a government informant. Released on bond, he failed to show up for his mandatory court appearance. Surveillance of the Weavers' cabin took place for months as the U.S. Marshal Service tried to determine the best way to take him in. On August 21, 1992, its carefully planned scouting mission resulted in a shoot-out in which fourteen-year-old Samuel Weaver and one of the most highly decorated marshals in the service were killed.

The next day, Vicki Weaver's head was shattered by a sniper's bullet as she stood on the porch of the cabin with a nine-month-old baby in her arms. The FBI snipers at Ruby Ridge were members of the bureau's military-style Hostage Rescue Team. During the standoff, the number and military capability of the FBI agents increased. Shots had been fired through the cabin and federal snipers were scanning the cabin and the perimeter for suitable targets. By the time of the shoot-out, more than a hundred vehicles, including armored personnel carriers and bulldozers, were brought into the area. More agents continued to show up as though they were descending on a military encampment. Lured by news reports on the siege a large collection of people converged on the FBI perimeter. These included members of militia organizations, religious extremists, and those holding hostile attitudes toward the government.

The siege lasted eleven days and ended with the surrender of Randy Weaver and his friend Kevin Harris, but the controversy continued several years afterwards. Eventually, the U.S. Department of Justice settled a lawsuit that had been initiated by the Weaver family. Without admitting wrongdoing, the government paid Randy Weaver and his daughters a little more than $3 million to settle a claim for the deaths of Vicki and Samuel Weaver. Top FBI officials claimed that they had not approved the unprecedented and illegal shooting of civilians without provocation.

In the performance of their duties, the police become important symbols of the established social order. While the badge and the uniform are emblems of authority in everyday life, they frequently become symbols of oppression and injustice to the disenchanted. While beliefs about police brutality are sometimes valid, they often become magnified in the realities constructed by those involved in acts of confrontation. The police themselves sometimes become objects of abuse and have to deal with their own inner feelings of fear in the face of open resentment and hostility. Police officers frequently lack guidelines for police procedure as novel situations develop and officers become objects of antagonism and distrust.

Further issues pertaining to civil rights, social control, and dissent were brought into focus with the episode involving the Branch Davidians at Waco, Texas, on February 28, 1993. The Branch Davidians had emerged from a schism of the Seven-Day Adventist Church and established a religious commune with David Koresh as their charismatic leader. Koresh had taken control of the commune, and his claim to be a reincarnation of Christ was accepted by his followers.

Koresh taught that the prophecies of the Bible were being fulfilled and that the Apocalypse would begin with the American army attacking Mount Carmel, the name given to the Branch Davidian compound. In preparation for the final days, the Davidians buried a school bus to be used as a bunker, stored a huge quantity of food, and developed an arsenal of impressive military weapons. The arsenal included assault weapons, both automatic and semiautomatic rifles, Beretta semiautomatic pistols, .50–caliber machine guns, and a large supply of hand grenades. The value of the weapons was estimated at about $200,000.

While freedom of religion and gun ownership are rights protected by the U.S. Constitution, the Bureau of Alcohol, Tobacco, and Firearms (ATF) became involved in the case because of reports about the noise associated with training both men and women to fire the weapons in the Branch Davidian arsenal. There were also rumors that weapons were being modified for military purposes and that chemical weapons were being developed. Concern on the part of law enforcement officials also derived from a series of articles in a local newspaper on "The Sinful Messiah." The newspaper articles were based on information from defectors who were willing to talk about what was going on in the compound. Defectors claimed that

Koresh severely abused children, had sex with minors, and practiced polygamy, all in the name of God.

The showdown between the government and the cult began on February 28, 1993, when ATF agents attempted to arrest Koresh on charges of possessing illegal firearms and explosives. The Branch Davidians had been tipped off about the plans and were ready. While there is uncertainty over who fired the first shot, a heavy exchange of gunfire took place over the next forty-five minutes. Twenty ATF agents were either killed or wounded, while there was an undisclosed number of casualties among the Branch Davidians. Although the ATF assault team had trained at the military base at Fort Hood, Texas, the firepower of their weapons could not match that of the religious cult. Following a negotiation of a cease-fire, the FBI took charge of governmental operations.

Over the fifty-one–day siege that followed, attempts were made by the FBI to negotiate a solution to the crisis. Although concerned that the Davidians might commit mass suicide, the FBI employed widespread harassment techniques, including playing loud, offensive music and turning off the electricity. After concluding that Koresh and his followers could not be persuaded to come out, the FBI planned a final assault on the compound on April 19, 1993. After being notified that a tear gas attack was imminent, the Davidians started shooting. The gas attack continued for several hours before tanks were used to smash into the buildings. Several fires started, quickly engulfing the compound with intense heat. About eighty members of the Branch Davidians perished along with their leader, David Koresh. Uncertainty remains over how the fire got started and who was responsible.

The incident at Waco was one of the most disturbing episodes in the history of federal law enforcement. In subsequent investigations and court proceedings, the FBI was exonerated. Responsibility for the disaster was placed exclusively on David Koresh and his followers. Yet the episode at Waco was regarded as clear evidence of state tyranny and repression by a wide range of militia groups and religious extremists. In their view, there was an egregious violation of the constitutional guarantees of freedom of religion and the right to bear arms.

Oklahoma City Bombing

Before his execution, Timothy McVeigh indicated that he had planted the bomb in front of the federal building at Oklahoma City to avenge the deaths at Ruby Ridge and Waco. The earlier episodes had become linked in public discourse over the rights of individuals and the imperatives of law enforcement. A great deal of anger was directed toward government agencies that were perceived as using excessive force against the Weaver family at Ruby Ridge and the Branch Davidians at Waco.

On April 19, 1995, a rented Ryder truck heavily loaded with explosives was detonated outside the Alfred P. Murrah federal building in downtown Oklahoma City. The car bomb virtually destroyed the federal building and severely damaged six other buildings in the vicinity. The explosion left 168 people dead and about 500 injured. The fatalities included nineteen children who had been in a day-care center on the second floor. Subsequently, a nurse was killed during the rescue efforts. It was the most serious episode of terrorism in the history of the United States.

The news coverage was extensive, and the nation responded as it had to other national traumas of the twentieth century. Fear and anger were combined with intense feelings of empathy for victims and their families. The concern was primarily with the way in which individuals could be blown to smithereens while involved in the most ordinary of daily pursuits. It was particularly disturbing that the damage was intentional and that it occurred in our own country. Oklahoma City did not seem to be a likely target for a terrorist act of this magnitude.

Prior to the Oklahoma City bombing, most of the acts of terrorism within the United States had been on a relatively small scale and were generally perceived to be ineffective in calling attention to a social cause or to any political objectives. But now the sense of safety and security Americans had about living in their society was diminished. Previous acts of terrorism by alienated individuals were insignificant by comparison. Public concerns were expressed in a clamor for decisive action in the quest to apprehend suspected perpetrators.

About ninety minutes after the blast, Timothy McVeigh was pulled over by a highway patrolman for driving a car without a license plate. McVeigh, a highly decorated soldier of the Gulf War, was arrested on traffic charges and for carrying a loaded semiautomatic pistol. When FBI agents inventoried the car, they found pages from right-wing books and magazines and a futuristic novel glorifying an anticipated racist revolution. It became clear that McVeigh was steeped in militant antigovernment ideology. Two days later he was charged with the Oklahoma City bombing.

After his military service, McVeigh had symbolically withdrawn his allegiance from the United States. He no longer paid income tax and drove his car without a driver's license. He carefully considered right-wing books on how to disappear from the government's view, go underground, and make bombs. He and an army buddy, Terry Nichols, provided psychological support for each other. Apparently, McVeigh suffered from an exaggerated sense of justice and felt that the federal government should be punished for what he saw as the slaughter of innocents at Waco.

Following his conviction, McVeigh was given an opportunity to make a statement before his sentencing. He used the occasion to claim that he had acted in retaliation for what happened at Waco and that he had timed the second anniversary, April 19, as the date for his retribution. McVeigh claimed, in effect, that he had declared war on a government that had declared war on its own people. He asserted that he and he alone was responsible for planning and carrying out the attack.

Serious doubts were raised by many people about the possibility that McVeigh alone could have developed such a complex bomb, loaded several thousand pounds of explosives in a rented truck, and detonated it without blowing himself up. He had not received any special training in explosives during his military service. Demolition and military experts expressed doubts about the possibility of a single bomb, of the type that was used, bringing down the federal building without supplementary demolition charges.

Terry Nichols was subsequently found guilty of being a co-conspirator with McVeigh in advocating and planning violent assaults on federal targets. They had become close friends during their military service because of their fondness for guns and their hatred for government. Both McVeigh and Nichols became avid readers of extremist right-wing literature, with a special emphasis on conspiracy theories of power and antigovernment literature. Although he was in another state at the time of the bombing, Nichols received a life sentence for his role as a conspirator in planning the attack.

Following the Oklahoma City bombing, strict security measures were initiated for federal buildings. Barriers were constructed to prevent unauthorized trucks or cars from entering the vicinity of buildings. The easy entry of citizens into federal buildings was terminated. Security systems, including armed police and metal detection systems, were installed. Even federal employees were required to go through security systems on their way to work.

Separately and in combination, the episodes at Ruby Ridge, Waco, and Oklahoma City became important symbolic referents for a wide variety of constituencies. Antigovernment activists imputed special meanings to these events, as did religious extremists, law enforcement personnel, authority figures, and people in general. Like other forms of terrorism, these events confirmed that we live in a dangerous world and that the safety and security of everyday life are not self-evident.

The Ruby Ridge and Waco incidents became symbols of government tyranny for militia groups and antigovernment activists. From the vantage point of their hostility to the government, the bombing of the federal building in Oklahoma City was defined as the first major victory in the war against federal law enforcement. The civilians who lost their lives were simply regarded as the casualties of war. The federal building was seen as a representation of the malevolent authority exercised by the FBI and other governmental agencies and thus suitable as a target for revenge.

A message was also sent to federal law enforcement officials about the potential consequences of an excessive use of force. Changes in approach were reflected in the subsequent eighty-one–day standoff in 1995 with a highly armed militia group in central Montana. The Montana Freemen had declared their 960–acre ranch a sovereign territory, which they had named "Justus Township." The Freemen had rejected the validity of government from the county and state to the federal level. They refused to pay taxes, license their cars, or to recognize the authority of the courts. All of the twenty-one men on the ranch had warrants out for their arrests, with the charges ranging from writing bogus checks for more than $1 million to threatening the life of a federal judge.

The federal agents were determined to avoid repeating what had happened at Ruby Ridge and Waco. Instead of a military assault, they slowly increased pressure by cutting phone lines, shutting down the electrical system, and not permitting friends or relatives to visit the ranch. Eventually, sixteen members of the group surrendered, ending the longest federal siege in modern history. While the news media and some of the American public regarded the caution used in Montana as a sign of weakness, it was becoming clear to law enforcement officials that an excessive use of force can intensify rather than reduce the problems of terrorism.

With the terrorist attack on the federal building at Oklahoma City, the subsequent destruction of the twin towers at the World Trade Center and the bombing of the Pentagon, the age of terrorism was fully launched. The vulnerability of our complex civilization was illustrated, and the world could never again be the same. The continuity of everyday life as it was known and understood could no longer be taken for granted.

As a monument to victims, survivors, and rescuers, the Oklahoma City National Memorial was constructed on a two-block square in the downtown area. A part of the memorial is dedicated to victims and consists of nine rows of chairs representing the nine floors of the building. Each empty chair is dedicated to one of 149 victims of the tragedy and thus symbolizes a missing person. To the side of the main memorial are nineteen smaller chairs symbolizing the children who were killed. On a section of the wall that remained standing, the names of survivors of the blast are etched. People who want to leave a note or a memento may use a chain-link fence on each side of the memorial. One of the notes hung on the fence read, "If memories were stairs, we would climb to heaven to be with you."

The memorial provides a peaceful and beautiful place for reflecting on the human condition and the meaning of the tragedy. Such reflections suggest our vulnerability and the mortality of each of us. The tragedy of death reaches its highest level of intensity when it is out of place. We all have notions about the proper time to die, after a long and useful life or as relief from the pain of a prolonged illness. To have a life ended abruptly by a terrorist bomb has no place in our conceptions of a just and orderly world.

The official brochure at the memorial describes the 1995 episode as "the largest terrorist attack in U.S. history." The monument to the victims at Oklahoma City provides an advance indicator of the even more serious terrorist attack to be confronted on September 11. The Oklahoma City bombing reminds us that the perpetrators were American citizens who lived here as alienated and disenchanted strangers in our midst. The two episodes remind us that misplaced idealism and fanaticism may generate a readiness to die for what is perceived as a sacred cause. The two events also reflect a lack of empathy for innocent victims. In combination, Oklahoma City and the World Trade Center confirmed the observation that the new world order may appropriately be designated "the age of terrorism."

Discussion Questions

1. In your view, what is the most plausible explanation for the shootings at Columbine High School? Please justify your answer.
2. What are the arguments for and against administering psychological tests to the entire population in order to identify potential killers?
3. In view of the right to legal abortion, how would you explain the recurrent violence directed toward abortion clinics?
4. Has the violence growing out of deep-seated racism in our society diminished in recent years? Please justify your answer.
5. Is there a need for special training of the police to offset any trends toward inappropriate and excessive use of force?
6. Should the picture postcards of lynchings have been placed in museums for public viewing? What accounts for the large number of people who waited in long lines to see the exhibit?
7. Was the eventual military assault on the Branch Davidian compound the only reasonable way to resolve the conflict? Please defend your answer.
8. If you were on a committee to design a memorial for the victims of the Oklahoma City bombing, what would you recommend?

11 • The Terrorist Attack of September 11

The initial responses to the events of September 11, 2001, were shock, disbelief, and incredulity. The tragic news from New York and Washington jolted Americans out of the sense of complacency that had developed following the end of the cold war. The historical experience was of such an extraordinary character that the unfolding of events could not be placed within the usual framework for understanding everyday life.

Two airplanes commandeered by terrorists crashed into the twin towers of the World Trade Center. Each of the planes contained 10,000 gallons of highly flammable fuel. The heat generated by the explosion approximated the energy output of a nuclear power plant, reaching temperatures as high as 2,000 degrees. The intense heat softened the steel columns, reducing their capacity to support the building.

Many of the 35,000 people who are usually in the towers by 9:15 A.M. had not yet arrived at work. Those who were there needed to get out as quickly as possible. Those above the impact area were not able to escape, and some jumped from the top floors rather than suffer death from the heat and flames. The first plane struck the north tower between the ninety-fourth and ninety-eighth floors, while the second plane struck between the seventy-eighth and eighty-fourth floors. There were approximately 5,000 to 7,000 people in each tower at 8:46 A.M., the time of the first strike. The towers collapsed in less than two hours after impact, allowing several people at the lower levels to get out of the buildings. Business representatives from 115 countries were among those who died in the two planes and in the attack on the twin towers. Bravery and heroism were reflected among the more than 200 firefighters and police officers who lost their lives helping people to evacuate the buildings.

The routine journey to work had become a journey to death and destruction. The deaths were seen as senseless events that should never have occurred by the standards of what is normal, natural, and just within the social realm. Anxiety levels were high among those who had an intimate friend or relative who failed to return from work and was presumed dead under the rubble at the World Trade Center. Photos of the missing were prominently displayed on bulletin boards near ground zero and subsequently published in New York newspapers along with brief biographical sketches.

Initially, the losses were estimated at almost double the fatalities at Pearl Harbor. Shortly after the collapse of the towers of the World Trade Center, the White House was evacuated. All incoming international flights to the United States were diverted to Canada. The primary elections in New York City were canceled. The headquarters of the United Nations in New York was fully evacuated. And the international airports in San Francisco and Los Angeles were evacuated and closed.

About half an hour after the attack on the World Trade Center, a third hijacked plane crashed into the west wall of the Pentagon in Washington, DC. The Pentagon and the World Trade Center were primary symbols of world dominance by the American economy and military. Although the Pentagon had been designed to withstand a terrorist attack, a section of it collapsed and burned upon impact of the plane. There were more than 20,000 civilian and military workers in the building at the time. The casualties included the 184 people at the Pentagon who died along with the 59 aboard the hijacked plane.

A national trauma of intense proportions was in the process of developing. All commercial planes were grounded throughout the country, and thousands of passengers were trapped in airports. Anxiety levels were high about how it would be possible to get home. In the absence of any immediate course of action, the nation became engrossed in reports from the news media. Few people had ever thought of the possibility of using a commercial airplane as a rocket or as a military weapon.

The trauma of the attack continued to unfold in a fourth hijacked plane over western Pennsylvania. In a series of cell phone calls, passengers aboard the plane learned about the tragedy of the World Trade Center. They suspected that the next target would be the White House or the nation's capitol building. The heroic efforts of the passengers thwarted the plans of the terrorists, even though they were not able to save themselves. They personally gave their lives in order to save the lives of other people. During their assault on the terrorists, the plane crashed in a field about eighty miles southeast of Pittsburgh.

The shock of the attack was soon followed by intense feelings of sadness and patriotism. The sadness grew out of the loss of lives and the conditions under which the deaths had occurred. The news media played upon the tragedy by elaborating on the experiences in New York and Washington and aboard the plane that crashed in Pennsylvania. Emphasis was placed on acts of heroism among those who had died as well as on those who had survived. Attention was also given to the impact of the casualties upon surviving family members, their communities of origin, and their close friends.

Uncertainty and fear developed over the possibility that the terrorist attack was a forerunner of additional calamities to come. The fear was intensified by the television coverage of the events surrounding September 11. Not only was there a rapid relay of information, but also extensive pictorial repetitions. For example, film depicting the planes flying into the World Trade Center and the subsequent collapse of the buildings was shown repeatedly. Such portrayals reflected a sense of danger and intensified feelings of personal insecurity.

If the objectives of the terrorists were to instill fear in the general population, they could not have been more successful. The fear response centered not only on the dangers inherent in commercial air flights, but also in the possibility that subsequent acts of terror would be directed toward contaminating urban water supplies, blowing up buildings, dynamiting bridges, or exploding bombs in subways. The prior sense of confidence in our infrastructure and its interdependency was called into question.

As a result of the intensity of emotional responses, individuals were not able to remain inactive or indifferent. Everyday life had been disrupted to such a magnitude that a great deal of repair work was required to integrate recent events with prevailing understandings of the modern world. In addition to becoming engrossed in reading newspapers, listening to the radio, and watching television news, individuals engaged in a great deal of discussion as they attempted to develop plausible explanations of how and why the event occurred. Several of our everyday assumptions about order and social stability were shattered.

Shattered Assumptions

September 11, 2001, was a day when the world changed. The distinction between "before" and "after" became ingrained in the consciousness of Americans—indeed, in the awareness of many countries of the world. The nation with unsurpassed military capability was demonstrated to be vulnerable to a terrorist attack that could be carefully planned and successfully carried out. Because of the trauma of the attack, the place of the United States among the nations of the world was changed, and the normality of everyday life could no longer be taken for granted.

One of the major assumptions shattered by September 11 was that the end of the cold war had provided Americans with an increased degree of safety and security. The tearing down of the Berlin Wall and the breakup of the Soviet Union were seen as offering prospects for the creation of a new world order. The United States emerged from the cold war as the world's only superpower, with a position of dominance in the realms of the military, the economy, science, technology, and perhaps even culture. In the new world order, the fear of nuclear annihilation from a military confrontation with another superpower receded into the background. There were no credible threats to the military and economic superiority of the United States. In effect, the end of the cold war marked a dialectical triumph of the Western style of liberalism over all other contending ideologies. America reigned triumphant and, while there were residual concerns about nuclear power, the post–cold war era delivered a sense freedom from fear of impending military destruction. But merely eleven years after the collapse of the Soviet Union, the terrorist attack of September 11 shattered Americans' assumptions about their military invincibility. The myth of U.S. superiority and invulnerability was dealt a severe blow, without the conventional weaponry of war.

The terrorist attack provided a dramatic illustration of the vulnerability of the nation that had the world's largest defense budget and unsurpassed military capability. It led to an awareness that the major threats to the security of the United States did not stem so much from the threat of adversarial nations as from alienated and disenchanted individuals. A relatively small number of individuals armed only with box cutters and a willingness to die had disrupted the world's most powerful nation.

A second major shattered assumption grew out of the everyday elements of trust that are necessary for a modern society. We necessarily assume that the water supplied by the city is safe to drink, that electricity will be there when we need it, and that we will be paid for the work we do when payday rolls around. The speed, efficiency, and safety of commercial aviation are very much a part of our everyday awareness. It is only through our trust of the many specialists upon which we increasingly depend that a modern society is workable.

The violation of the trustworthiness of everyday life on September 11 resulted in feelings of personal vulnerability. The vulnerability was reflected in uncertainty over the scope of the attacks that had been planned as well as uncertainty over when and where the next attack would occur. Anxiety levels intensified as passengers were exposed to close scrutiny at security checkpoints in airports, as guards were increased at bridges and subways, and as passes were required for entering public buildings. The increased importance of internal security was recognized through the creation of a new cabinet post in the federal government.

The interdependency that promotes the efficiency of a modern society also reflects its vulnerability. It is for this reason that terrorism has a special appeal to the disenchanted who have only limited resources. A direct military confrontation is untenable in light of the overwhelming capacity of the modern state for waging warfare. But what the disenchanted can do is disrupt a social system and instill terror within the general population. Given the random killing of innocent civilians, no one can be completely sure that they will not be victimized.

Drawing on the theory of "the social contract," we may observe that a related shattered assumption of September 11 was that our own understanding of the world is likewise accepted and applied by other people. As humans we are dependent on each other, both within our own society and within the global community. This requires that we use common frames of reference as a basis for interaction. If we cannot assume that those with whom we interact share our values, norms, morality, and rules of law, we would be incapacitated. If this set of assumptions breaks down, we are faced with a crisis. Confusion, bewilderment, and disbelief were prominent among the responses to the terrorist attack.

Throughout the country, Americans raised the question "why do they hate us?" While most Americans thought they were admired and respected by the rest of the world, this assumption turned out to be in error. Americans thought of themselves as the ones who had liberated Europe from the tyrannical domination of Nazi Germany. They saw their benevolence as reflected in the Marshall Plan, which had helped to rebuild countries devastated by the destruction of World War II. They also saw themselves as providing leadership for the free world throughout the cold war. Americans were puzzled by the strong sentiment of anti-Americanism that surfaced even among the European allies that had cooperated with the United States over the past fifty years.

An assumption about the fondness for American culture among the nations of the world was also shattered. The secular and sensual lifestyles reflected in modern movies and television programs turned out to be particularly offensive to religious fundamentalists in many parts of the world. The traditional norms and values of many Islamic societies conflict with the individual freedom and hedonistic values depicted in American popular culture. Yet the satellites that circle the globe several thousand miles above the equator make American television available to the rest of the world. Political boundaries are permeable, and there is nothing Islamic or other countries can do to prevent the sexual themes of soap operas and other forms of popular culture from being available to their viewers. Through Hollywood, television, and other forms of popular culture, the United States is seen as reflecting the degeneracy and decay of Western civilization.

In small groups and intimate conversations all over the country, Americans raised questions about the intentions, decisions, actions, and motives of the terrorists in shaping the course of events. Notions about evil, religious fanaticism, political extremism, and hidden conspiracies loomed large in individual and collective attribution of causality. The scope of the shattered assumptions required Americans to modify and refine their national identity. Both deciding on what it means to be an American and locating the place of the United States among the nations of the world are issues still in progress and far from being resolved.

Causal Explanations

Causal explanations, even if erroneous, impose order on what otherwise would appear to be random, haphazard, and meaningless events. Initial attributions drew heavily upon the theme of evil in attempts to make sense out of what had happened. As an embodiment of evil, Osama bin Laden was assumed to be the mastermind in back of the attack. The training of terrorists and the mobilization of resources for an assault on American institutions had accompanied his declaration of jihad (holy war) against the United States.

Osama bin Laden, the son of one of Saudi Arabia's wealthiest families, became the coordinator of al Qaeda, an international terrorist organization. In the decade prior to September 11, he had masterminded and financed several terrorist operations to express his anti-American, anti-Western, and anti-Israel sentiments. Throughout this period, he made frequent references to what he perceived as an American crusade against Islam, issued a religious edict calling for the killing of Americans, and stated the objective of removing the Western infidels from Muslim countries.

To emphasize the theme of evil, comparisons were made between bin Laden and Adolf Hitler in public discourse within the United States. The comparison reduced the complexity of events and provided a public framework for clarity and understanding. However, the concept of evil with its demonic overtones has to a very large degree disappeared from academic discourse in modern society. The current emphasis on cultural relativism and pluralism has resulted in discomfort with such terms as "bad," "immoral," and "evil." While the concept of evil lacks precision, it usually refers to intentional acts of destructive or harmful behavior perpetrated by a person or a group. The individual evildoer is seen as unrepentant, remorseless, and lacking in any redeeming social value. Persons engaging in evil acts are assumed to be inhuman, beastly, and lacking in empathy for their victims.

Invoking the notion of evil has a labeling or name-calling quality. It is interesting to note that Islamic extremists promoting a jihad against the United States draw upon a similar vocabulary. Bin Laden denounced the United States as an embodiment of evil, suggesting that all goodness is on his side.

Underlying the war on terrorism and the holy crusade of Islamic jihad, there are attitudes of reciprocal distrust and demonic name-calling.

Others qualified the designation of evil by maintaining that the terrorists were not so much evil as misguided religious extremists. As religious extremists, they were regarded as idealists who believed in the rightness of what they were doing. For example, in an address to his followers in 1998, bin Laden observed that his brand of terrorism was commendable for it was a religious war directed at tyrants and the enemies of Allah. The brand of religion espoused by bin Laden provided a sense of meaning and direction for acting in accordance with mandates received from God.

As true believers, terrorists achieve a sense of exhilaration and self-fulfillment through their dedication and their willingness to die for a holy cause. Suicide as an extreme form of personal sacrifice becomes a form of self-actualization. Americans trying to understand the September 11 attacks drew upon their memories of similar forms of extremist behavior. Older Americans were reminded of the Japanese kamikaze fliers of World War II who dived their planes into American ships and were willing to lose their lives in the process. The willingness of young people to voluntarily sacrifice their lives for a holy cause is appalling to most Americans.

Few are able to adequately understand the motives of religious extremists who are willing to die for a cause. With the increasing secularization of modern society, deep commitments to any form of sacred values have become limited. Yet it is important to note that there are more people in the world who die from suicide each year than from all of the wars that are fought. The World Health Organization (WHO) reports that suicide is the third biggest cause of death among people aged fifteen to thirty-four worldwide. From an individual's standpoint, it would seem preferable to voluntarily sacrifice one's life for a holy cause than to take one's life out of a sense of despair. The suicide terrorists of 9/11 may very well have believed that following their violent deaths they would go directly to heaven.

A more sophisticated explanation of the terrorist attack focused on the process of globalization. In this view, the United States symbolized advanced forms of modernization. The epic clash of civilizations was reflected in the terrorists' selection of the Pentagon and the World Trade Center as the objects of attack. The United States was merely representative of Western economic and cultural domination of the rest of the world. Traditional, sacred values were seen as threatened by the onslaught of Western values that were being imposed on the rest of the world. The terrorist attack was then a response to the clash between the lifestyles and values of Western and Islamic civilizations.

Americans were divided over the acceptability of the prevailing explanations of the terrorist attack of September 11. Such descriptions of the traumatic event as a conflict between good and evil, as an expression of religious fanaticism, or as a clash of civilizations were acceptable to some but rejected by others. Even the war metaphor was questioned because it implied armed aggression and hostility between clearly identifiable nations. Explanations receded into the background as political officials sought policies to prevent another terrorist attack from occurring.

The War on Terrorism

The intensity of the fear and anger among Americans resulted in a call for a militant line of action. Americans were outraged and determined to go after the terrorists. Nothing could be done directly about the suicide bombers, but a great deal could be done about the extremist leaders and organizations that had planned and orchestrated the attack on the United States.

Under the known leadership of bin Laden, the objectives of the terrorists were to maximize the number of people killed, to maximize the societal disruption, and to destroy major economic, military, and political symbols of the world's uncontested superpower. The new forms of terrorism stemmed from religiously inspired groups that lacked any firm connections to a specific national state. Since their organization was global in scope, their activities were not subjected to the usual state sanctions for criminal conduct. Within a religious framework, the leadership of global terrorism had the capacity to draw upon a relatively large number of young adults who are willing to volunteer for suicide missions.

In order to locate and destroy terrorists, it became necessary to take military action against those nations that harbored and provided financial support for them. It was within this context that Americans launched an assault against the terrorist organizations located in Afghanistan. The organization of al Qaeda under the leadership of bin Ladin had found a sanctuary in Afghanistan. The Taliban leaders who had gained control of the country gave al Qaeda a high degree of freedom for training and indoctrinating terrorists. They also permitted importing weapons, raising funds, and forging ties with other jihad groups and leaders. The general headquarters of international terrorism had been established for planning and carrying out attacks on the United States and other countries.

Initially, congress had supported President George W. Bush in his declaration of "war on terrorism." Such a designation served to indicate that those in positions of power were taking decisive action. The United States was becoming engaged in a permanent war without a clearly identifiable enemy. There were no battle lines, as there had been in World War II and Korea, and there were no definitive gauges that would indicate when the war was over. The country was engaged in a new kind of war, and the war designation was drawn upon to mobilize society by promoting national solidarity and a sense of patriotism.

In his State of the Union address in January 2002, President Bush designated as "evil" those enemy nations that were devoting their resources to the development of weapons of mass destruction. He applied the term "axis of evil" specifically to Iraq, Iran, and North Korea. Such a designation was based in part on those nations' presumed support for the terrorist attacks and in part on their research programs to enhance their capacity for waging chemical, biological, and radiological warfare. Shock at the president's remarks derived in part from his use of the term "axis of evil" and in part from the expectation that he was presenting justifications for launching air strikes at targets within the countries regarded as rogue nations. Placing the emphasis on rogue states may have served as a substitute for the inherent difficulty of locating and destroying terrorist networks.

Developing weapons of mass destruction was a part of the legacy of the cold war. Both the United States and the Soviet Union had developed large stockpiles of highly lethal military weapons. The possibility of developing such weapons had become common knowledge on a worldwide basis. The fear response in the United States grew out of a concern that in future attacks much more lethal weapons could be used to produce a much greater destruction of life and property.

Although terrorists lack the resources necessary for developing sophisticated nuclear weapons, they do have the capacity for developing dirty bombs. A dirty bomb is a conventional explosive device, of the type used in the Oklahoma City bombing that is packed with radioactive substances. In an explosion, the radiation could become airborne and spread contamination, injury, and death over a large area. While such a weapon is limited in its effectiveness, it has an enormous capacity for instilling fear in a large population.

Both American and Soviet scientists who once worked on germ weapons are now also concerned with control over this deadly threat. The possibility of a serious bioterrorist attack was suggested by the emergence of an anthrax scare in October 2001. Five people were killed and seventeen others were made ill by letters containing anthrax spores sent to news media and several government offices. Although the panic that followed was an overreaction, there was general agreement that the possibility of a bioterrorist attack should be taken seriously. If the objective of suicide terrorist is only to kill people, the use of germ warfare could be very effective.

Since the anthrax scare was only a month after the attack on the World

Trade Center, it was initially thought to be a component of the international terrorist attack. However, no connection to international terrorism was ever established, and some people came to the conclusion that the perpetrator was a disenchanted research scientist in the United States. If so, the anthrax episode would resemble the domestic terrorism of the unabomber variety. As a result of uncertainty over future bioterrorism, all soldiers on assignment in Iraq received an anthrax vaccination along with their smallpox vaccination.

American intelligence reports suggested that Iraq was actively engaged in the production of weapons of mass destruction and that these weapons could be made available to terrorists. President Bush's appeal to the United Nations for an endorsement of his plans for air strikes and a ground invasion of Iraq failed to meet with approval. The United Nations inspectors had not found any evidence of weapons of mass destruction in Iraq and requested more time before the United States and its allies launched a military attack. While the United States did have some allies in the invasion and occupation most of the Western democracies, including those that had been close supporters of the United States since World War II, were opposed to the military action against Iraq. References to the United States as the world's leading rogue nation became prominent in Europe. In spite of opposition from democratic allies, the United States implemented its plans to launch a preemptive strike against Iraq.

A preemptive strike is based on what is presumed to be the motives, intentions, and plans of an enemy nation. Why wait for another Pearl Harbor in which an enemy might use weapons of mass destruction against the United States? Since the United States is the world's only military superpower, why not go ahead and crush an enemy before it strikes first? To do so would set an example of the futility of any other nation following the course of action under way in Iraq.

The military invasion of Iraq was swift and decisive. Just six weeks after the start of the war the president of the United States announced "Mission Accomplished" aboard an aircraft carrier. However, dismantling one of the world's largest armies, from the standpoint of manpower, did not mean that the war was over. There was widespread looting following the collapse of the authority structure in Iraq. Guerrilla warfare sporadically erupted and led to intense fighting with the army of occupation.

Americans were in the process of becoming more highly divided than at any time since the Vietnam War. No weapons of mass destruction were found in Iraq, and there was no evidence that Iraq had provided support for the terrorist attack of September 11. It became apparent that no adequate plans had been made for either nation building or for the occupation of Iraq after the invasion was over. Many of the soldiers in the National Guard units sent

---

Box 11
Symbolic Event: Prisoners as Enemy Combatants

The publication of pictures revealing cruelty and unusual punishment of Iraqi prisoners by American soldiers at the Abu Ghraib prison outside of Baghdad was shocking to many Americans and even more so to the rest of the world. The humiliation and abuse included stripping prisoners of their clothes, stacking them on top of each other in the nude, and forcing them to engage in sexual acts. An exceptionally offensive picture showed a naked prisoner being led by a female guard with a leash around his neck. The photographs revealed what human rights activists had long expected. Some of the forms of humiliation, fear, and physical deprivation that had been used by American interrogators in Afghanistan and Guantánamo were now being applied in Iraq. Indignant Americans clamored for investigations to establish responsibility for these atrocities.

The torture of prisoners of war to extract information from them was banned by the Geneva Convention in 1949, which had been endorsed by the United States. Some people were reminded of Nazi Germany and the former Soviet Union. In such totalitarian societies, individuals designated as enemies of the state were tortured without mercy for information before they were killed. But as a self-proclaimed civil society, the United States is bound by the rule of law and by the United Nations Universal Declaration of Human Rights. Initially, the Defense Department attempted to dismiss the abuse as "criminal misconduct" by a small number of individual soldiers. However, subsequent investigations revealed that the several hundred cases of known abuse may have been deeply embedded in U.S. policies for waging the war on terrorism.

---

to Iraq felt that they were not adequately trained for the nuances of an army of occupation in a hostile land.

The denial of prisoner of war status to the captives held in Afghanistan, Guantánamo, and Iraq became an additional contentious issue both within the United States and in other countries. The United States was committed to international agreements on the treatment of prisoners of war. But since the prisoners were not wearing uniforms and were not representatives of a state-sponsored military unit, they were regarded as terrorists or international criminals. Since they did not have American citizenship, detainees were not entitled to the protection of civil liberties guaranteed by the U.S. Constitution. This meant that they could be held indefinitely without any charges brought against them and without a trial by jury or an opportunity to state their case in court.

By executive order, the prisoners from Afghanistan had been designated as "enemy combatants." In the absence of prisoner of war status, they were not entitled to the humane treatment specified by the Geneva Convention.

The designation as "enemy combatants" was for the purposes of forceful interrogation. The detainees might have insider information on how and when the next terrorist attack would occur or on the logistics of leadership, financing, and the location of terrorist organizations. This was the justification for a policy of "forceful interrogation" that would permit U.S. military experts to use coercive methods behind closed doors for obtaining much-needed information.

If there were certainty that the torture of enemy combatants would prevent a future attack of the magnitude of September 11, then most Americans would very likely endorse such extreme procedures. If there were a strong suspicion that a detainee had information on bombs that had been strategically planted in buildings around the United States, few would insist on restraints in obtaining this information. But such certainty is extremely unlikely. From all we now know, the information extracted from detainees has been very meager and of limited value.

The United States had been led to believe that Americans would be welcomed as liberators in freeing Iraq from the capricious rule of Saddam Hussein. Further, it was expected that with the introduction of democracy, Iraq would become a model for other nations in the Middle East to emulate. Instead of fulfilling these expectations, the American invasion was followed by chaos, despite an impressive voter turnout in the Iraqi elections of 2005. U.S. armed forces were faced with a well-organized, extremely violent insurgency and the demand by many civilians that Americans get out of Iraq.

Homeland Security

The United States was not prepared for the kind of destruction that occurred on September 11. The perpetrators were hidden and unknown even as the nation looked deeply into events in order to determine what had happened. The central leadership of the Bush administration was also caught off-guard as it sought to comprehend the source of the tragedy. It became important to recognize the contours of a new and even more serious threat than was suffered in the previous terrorist attack on the World Trade Center in 1993, the two embassy bombings in Tanzania and Kenya in 1998, and the crudely executed attack on the USS *Cole* in the Gulf of Oman in 2000.

The September 11 terrorist attack provided a dramatic illustration of the permeability of national borders. With the scientific and technological sophistication of the modern world, movement across national borders can be achieved with very little difficulty. Much of the 5,000–mile border between the United States and Canada is unprotected. Large sections of the Mexican-U.S. border can be crossed with very little difficulty. Further, the many ways that people can legally cross borders as students, tourists, business travelers, and workers truly reflect the interdependency of a globalizing world.

The USA Patriot Act of 2001was quickly passed by Congress after September 11 without serious debate and without most members of Congress actually reading it. The new law seriously compromises the constitutional basis for American democracy by placing severe restrictions on civil liberties. Law enforcement officials now have the authority to monitor telephone conversations, e-mail communications, and bank records without anyone's permission or knowledge. Libraries and bookstores are required to give information on the purchases and reading habits of individuals when requested to do so by federal security agents.

Certain aspects of the First Amendment right to freedom of speech, including the right to criticize the government without fear of punishment or indefinite detention have been compromised. Criticism of the policies of government can be regarded as a subversive activity, as unpatriotic, and as aiding and assisting the enemy. Anyone who questions the motives or policies of the government in fighting terrorism runs the risk of being labeled a terrorist, a terrorist sympathizer, or an enemy combatant.

Homeland security legislation permits law enforcement officials to arrest suspects and hold them in prison for an unspecified time without the benefit of an attorney and without specific charges being brought against them. American citizens might have their names added to the "no fly" list submitted to airlines without any way of knowing how their names got there or how to have them removed. Average citizens are without protection against unreasonable search and seizure. Secret warrants can now be issued for a search of private homes and for a confiscation of property whether the owner is at home or not.

All these restrictions on civil liberties, which would have been illegal only a few years ago, represent some of the many consequences of pursuing an all-out war on terrorism at home as well as abroad. The most tenuous connection to a "terrorist organization" or a "terrorist state" can now lead to serious federal charges, reminding many Americans of the guilt by association during the days of McCarthyism. In retrospect, what is most surprising is that the many compromises of civil liberties were passed by Congress without debate and without the opportunity to negotiate amendments. The very designation of these provisions as the "Patriot Act" implied that those who opposed them were traitors or unpatriotic.

Hundreds of immigrants to the United States were subjected to lengthy detention without notification of their families. Some of the detainees were subjected to physical and verbal abuse, and hundreds were deported for such minor offenses as visa violations. There were no specific terrorist charges against any of the detainees. The arbitrary and capricious exercise of power had become a part of the law enforcement process in the age of terrorism.

As a result of the concern for protecting American civil liberties, hundreds of municipalities scheduled open forums and debates to explore the implications of the Patriot Act. As a result of these deliberations, more than 200 local and state resolutions were passed to condemn what were regarded as flagrant violations of the U.S. Constitution. Several local law enforcement agencies went on record as promising to refuse to cooperate with an enforcement of the Patriot Act.

The extensive measures that have been taken to circumvent future terrorist attacks serve several purposes. Such measures are regarded by some as providing strong and effective leadership in dealing with a serious problem. Those holding this view believe that our personal and collective safety is improved through the strong measures that our government has taken. Others believe that there are serious limits to the practicality and affordability of such attempts to prevent terrorism from ever occurring. For example, screening the millions of passengers who daily ride such forms of public transportation as Amtrak, subways, buses, and commercial airlines would be an enormous and extremely costly task. The probability of finding one individual or small group of terrorists embarked on a destructive suicide mission is limited.

Upon signing the Homeland Security Act of 2002, President Bush observed that "the front of the new war is here in America." The act created a new cabinet-level agency that was given administrative control over border protection, public transportation, public health, and counterterrorism measures. This new agency was also given many of the same information-gathering and surveillance powers given to the FBI and the Department of Justice under the Patriot Act. The underlying assumption seemed to be that there are hidden enemies in our midst who must be vigorously pursued and incapacitated in order to prevent another terrorist attack from occurring.

The lack of national debate over homeland security legislation did not mean that Americans were willingly giving up their civil liberties. Instead, it was more nearly an indicator of the ascendance of the fear of terrorism in American consciousness. Without public discussion on issues directly related to national security, the latent anxieties over civil liberties surfaced in other ways. For example, Americans developed a deep interest in reading about the nation's founders and the conditions surrounding the creation of the U.S. Constitution. Biographies of the founders became best sellers. For the most part, these books idealized such men as Franklin, Washington, Adams, Madison, and Hamilton. Following the American Revolution, the creation of a new and workable government was a challenge of monumental proportions. The architecture of the Constitution grew out of the rationality of the Enlightenment and the recognition of the need to work out creative solutions to deep-seated conflicts and competing interests. It was the commitment of an entire generation to promoting individual liberty and creating a secular civil society that shaped the political culture and the collective identity of the new nation.

The concerns growing out of collective fear have tested the nation's commitment to basic freedoms many times. Early in the history of the nation, the Alien and Sedition Acts permitted censorship, imprisonment, and deportation of those critical of the government. The administration of John Adams became historically tarnished through its use of fear to suppress dissent and the freedom of speech. Restrictions on civil liberties occurred during the Civil War, during the Red Scare of the 1920s, with the internment of Japanese Americans during World War II, and with McCarthyism during the 1950s. In each of these historical cases, civil liberties were restored either by court order or by the passing of the national emergency. What is not presently known is the degree to which the current suppression of civil liberties might, unlike the past cases, become a permanent part of America's political culture.

The Culture of Fear

Before the terrorist attack of September 11, numerous books and journal articles suggested that a culture of fear had developed in the United States. The collective perceptions of risk and danger stood in sharp contrast to the primary emphasis on mastery and control in the scientific, technological, and organizational spheres of society. Popular culture and mass entertainment, as well as the news media, pointed toward the mishaps, tragedies, and dangers inherent in social living.

A casual inventory of everyday fears before 9/11 would have been a very long list. The health field included fears about the safety of the water we drank, the food we ate, and the air we breathed. The fear of AIDS, Ebola, and mad cow disease suggested the importance of taking extraordinary measures in everyday life. Perceptions that human beings were not in control of the consequences of their own actions surfaced in the fear of nuclear power plants and in the fear of exposure to radiation from the use of computers. Because of the fear of criminal victimization, enormous resources went into the construction of prisons. The list could go on and on.

The collective fear generated by the terrorist attack of 9/11 built upon and extended the culture of fear in our society. Many of the measures intended to increase the level of national safety and security have had the reverse effect at the individual level. For example, color-coded alerts from the FBI and Homeland Security can contribute to increased levels of fear. At airports, travelers are required to produce a photo ID to establish their identity, to remove their shoes and their belts, and to empty their pockets. They are also required to prove that their laptop does not contain a bomb and to send their briefcase or pocket book through a machine to prove that it does not contain a weapon. Any comment regarded as offensive by the security officers may provide a basis for detention, special treatment, and a missed flight. The message of these procedures serves as a reminder that we are living in a dangerous world and that travel on any specific flight without extraordinary precautions may turn out to be a lethal undertaking.

The consequences of high levels of fear, sustained over a long period of time, are likely to be maladaptive. The sense of vulnerability leads to a preoccupation with defensive measures, avoidance behavior, and restrictions on freedom of movement. It is out of collective fear that paranoia is directed toward neighbors and hate crimes are directed toward strangers and immigrants. It may be that terrorism can induce a country to scare itself into a state of paralysis. If so, the primary enemy may not be the terrorists so much as the fear that we have created for ourselves. Intensifying the level of fear within the general population cannot, in and of itself, be an effective strategy for defeating the terrorists.

The attempt to promote national security by increasing defense expenditures for sophisticated military weapons is an exercise in futility. The defense expenditures of the United States already exceed those of the world's fifteen next-largest defense budgets put together. With its awesome weapons of mass destruction, the United States can quickly crush any nation it regards as an enemy. Yet this unsurpassed military capability cannot protect it from an international terrorist attack within its own borders. As it demonstrated in Iraq, the United States has the capacity to strike down a designated rogue nation while terrorist cells with their shifting networks of membership and leadership can remain in existence.

The global character of modern terrorism requires us to recognize that the incubation of terrorist plans and strategies may originate at any place in the world. We saw on September 11 the kind of damage to our society that could be inflicted by the clandestine activities of only a small number of individuals with very limited resources. Preventing a terrorist attack from ever occurring is beyond the capability of either our intelligence-gathering agencies or our military institutions. In a world that has become interdependent, we may not be able to increase our sense of safety and security by enhancing our military sophistication.

Most people are aware that there is no place to hide from the risks and dangers of the modern world. The rhetoric of mastery and control over events is necessarily a part of the political process for instilling confidence in a nation's leadership, but its fraudulent character is apparent to many people. Increased governmental surveillance of the personal lives of individuals will not eliminate the threat of terrorism. A suspension of the civil liberties guaranteed by the U.S. Constitution will neither increase our sense of national security nor prevent unidentified individuals from smuggling weapons of mass destruction into the United States.

We know from anthropology that human beings have a remarkable capacity for creating and adjusting to a wide range of cultural conditions. However, there are limits. We do not know, for example, the long-range effects of intense and prolonged levels of fear on the general population. We have no way of knowing what the full range of these effects will be, but there is a very high probability that they will be deleterious. Neither the creativeness of modern civilization nor the well-being of individuals can long endure under extreme conditions of collective fear. Democracy and civil liberties may very well be among the first accomplishments of civilization to go.

Discussion Questions

1. How would you account for the strong sense of patriotism and national unity following the terrorist attack on September 11?
2. Is it possible to prevent another terrorist attack of the magnitude of the one that occurred on September 11? Why or why not?
3. Are the suicides of Islamic terrorists a form of self-destruction or self-fulfillment? Please justify your answer.
4. Are there any conditions in which the use of torture is justified in the interrogation of prisoners? Why or why not? Under what conditions does a forceful interrogation of prisoners constitute a violation of basic human rights?
5. Were there adequate justifications presented to the United Nations and to the American people for the invasion of Iraq? Why or why not?
6. Will the temporary compromise of our civil liberties become a permanent part of our political culture? Why or why not?
7. Is the fear of terrorism a realistic concern, or has there been an overreaction in our society? Please justify your answer.
8. Does the fear of terrorism build upon a "culture of fear" in our society? Why or why not?

III
Epilogue

12 • Collective Memory

One of the basic lessons derived from a review of national traumas is that the social order is fragile and subject to disruptions in unexpected ways. We may desire stability and coherence in the world around us, but at the same time we are required to cope with unwanted events of an extraordinary magnitude. Both triumphs and tragedies are inherent in social living. The triumphs verify the assumption that plans can be made and implemented, while the traumas remind us that hopes and intentions have their limits.

Superimposed on the lifestyles of the twentieth century were serious troubles. Extremes were evident in the shifts from economic abundance to severe economic hardships, from military unpreparedness to the capacity for annihilating all human life on this planet, from an intense fear of communism to political indifference toward the communist label. The extremes were also reflected in the shifts from sanctifying of political leaders to regarding them as criminals, and from the elation of landing human beings on the moon to the space shuttle *Columbia* breaking apart on reentry to the earth's atmosphere. Sharp contrasts thus surfaced in the experiences of Americans and in the attitudes they held about their recent past. Some people reflected on past accomplishments and developed a sense of pride in their country; others focused on traumas, assumed that there would be historical repetitions, and became pessimistic about the future.

The social significance of traumatic events stems from collective debates over the causes, conditions, and consequences of the chaotic forces that impinge upon our consciousness. In the trauma phase of an event, basic questions are raised, such as "How did it happen?" "Why did it happen?" and "What is going to happen next?" With the passing of time, however, the boundaries around specific events weaken as the events are placed within the general fabric of social life. In the telling and retelling of the stories of our past, the events in question become stereotyped and selectively distorted as they become embedded in collective memories.

We usually think of memory as the retrieval of information that is stored in the brains of individuals. However, in the final analysis, memory is a collective phenomenon. The human brain is certainly central to what we associate with being human. After all, it is the complexity and the sophistication of the human brain that sets us apart from all other animals. The contents of the human brain are primarily social in character. It is through the use of language and other symbols, and through our interactions with others, that we construct the possibilities and the limits of the world around us. Images of us and of our external environment are shaped by memories that are passed on by legions of men and women we have never known and never shall meet.

Individual memories are shaped disproportionately by lived experiences, while collective memories are represented in the full inventory of historical experiences that are drawn upon for contemporary sources of meaning. The task of the individual is to find his or her place within the broader scheme of human affairs. A primary task of a nation is to rework the data from the past in order to shape a contemporary identity.

Before the invention of the printing press and the widespread use of the written word, collective memories were transmitted primarily by means of oral history. Through the myth-making process, group experiences were passed on from one generation to the next. Stories were told about heroic times and the moral foundations of society. Some degree of social continuity was provided by oral traditions in which narratives were often embellished in order to have more dramatic effects on listeners. New generations were provided with frames of reference for deciding what to do, or what not to do, in given situations. Then as now, mythical accounts provided the ingredients for shaping a collective identity.

Today, we have newspapers, formal documents, photographs, computers, and other sophisticated devices for storing information that may be retrieved when the need arises. Recorded history provides us with access to information about the problems of the past, the attempts that were made to solve those problems, and the outcomes that resulted. Collective memories thus serve as a storehouse of knowledge that goes far beyond the information that is directly stored in the brains of living men and women. The importance of the data from the past, however, is not self-evident. It must be interpreted, given credibility, and constructed along lines that give it applicability to present concerns.

Humans thus take an active part in determining what their collective memories will be. Events are fashioned through a filtering of experiences. Some experiences are dismissed, while others are elaborated and given high levels of significance. Selective inattention and forgetting are ways of minimizing the risk of cluttering memories with information that is perceived to be trivial or irrelevant. In contrast, we tend to remember what we sense is important for us to remember. Individually and collectively, we seek to repeat those activities that were rewarding to us in the past and to avoid those activities that were associated with pain and suffering. Memories of how a social system was damaged by a traumatic event serve as a reminder of what to avoid in the future.

In publicly held attitudes and in the decisions of policy makers, national traumas frequently serve as negative frames of reference. The stories of these traumas remind us of our mistakes and suggest how to avoid similar mistakes in the future. These stories include, for example, how unresponsive government officials were to the intensifying hardships of the Great Depression, how Americans were unwilling to prepare for war at a time when advance preparations were necessary, how we were caught off-guard at Pearl Harbor, how close we came to nuclear war during the Cuban missile crisis, how we got caught in the quagmire of Vietnam without any satisfactory way out, and how the misuse of power led to the forced resignation of President Nixon. Dramatic messages are received from the past and may help the nation to avoid or to minimize such problems in the future.

Collective memories may be thought of as a storehouse of information on how problems were confronted and solved in the past. For example, the mobilization of resources to develop the atomic bomb became a grandiose model of what is possible when there is a concerted effort to solve some identifiable problem. Landing people on the moon and eradicating smallpox worldwide were additional spectacular accomplishments that were recorded among recent memories. Collective memories thus incorporate not only the tragedies of the past, but also extraordinary heroic accomplishments. Identifiable problems are seen as amenable to solution through collective action.

National traumas also provide the raw material for shaping national identities and revitalizing values for promoting the collective good. To provide some assurance that the past will be remembered properly, acts of commemoration are directed toward the creation of national shrines, monuments, memorials, and holidays. These creations build upon echoes from the past and facilitate the memory process for current and future generations. To take their proper place in the fabric of social life, traumatic events need to be selectively remembered. Those aspects of the past that were embarrassing to the nation or lacked relevancy for the moral foundations of society tend to be ignored.

National traumas provide the raw material for a vast amount of cultural elaboration. The hundreds, even thousands, of books, movies, and television productions devoted to national traumas reflect the many ways in which Americans remember their past. Like all other societies, our society must pass its heritage from one generation to the next and prepare people for the challenge of changing conditions. The expanding scope of the entertainment industries in serving this function is evident. Collective memories are drawn upon to tap a responsive chord in mass audiences. The attitudes, emotions, and predispositions of the viewers and readers shape and refine the contents and the entertainment value of the productions.

As new generations confront the problems of their time and place, the inventory of data from the past is reevaluated. Some experiences from the past become embellished and elaborated in attempts to give them contemporary relevance. Other experiences are forgotten or ignored because they are no longer perceived as useful. It is perhaps because of the human life cycle that societies retain their innovative potential. New members are added to a social system and existing members die. Through the replacement of members, societies take on dynamic qualities reflected in the opportunities provided for new beginnings.

Generational Effects

The members of a generation are influenced disproportionately by what was happening historically during their formative years. While we cannot say with precision what the boundaries for the formative years are, they would seem to be primarily the years of late adolescence and early adulthood. These are the years in which major life decisions are made at the individual level about continuing one's education, selecting a career, entering the labor force, getting married, and becoming a parent. The large number of decisions in early adulthood places individuals in a position of hyperreceptivity to the events that are occurring in their communities and in the nation. Personal encounters with national traumas during the formative years tend to have a disproportionate effect on any given generational unit.

Sociologists have observed that for an event to have a generational effect it must have an enduring place in the memories of those who experienced it during their formative years. The emotional impact of the event must be of a sufficient magnitude that it is remembered in a similar way by a large number of people. Further, the event must generate a sufficient level of public attention that people feel a pressing need to develop attitudes and beliefs about it. Using these criteria, the historical events of the twentieth century that have had the most enduring effects on generational memories are the Great Depression of the 1930s, the epic struggles of World War II, the assassination of President John F. Kennedy, the civil rights movement, and the collective frustrations of the Vietnam War. Other traumas had intense emotional impact on the nation, but were of shorter duration and had less lasting effects in collective memories.

Drawing on a national sample, a University of Michigan study in 1989 found generational effects in perceptions of the most important historical events in their personal memories. The events most frequently mentioned were those that had occurred during the subjects' early adulthood. Americans in their fifties, sixties, and older more frequently mentioned the Great Depression and World War II, while younger Americans more frequently mentioned the Vietnam War and the assassination of President Kennedy. Perceptions of consequential historical events are thus most likely to include events that occurred during an individual's impressionable years.

Those entering into early adulthood during the Great Depression had direct experiences with high rates of unemployment and economic hardships. Knowing what scarcity was like, they became disproportionately oriented toward saving, investment, and the accumulation of assets. This generation did not take the economic prosperity of the post–World War II era for granted but saw it as an opportunity to increase their sense of economic security. An increase in income level was seen as an opportunity to prepare for the lean years that might lie ahead. Swings in the business cycle were recurrent concerns, since there was no way of knowing in any given case how far the recession swing would go. Building assets became associated with both a perception of personal accomplishment and a sense of economic safety and security. For many of this Depression generation, saving was not so much a means for accumulating assets in order to enjoy the good life later on, but a meaningful goal in itself. Perhaps more than previous generations, this generation was interested in building assets in order to achieve personal financial security and to pass on assets to the next generation to provide for the financial security of children and grandchildren.

In contrast, the generation entering early adulthood during the 1950s and 1960s had direct experiences with economic abundance and tended to take access to the good life for granted. They tended to see the older generation as overly materialistic and money-oriented. They were more concerned with following impulse, seeking self-actualization, and making free use of consumer credit. "Spend now and pay later" became an accepted point of view for this privileged generation, and hedonistic behavior tended to take priority over long-range financial planning.

Collective memories frequently are drawn upon to support a political position or to document the urgency of avoiding a particular line of action. For example, the debates in the U.S. Senate over the Gulf War reflected generational effects. Older members of the Senate drew upon their experiences with World War II, saw a similarity between Saddam Hussein and Adolf Hitler, and argued against any form of compromise or appeasement. Nothing short of a direct, forceful military response to Iraq's invasion of Kuwait was seen as adequate. In contrast, Vietnam veterans in the Senate were concerned about the long-range implications of U.S. involvement, predicted heavy American casualties, and maintained that we lacked any set of guidelines on how to withdraw. Memories of both World War II and the Vietnam War were thus implicated in the debates over contemporary policy options and alternatives. Some subsequently saw the use of American military might against Iraq as a demonstration of how we should have fought the war in Vietnam. In this respect, the significance of collective memories lies less in their accuracy than in the meanings they have for their adherents.

The emotional impact of generational experiences became evident in media interviews with veterans on the fiftieth anniversary of the D-day invasion of Europe. Placing emphasis on individual soldiers who had played a role in the historic invasion of Normandy, a major turning point of World War II, humanized the event. Stories about the tenacity of the fighting, the scope of the fatalities, and the trauma of war were openly expressed in newspaper and television reports. On this ceremonial occasion, tragedies in the personal lives of individuals were linked with the historical encounter. The anniversary commemoration permitted veterans to express pent-up emotions and to remind new generations of the sacrifices made by those who preceded them in a time of serious troubles.

The significance of the divisions along generational lines has been intensified as a result of the fact that people live longer and many dramatic changes in the U.S. population occurred during the course of the twentieth century. For example, fertility declined, life expectancy at birth increased by more than twenty-five years, and the median age of the population increased. These demographic changes sharpened the contrasts in generational experiences and intensified the fragmentation of the social realm.

The more recent generations are notorious in their disregard for the long reach of their historical past. Henry Ford's comment that "history is bunk" is a sentiment shared by many young adults. There is a sense of comfort in putting bad times behind us and thinking positively about both the present and the future. One college student spoke for her generation when she said: "All this talk about the American institution of slavery and other atrocities in American history just makes me feel sad. I was not alive then and did not have anything to do with such practices. Besides, we don't do that kind of thing anymore. I would prefer not to hear about it."

While generations are regarded as composed of those who experienced historical events in a similar way, there are qualifications that need to be added to this view. There are few, if any, societal events that are experienced in a similar way by all segments of the population. Instead, events are surrounded by multiple realities that vary in systematic ways among subgroups of the population. The responses of men are frequently different from those of women, and the responses of young adults are often different from those of people who are middle-aged and older. The responses also vary by race and ethnicity, by social class, and by a variety of other social locations that define the place of the individual within the social system. Further, religious and political ideologies provide ready-made frameworks that may be applied to the unfolding of events.

Depressive disturbances persist for those individuals who are exposed directly to traumatic events. When a trauma becomes national in scope, however, both the needs of individuals and the needs of the social system must be addressed. At the level of the social system, there is a need to give some form of enduring recognition to traumatic events. People seek some higher level of meaning for the tragedies that were suffered, thus enhancing collective values and ideals. The needs of the social system are addressed through such forms of commemoration as the creation of monuments, memorials, sacred shrines, and holidays.

Commemoration

The act of commemoration is a formal means of giving recognition to the importance of past events and designating them as worthy of collective remembrance. Symbolic representations of past events are designed to give special recognition to great men and women, to heroic undertakings, and to personal sacrifices for the benefit of the nation. The act of commemoration is essentially a means of rejuvenating cultural values and promoting images of society as a moral community. For this reason, the commemoration of public events endows them with sacred meanings and results in a blending of national sentiments with religious ideologies.

In the process of commemoration, a mixture of selective recall and selective distortion tends to operate. War monuments and memorials, for example, are forms of commemoration that typically gloss over the tragedies and horrors of war. The urge to find some higher meaning for war experiences leads to justifications for the sacrifice and the loss. The horror of war is displaced by an emphasis on its glory. Encounters with death and destruction are camouflaged by an emphasis on the sacred task of defending the nation. The speeches at sacred shrines on Memorial Day, the Fourth of July, and Veterans Day are all designed to enhance patriotic values through the glorification of war. Emphasis is placed upon the men and women who "voluntarily" sacrificed their lives for their country. The underlying message seems to be that Americans should be willing to make personal sacrifices for promoting the collective good.

In contrast to previous wars, the proper way to remember the Vietnam

War was problematic for Americans. The casualties and atrocities of the war and the errors in political judgment were so painful that most Americans simply wanted to forget about it and move on. Yet the trauma of the war was so intense that it could not be swept aside. Forgetting about it, or denying that it occurred, was not a reasonable option. The mistakes of the war had become a part of the American experience. It was the pressure from the veterans themselves that resulted in the creation of the Vietnam Veterans Memorial. The subtle symbolism of the memorial captures the trauma of the war and permits the millions who visit the wall each year to reflect in their own way on the lessons and meanings of war.

Memories of World War II and the Vietnam War are still vivid in American consciousness, while the Korean War has been described as "the forgotten war." It may be that we remember the wars that provided us with glorious victories or embarrassing defeats, but a war that provides us with a stalemate is hardly worth remembering. When the Korean War ended, the boundary between North Korea and South Korea was drawn at about the same place it had been drawn when the war started. The war was not looked upon as a "real" war, but only as a "police action" under the auspices of the United Nations. Despite the fierce battles and the 50,000 American fatalities, the Korean War never became a trauma to the nation. Thus, it is not the objective consequences in terms of pain and suffering that make an event worth remembering, but its impact on the institutional structure of society. During the Korean War, the United States was neither threatened by an external invasion nor deeply divided in opinion. It was a war that provided very little to celebrate or to memorialize.

National monuments and memorials are experienced as sacred places by the millions of Americans who visit them each year. The Vietnam Veterans Memorial, Kennedy's gravesite at Arlington Cemetery, the Tomb of the Unknown Soldier, the Lincoln Memorial, Civil War battlegrounds, Pearl Harbor, and the Little Big Horn are among the most frequently visited tourist attractions each year. While by purely objective criteria, these are mundane places with nothing particularly special about them, the meanings imputed to them are of a different order. For example, studies of tourists at the Vietnam Veterans Memorial indicate that most of the visitors have an intensely emotional reaction resembling a sacred or religious experience. They see themselves in the mirrored reflections on the wall, and whether they opposed or supported the war, they are not able to remain indifferent or unaffected.

A less successful commemoration is reflected in the World War II memorial dedicated in the summer of 2004, nearly sixty years after the war ended, and most of the 15 million men and women who served in uniform were no longer alive. The memorial has been criticized for not adequately representing the extensive sacrifices made by a generation of Americans. It lacks the themes of courage and bravery captured so well in the monument in Arlington Cemetery on the flag raising at Iwo Jima. It also lacks the emotional impact of the USS *Arizona* at Pearl Harbor. Others have criticized the memorial for taking up two and a half acres in the National Mall, restricting the aesthetic appeal of open space between the Lincoln Memorial and the Washington Monument.

The challenge of appropriate memory has been evident in the many controversies over the forms of representation for September 11. The controversies involve property rights, commercial interests, architectural designs, and sacred sentiments. Some argue that the destruction of the twin towers left a large gap in the New York City skyline that should be filled with new high-rise structures. While re-building the World Trade Center may be expedient for commercial reasons, ground zero has taken on special meanings in the life of the nation.

The intense heat vaporized many victims at the World Trade Center. No evidence of their remains has been found for permitting closure to the grief and mourning. In effect, ground zero has become a sacred place, not only for family and friends of the victims, but for the entire nation. To ignore these sentiments in the construction of high-rise commercial buildings seems insensitive. The effect of visiting ground zero is evident in the emotions displayed on the faces of thousands who make a pilgrimage to the sacred site each year.

The meaning of the site to the nation is reflected in the large gatherings and commemorative rituals on the anniversary of the attack. The ceremonies on September 11, 2004, for example, included recognizing the heroism of firemen and policemen, a ritualistic reading of the victims' names, and projecting two beams of light upward toward infinity to symbolize the missing towers. The negative space in the New York City skyline generated uneasiness as well as remembrance of the extraordinary tragedy of the terrorist attack. Participants were reminded of human fallibility and the tragic interruption of ordinary time by the epochal national trauma.

Only a small percentage of Americans make a deliberate pilgrimage to national shrines. More often, a visit to a sacred shrine is a bonus to a trip or to a vacation. Americans visit monuments, memorials, shrines, and museums when convenient. If one is driving across Interstate 90, a side trip to Mount Rushmore, to the saloon where Wild Bill Hickok was killed, or to the Custer battleground at the Little Big Horn becomes simply a way of breaking up the monotony of the trip. However, beneath the superficiality of these visits, there are important latent meanings that are evoked.

The meanings assigned to the Little Big Horn, for example, are richly varied for the many tourists who stop there. For some, the Custer battle-ground evokes reflection on what is perceived as an American policy of geno-cide toward an indigenous people. For others, the battleground elicits images of Custer as a hero or as a villain; for yet others, it is seen as the site of a major military victory by Native Americans who were attempting to protect their tribal lands. In some cases, the reflections may be as specific as imagin-ing the stench of the decayed corpses that were handled by those assigned to the burial detail. Linking personal lives with historical events is thus a selec-tive process.

We may ask why people go through the inconvenience of long-distance travel to visit memorials in remote places. We could learn about historical places and events by reading about them, by watching videos, movies, or television programs, or by surfing the Internet. Why travel rather than use other forms of information-seeking behavior? A partial answer is that being there provides a more authentic experience than can be derived from reading a book or watching television. Books are abstract, and the television experi-ence is vicarious and illusory in a way that direct encounters are not. While television is much more than moving dots on an electronic screen, it pro-vides only an incomplete experience.

The quest for authentic experiences and knowledge bears an affinity to the religious pilgrimages and the sacred journeys that were common in other times and places. The pilgrimages of the past, like those of today, offered opportunities for establishing a sense of personal connection with a set of ultimate values. The sacred journey facilitates separating the genuine from the spurious, the reality from the illusion, and the authentic from the inau-thentic. People need to actively participate in a meaningful cosmos. Both the needs of the soul and the needs of the body must be satisfied.

At the conscious level, we have rejected the sacred and mythical nature of the world we live in. In doing so, however, we have missed something. The human spirit requires more than work schedules and the materialistic con-sumption of consumer goods. The world is becoming increasingly interde-pendent, and if we are to find an adequate sense of meaning within it, we must extend our awareness of places and events that are geographically sepa-rated from the mundane aspects of everyday life.

In contrast to the travel required in visiting monuments and shrines, the commemoration of historical events by people dispersed throughout the coun-try is promoted through the creation of national holidays. Not only does a holiday permit commemoration throughout the nation, it also provides a struc-ture for selectively remembering the traumas and glories of the past. Dwell-ing routinely on tragic events would reflect a morbid form of anxiety and would be regarded as pathological. Yet those events that had an extraordi-

---

Box 12
Symbolic Event: American Rememberance of the Holocaust

American soldiers who took part in the liberation of the Nazi death camps were shocked at what they discovered there. There was no term in our vocabulary to adequately describe what they saw. The term "atrocities" had been applied to the inhumane treatment of prisoners by the Japanese in the Bataan death march. Subsequently, in the trial of Nazi war criminals, the term "crimes against humanity" was employed. The systematic persecution, coercion, and eventual murder of 6 million European Jews subsequently came to be described by drawing upon the new term "genocide."

Over time, the mass killings came to be regarded as a unique form of evil in the human experience. They also came to be designated as a world historical event and as a universal event that belongs to all of humanity. The systematic murder of 6 million Jews dramatically illustrated what human beings are capable of doing to each other. It was through universalizing the tragic event that it came to be designated as the "Holocaust." The trauma of the Jewish people became a trauma of all mankind.

Raising the Holocaust to the status of a dominant myth challenges both the ethical and the instrumental basis for modernity. Collective guilt, obedience in following orders, the use of technology in the killing process, and modern forms of transportation have all been implicated in observations on the Holocaust. Both the promise and the pitfalls of the human condition generate a collective need for remembrance. Museums are created to challenge all of us to experience the tragedy and to seek redemption.

The United States Holocaust Memorial Museum was created to link the collective memory of the American people with the Holocaust. Its location adjacent to the Mall in Washington, DC, provides a connection to other components of the American repertoire of memory. The long lines that formed following the opening of the museum in April 1992 exceeded everyone's expectation. The intense emotional experience of visitors to the museum serves as a reminder that evil is inside all of us and in every society. We thus all become victims as well as perpetrators as we relive the questions "How did it happen?" and "Why did it happen?"

---

nary emotional impact on the society cannot be easily dismissed or completely ignored. For this reason, special anniversaries are set aside as times for reflection on the events in question. Reflection is especially necessary for those events that remain unsettled or incomplete.

The designation of Martin Luther King's birthday as a national holiday, for example, was a way of giving formal recognition to the importance of social justice in the life of the nation. The personal charisma of King came to be associated with a willingness to die for a broader social cause if it becomes necessary. On the anniversary of his birth, the news media selectively reproduce his speeches, show photographs of civil rights demonstrations and marches, and reflect on contemporary issues of social justice. In this respect, the holiday is also a holy day as Americans reflect on the dominant values of their society and the contradictions inherent in modern social living.

In contrast to remembering King on the date of his birth, President John F. Kennedy is remembered on the date of his death. Besides commemorating his accomplishments, remembering Kennedy is more about reflecting on his unfulfilled potential. Perceptions of his youthfulness and his idealism promote speculation on how the world would have been different had he lived. Freed from the realities of practical politics, the imagery of Kennedy has a dream-like quality about it. As a central public figure of the twentieth century, Kennedy provides a model that enables individuals to reflect on their own hopes and aspirations. The imagery evokes human emotions, which intensify and gain concrete focus. Some believe Kennedy would have circumvented the quagmire of the Vietnam War, negotiated a settlement of the arms race with the Soviet Union, normalized relationships with Cuba, and advanced the cause of civil rights. Remembering Kennedy thus taps into personal hopes for a better world.

The national preoccupation with Kennedy, however, goes far beyond the loss of his leadership potential. While the collective quest for a resolution of the mystery of his death has a somewhat morbid quality about it, there appears to be a genuine national interest in knowing more about the circumstances surrounding his assassination. Americans who accepted the conclusions of the Warren Commission that Lee Harvey Oswald acted alone in killing the president have been able to complete the mourning process, bury the event deep in their generational memories, and put the event behind them. Americans who reject the report of the Warren Commission, however, still suffer from some degree of trauma. The six seconds in Dallas are replayed over and over in their memories. The excavation of new evidence and the creation of new explanations only serve to reinforce and perpetuate feelings of disturbance and uneasiness. These concerns are likely to dissipate only after the death of the generation that was so deeply moved by the emotional trauma of Kennedy's death.

The past is a time that has vanished; we visit there only intermittently, and we generally do not wish to linger there for very long. Nevertheless, newsgathering agencies always seem to remember anniversaries of traumatic events. From only a casual review of newspapers, it becomes evident that anniversaries are important to Americans as a time for reflection on traumatic events. Newspaper accounts not only provide a brief description of the trauma on its anniversary but also reproduce photographic images of the event and publish comments made by those who experienced it directly. The emphasis is not so much on the lessons taught by the trauma as on the continued recognition of the emotional impact it had and the place it selectively holds in the memories of individual men and women.

Popular Culture and Mass Entertainment

In popular culture and mass entertainment, collective memories are reflected in the many ways stories are told to new generations about their historical past. In movies, television programs, and fictional writings, storytelling takes an embellished form. Whatever events occurred in the past are now immobilized, and those who tell stories about them are free to shape them as they wish. The constraints surrounding events as they unfolded no longer apply. To the reading and viewing audience, plausibility is more important than historical accuracy.

Seeking both to entertain and to inform, the storytellers reconstruct previous events and selectively bring them into focus; the gaps are filled in; the stories are humanized and embellished with extraordinary forms of drama. In mass entertainment, specific imagery becomes highly focused and events are experienced as only fragmentary. The raw materials that may be drawn upon are infinitely variable.

The scope of events and the range of activities that can become objects of interest are substantially greater than they used to be. Remote places and happenings intrude into consciousness with increased frequency, and accordingly the activities of everyday life become refocused and extended. In this process, memories of traumatic events permit a blending of fact with fiction, of reality with illusion and facade. The public displays that bombard our senses every day serve as models of what to do, how to live, and what is possible. The trivial and the incredible tend to be dramatized, and the search for a collective identity becomes a never-ending quest.

The television industry is geared toward promoting a sense of community by creating products that will have universal appeal, regardless of race, class, gender, or religion. In developing an appeal to the largest viewing audience, the common language becomes spectacle through the use of violence and destruction. These grab the attention, transcend the mundane quality of everyday life, and are enhanced through the visual effects that can be created by modern technology. It is within this context that the audience becomes the primary determinant of the content of what is produced and also the judiciary that shapes the commercial success of any given production. The linkage of memory with symbolic events provides the raw materials for the construction of both personal and collective identities.

In the realm of mass entertainment, the past becomes a form of constructed memory, since the factual details of what actually happened in history are often neither known nor knowable. We may never know in a definitive sense why we were caught so disastrously unprepared at Pearl Harbor, what actual circumstances surrounded the assassination of President Kennedy, or how close we came to nuclear war during the Cuban missile crisis. Through the use of imagination and through drawing upon the predisposition of reading or viewing audiences, collective memories are elaborated and embellished. Historical events are treated both as symbolic events and as pseudoevents that reflect the problems and challenges of contemporary living. Under these circumstances, history becomes a form of remembering in which the mixture of fact and fiction is of less concern than the stimulus and entertainment value of the production.

The intent of mass entertainment is not to provide a message, as communication is usually understood, but to trigger a response in the viewing audience. In a successful television production, the viewers are drawn into the performances as they identify with the characters portrayed and the situations created. In this process, the realities of the technology by which television is produced are of little concern or interest to most of the viewers. The script writing, the rehearsals, the stage props, the photography, and the moving dots of light on an electronic screen recede into the background as viewers become engrossed in the symbolic events portrayed. The attitudes, emotions, and predispositions of the viewers shape and refine the contents and the entertainment value of television productions.

The large pool of moviegoers and television watchers judges the entertainment value of cultural productions. The decisions made by millions of people acting as individuals and out of self-interest determine the kinds of entertainment made available. A veto power over television productions may be exercised by simply switching to another channel or by deciding not to watch television at all.

While our language separates time into past, present, and future, our experiences tend to unify them as we reflect on the character of symbolic events. The realities of the past take on special meanings through our current perceptions of them, and the future becomes a mixture of present fears and aspirations. In media entertainment, the audience experience of the time dimension may be described as "everywhen." There were certain events that happened in the past, could still happen today, and can happen again in the future. The time dimension becomes blurred, a form of eternal dream time in which individuals travel psychologically to remote places and respond to the activity of people who represent both the living and the dead.

The traumas of the past provide reference points for assessing the quality of life in the present. While the emotional impact of the traumas of the past can be experienced only vicariously by more recent generations, they do provide cognitive frameworks in stereotypic form for shaping what are perceived as the dangers and the opportunities of the human condition. A sense of comfort may develop through recognizing that contemporary troubles may be small in comparison to the difficulties people faced in the past. In this respect, collective memories provide individuals with frameworks for locating their present lifestyles along a continuum somewhere between the best possible and the worst possible of all social worlds.

Historians are frequently appalled by the inaccuracies and distortions in the portrayal of past events in mass entertainment. After all, historians are professionals who have been given the responsibility of constructing accurate records of past events and thus keeping the nation informed about itself. Historians are necessarily concerned with the accuracy of the story that is told in a way in which others are not. They are the keepers of "authentic" and "official" versions of the past. Their professional code of ethics requires objectivity and accuracy, and their work is subjected to professional scrutiny and evaluated by peers.

Trusteeship over the official versions of history properly falls within the jurisdiction of professional historians. But even here, it is evident that we do not live in a world of solid fact. The rewriting of history stems less from new forms of evidence than from attempts to develop new perspectives and new understandings of past events. The lessons of history are never direct and self-evident. Their meanings must be constructed anew by each generation as it confronts the changing circumstances of its time and place. While the actual occurrences of historical events may be frozen in the past, the new meanings they are given become a part of the dynamics of any given society. The rewriting of history is often an attempt to place past events within the living framework of contemporary concerns.

The authority of popular culture productions to claim historical accuracy was brought into sharp focus with Oliver Stone's 1991 movie, *JFK*. Both journalists and historians were appalled at Stone's mixture of a documentary format with fictional drama without any guidance for the viewing audience. To add authenticity to the movie, documentary footage included visual images of events surrounding the motor cavalcade through Dallas. In addition, Stone's movie included newsreel footage of Jack Ruby's murder of Lee Harvey Oswald, and the Abraham Zapruder home movie film. The twenty-six–second, eight-millimeter silent film of Zapruder has remained the primary historical documentation of the assassination. Through weaving music with cinematic techniques, Stone's film presented conspiracy theories that implicated the CIA, the FBI, Castro, and Lyndon Johnson. The movie was designed to remove all doubts about the validity of conspiracy theories holding that Lee Harvey Oswald did not act alone.

The film left the audience with the belief that Oliver Stone's version of the Kennedy assassination was an authentic historical account of what really happened. Indeed, Stone claimed that his film did present "a version of historical truth." Such a claim for a cinematic production undermined the authority of mainstream journalists, historians, and others who have a professional stake in upholding the accuracy of the historical record. Stone's film and the nation's continued preoccupation with the factual details surrounding the assassination of Kennedy bring into sharp focus the many issues connected with the process of collective memory.

The assassination became a major symbolic event in the life of the nation, and the many constructed truth claims collided with each other. Contradictions and ambiguity in communal understandings provided the raw materials for an artistic embellishment of events. Reality does not stem so much from the objective qualities of traumatic events as from the symbolic meanings that are imposed upon them. We create the world through our perceptions of it and then seek to maintain that world in a manner consistent with our beliefs about it. It is through such symbolic constructions that we are provided with usable frameworks for shaping our memories and organizing them into coherent systems of meaning.

Who are the keepers of collective memories? In the final analysis, we all are. The intersection of personal biography with historical events is crucial to the multifaceted process of knowing who we are and what we are to become. Determining where we are, how we got to where we are, and where we are headed as we move into the future is basic to personal and collective identities. The task of the individual is to find his or her place within the broader scheme of human affairs. In this process, some see themselves as located at the center of what is happening in their time and place. Others see themselves as located on the periphery of the consequential events of their society. Some seek to become active participants in shaping the social and political climate of their society; others prefer to remain politically apathetic and to pursue their own self-interests.

Links Between the Past and the Future

The human predicament is that we are caught up in a contemporary setting that is necessarily fragmented from both the past and the future. The future is unknowable, and the past in all its many details and nuances is lost to us. Yet we attempt to reduce the uncertainty of past events by drawing upon historical fragments that are embellished and taken out of context. Our sense of certainty about what happened in the past can rest only on incomplete information. The immutable character of the past precludes altering the course of events that did occur. We cannot rerun the Civil War, the Japanese attack on Pearl Harbor, or the Cuban missile crisis. We can only modify these events by using our imagination and speculating on what might have been. Prominent among such speculations are notions about how the outcomes would have changed had the decisions of key participants been different.

In reflecting on traumatic events, people tend to raise "what if" questions. What would have happened if Hitler's army had invaded England instead of fighting a two-front war against the Soviet Union? How many American lives would have been lost if President Truman had decided against dropping the atomic bomb on Japanese cities? If Kennedy had not been assassinated, would he have negotiated a settlement of the cold war? How would the world be different if Charles Lindbergh had been elected president of the United States in 1940? While such questions have a parlor game appeal, they reflect an emphasis upon the importance of contingencies as well as decision making in shaping the historical process.

The selectivity of historians in their narratives of the past has been of special concern to subgroups of the population whose experiences have been ignored or downplayed. The modern consciousness of African Americans has called for a new look at the ways in which history has been written in the past. Traditional narratives by professional historians focused disproportionately on the experiences of the dominant group and were designed to reinforce the interests of the ruling class. For example, very little attention was given to the brutality of the institution of slavery from the vantage point of the victims. The rewriting of history is designed to give explicit recognition to the noteworthy accomplishments of African Americans. Historical corrections are necessary to set the record straight and to provide a basis for appreciating the black heritage within the context of a pluralistic society.

Collective memories have also been of recent concern to feminists who maintain that women are seriously disadvantaged by the ways in which history has been reported. While women constitute more than half of the population, their experiences have been underrepresented in historical accounts. To correct the selectivity of historical reporting, there has been an explosion of publications about the part women have played in the historical process. Rather than seeing women as subordinate to men in a patriarchal society, feminist historians now pay attention to the important roles women have played in societal development. The new consciousness of women grows out of the quest for social justice, out of an interest in broadening the scope of historical analysis, and out of a desire to promote the opportunities for women to participate in the political and economic life of the nation.

The philosopher George Santayana once said, "Those who do not learn from history are condemned to repeat it." Properly learning from history, however, is a difficult task. The proper way to remember becomes both a psychological and a political question. For example, why have both the media and the public in general become preoccupied with the deaths of Marilyn Monroe, Elvis Presley, President Kennedy, and Princess Diana? Heightened emotional arousal and intense identification have accompanied the troubled lives and tragic deaths of these celebrities. By way of contrast, there has not been a comparable level of identification with the millions who died in the Nazi Holocaust, the Soviet purges, or the flu epidemic of 1918–1919. The famous dead become our new saints by transcending the limits of earthly existence. It is through collective myths that we share our common humanity and gauge our mortality.

In the final analysis, collective memories may be understood as forms of myth making. Their significance lies less in their accuracy than in the meanings they have for adherents. From an objective standpoint, there is a wide gap between the pictures in our heads and the world outside. There will always remain an external world that exists independently of our perceptions of it. We construct the world into systems of meaning that can be drawn upon when the need arises. The creation of myth is pragmatic because accounts of tragic events are drawn upon for self-serving purposes. Myths are useful in sustaining personal identities and commitments as well as in supporting a political policy or in documenting the urgency of avoiding a particular line of action. As forms of myth, however, collective memories also become endowed with sacred meanings as they are drawn upon to embellish perceptions of society as moral community.

Discussion Questions

1. What are some of the major ways that individual memory differs from collective memory?
2. Discuss the importance of modern forms of technology for the storage and retrieval of information about the past.
3. What are generational effects and how do they influence the political culture of a nation?
4. What was the basis for the controversy over the design and construction of the Vietnam Veterans Memorial?

5. Discuss the importance of visual images and photography for collective memory.
6. To what extent do popular culture and mass entertainment shape modern forms of collective memory?
7. Drawing upon Oliver Stone's movie *JFK*, discuss the controversy over the issues of accuracy and authenticity in film productions.
8. If you were appointed to a committee to design a memorial commemorating 9/11 at ground zero, what would you recommend? Why?
9. What is meant by George Santayana's comment that "those who do not learn from history are condemned to repeat it?"

Bibliography

Chapter 1

Balsiger, David, and Charles E. Sellier Jr. 1977. *The Lincoln Conspiracy.* Los Angeles: Schick Sun Classic Books.

Becker, Ernest. 1968. *The Structure of Evil.* New York: George Braziller.

Berger, Peter L. 1977. *Facing Up to Modernity.* New York: Basic Books.

Berger, Peter L., Brigitte Berger, and Hansfried Kellner. 1973. *The Homeless Mind: Modernization and Consciousness.* New York: Vintage Books.

Brown, Roger, and James Kulik. 1977. "Flashbulb Memories." *Cognition* 5:73–99.

Browne, Ray B., and Arthur G. Neal. 2001. *Ordinary Reactions to Extraordinary Events.* Bowling Green, OH: Bowling Green State University Popular Press.

Cantril, Hadley. 1966. *The Invasion from Mars: A Study of the Psychology of Panic.* New York: Harper and Row.

Curry, Richard O., and Thomas M. Brown, eds. 1972. *Conspiracy: Fear of Subversion in American History.* New York: Holt, Rinehart, and Winston.

Douglas, Mary, and Aaron Wildavsky. 1982. *Risk and Culture.* Berkeley: University of California Press.

Eber, Elisabeth Dena, and Arthur G. Neal, eds. 2001. *Memory and Representation.* Bowling Green, OH: Bowling Green State University Popular Press.

Fein, Helen. 1993. *Genocide.* Newbury Park, CA: Sage.

Frankl, Viktor E. 1965. *Man's Search for Meaning.* New York: Washington Square Press.

Gans, Herbert J. 1979. *Deciding What's News.* New York: Pantheon Books.

Goffman, Erving. 1963. *Behavior in Public Places.* New York: Free Press.

Herman, Judith Lewis. 1992. *Trauma and Recovery.* New York: Basic Books.

Janoff-Bulman, Ronnie. 1992. *Shattered Assumptions: Toward a New Psychology of Trauma.* New York: Free Press.

Kennedy, Paul. 1993. *Preparing for the Twenty-First Century.* New York: Random House.

Lifton, Robert Jay. 1973. *Home from the War.* New York: Basic Books.

Lipsky, Michael, and David J. Olson. 1969. "Riot Commission Politics." *Transaction* 6 (July–August): 8–21.

Mirowsky, John, and Catherine E. Ross. 1989. *Social Causes of Psychological Distress.* New York: Aldine de Gruyter.

Neal, Arthur G., ed. 1976. *Violence in Animal and Human Societies.* Chicago: Nelson Hall.

Nisbet, Robert A. 1953. *The Quest for Community.* New York: Oxford University Press.

Parenti, Michael. 1993. *Inventing Reality: The Politics of News Media.* New York: St. Martin's Press.

Power, Samantha. 2002. *"A Problem from Hell": America and the Age of Genocide.* New York: Perseus Books.

Shibutani, Tamatsu. 1966. *Improvised News.* Indianapolis: Bobbs-Merrill.

Slaby, Andrew E. 1989. *Aftershock: Surviving the Delayed Effects of Trauma, Crisis, and Loss.* New York: Villard Books.

Warner, W. Lloyd. 1962. *American Life: Dream and Reality.* Chicago: University of Chicago Press.

Weinstock, Jeffrey Andrew. 2002. "Mars Attack! Wells, Welles, and Radio Panic: Or the Story of the Century." In *Ordinary Reactions to Extraordinary Events,* ed. Ray B. Browne and Arthur G. Neal. Bowling Green, OH: Bowling Green State University Popular Press.

Wilson, John P. 1989. *Trauma: Transformation and Healing.* New York: Brunner/Mazel.

Chapter 2

Allan, George. 1986. *The Importance of the Past.* Albany: State University of New York Press.

Bellah, Robert N. 1975. "Civil Religion in America." In *Life Styles Diversity in American Society,* ed. Saul D. Feldman and Gerald W. Thielbar, pp. 16–34. Boston: Little, Brown.

Berger, Peter L. 1967. *The Sacred Canopy.* Garden City, NY: Anchor Books.

Chapman, William. 1991. *Inventing Japan: The Making of a Postwar Civilization.* New York: Prentice-Hall.

Durkheim, Emile. 1961. *The Elementary Forms of the Religious Life.* New York: Collier Books.

Grainge, Paul, ed. 2003. *Memory and Popular Film.* New York: Manchester University Press.

Hamilton, V. Lee. 1978. "Who Is Responsible? Toward a Social Psychology of Attribution." *Social Psychology* 41:316–327.

Hiller, Harry H. 1986. *Canadian Society: A Macro Analysis.* Scarborough, Ontario: Prentice-Hall Canada.

Janis, Irving L. 1989. *Crucial Decisions: Leadership in Policymaking and Crisis Management.* New York: Free Press.

Landsberg, Alison. 2004. *Prosthetic Memory: The Transformation of American Remembrance in the Age of Mass Culture.* New York: Columbia University Press.

Leone, Bruno. 1986. *Nationalism: Opposing Viewpoints.* St. Paul, MN: Greenhaven Press.

Lipset, Seymour Martin. 1963. *The First New Nation: The United States in Historical and Comparative Perspective.* New York: Basic Books.

Lowenthal, David. 1985. *The Past Is a Foreign Country.* New York: Cambridge University Press.

Maier, Charles S. 1988. *The Unmasterable Past: History, Holocaust, and German National Identity.* Cambridge, MA: Harvard University Press.

Manschreck, Clyde L. 1971. *Erosion of Authority.* Nashville: Abingdon Press.

Moorhead, G., R. Ference, and C. Neck. 1991. "Group Decision Fiascoes Continue: Space Shuttle *Challenger* and Revised Groupthink Framework." *Human Relations* 44:539–550.
Naveh, Eyal. 1993. "'He Belongs to the Ages': Lincoln's Image and the American Historical Consciousness." *Journal of American Culture* 16:49–57.
Niemi, Robert. 1993. "JFK as Jesus: The Politics of Myth in Phil Och's Crucifixion." *Journal of American Culture* 16:35–40.
Reischauer, Edwin O., and Marius B. Jansen. 1995. *The Japanese Today: Change and Continuity.* Cambridge, MA: Belknap Press.
Simon, Yves R. 1980. *A General Theory of Authority.* Notre Dame, IN: University of Notre Dame Press.
Udoidem, S. Iniobong. 1988. *Authority and the Common Good in Social and Political Philosophy.* New York: University Press of America.
Vaughan, Diane. 1996. *The* Challenger *Launch Decision: Risky Technology, Culture, and Deviance at NASA.* Chicago: University of Chicago Press.
Warner, W. Lloyd. 1953. *American Life: Dream and Reality.* Chicago: University of Chicago Press.

Chapter 3

Allen, Frederick Lewis. 1940. *Since Yesterday: The 1930s in America.* New York: Harper and Row.
Amenta, Edwin, and Sunita Parikh. 1991. "Capitalists Did Not Want the Social Security Act." *American Sociological Review* 56:124–132.
Bakke, E. Wright. 1940. *Citizens Without Work.* New Haven, CT: Yale University Press.
Bendiner, Robert. 1967. *Just Around the Corner: A Highly Selective History of the Thirties.* New York: E.P. Dutton.
Bergman, Andrew. 1971. *We're in the Money: Depression America and Its Films.* New York: Harper Torchbooks.
Bernstein, Irving. 1985. *A Caring Society: The New Deal, the Worker, and the Great Depression.* Boston: Houghton Mifflin.
Bird, Caroline. 1966. *The Invisible Scar: The Great Depression and What it Did to American Life, from Then Until Now.* New York: David McKay.
Brunner, Karl, ed. 1981. *The Great Depression Revisited.* Boston: Martinus Nijhoff.
Buss, Terry F., and Stevens Redburn. 1983. *Mass Unemployment: Plant Closings and Community Mental Health.* Beverly Hills, CA: Sage.
Cohen, Robert, ed. 2002. *Dear Mrs. Roosevelt: Letters from Children of the Great Depression.* Chapel Hill: University of North Carolina Press.
Elder, Glen H., Jr. 1974. *Children of the Great Depression.* Chicago: University of Chicago Press.
Feather, Norman T. 1990. *The Psychological Impact of Unemployment.* New York: Springer-Verlag.
Galbraith, John Kenneth. 1988. *The Great Crash of 1929.* Boston: Houghton Mifflin.
Garraty, John A. 1987. *The Great Depression.* New York: Doubleday Anchor.
Goldston, Robert. 1968. *The Great Depression: The United States in the Thirties.* Greenwich, CT: Fawcett Premier.
Hobson, Archie, ed. 1985. *Remembering America: A Sampler of the WPA American Guide Series.* New York: Columbia University Press.

Kamorovsky, Mirra. 1940. *The Unemployed Man and His Family.* New York: Dryden Press.

Klingaman, William K. 1989. *The Year of the Great Crash.* New York: Harper and Row.

McElvaine, Robert S. 1984. *The Great Depression.* New York: Times Books.

Mitchell, Broadus. 1947. *Depression Decade.* Vol. 9 of *The Economic History of the United States.* New York: Rinehart.

Nash, Gerald D. 1979. *The Great Depression and World War II.* New York: St. Martin's Press.

Newman, Katherine S. 1988. *Falling from Grace: The Experience of Downward Mobility in the American Middle Class.* New York: Free Press.

Recken, Stephen L. 1993. "Fitting-In: The Redefinition of Success in the 1930s." *Journal of Popular Culture* 27 (winter): 205–222.

Rollins, Alfred B. Jr., ed. *Depression, Recovery, and War: 1929–1945.* New York: McGraw-Hill.

Shannon, David A., ed. 1960. *The Great Depression.* Englewood Cliffs, NJ: Prentice-Hall.

Sternsher, Bernard. 1970. *Hitting Home: The Great Depression in Town and Country.* Chicago: Quadrangle Books.

Uys, Errol Lincoln. 2003. *Riding the Rails: Teenagers on the Move During the Great Depression.* New York: Routledge.

Ware, Susan. 1982. *Holding Their Own: American Women in the 1930s.* Boston: Twayne.

Watkins, T.H. 1993. *The Great Depression: America in the 1930s.* Boston: Little, Brown.

Wolters, Raymond. 1970. *Negroes in the Great Depression.* Westport, CT: Greenwood Press.

Chapter 4

Adams, Michael C. 1985. *The Best War Ever: Americans in World War II.* Baltimore: Johns Hopkins University Press.

Akizuki, Tatsuichiro. 1981. *Nagasaki 1945.* New York: Quartet Books.

Benedict, Ruth. 1989. *The Chrysanthemum and the Sword: Patterns of Japanese Culture.* Boston: Houghton Mifflin.

Brokaw, Tom. 2004. *The Greatest Generation.* New York: Random House.

Bundy, McGeorge. 1988. *Danger and Survival: Choices About the Bomb in the First Fifty Years.* New York: Vintage Books.

Daniels, Roger. 1975. *The Decision to Relocate the Japanese Americans.* Philadelphia: J.B. Lippincott.

Daniels, Roger, Sandra C. Taylor, and Harry H.L. Kitano. 1994. *Japanese Americans: From Relocation to Redress.* Seattle: University of Washington Press.

Goodwin, Doris Kearns. 1994. *No Ordinary Time: Franklin and Eleanor Roosevelt: The Home Front in World War II.* New York: Simon and Schuster.

Grodzins, Morton. 1949. *Americans Betrayed: Politics and the Japanese Evacuation.* Chicago: University of Chicago Press.

Hoehling, A.A. 1963. *The Week Before Pearl Harbor.* New York: W.W. Norton.

Hoopes, Roy. 1977. *Americans Remember the Home Front.* New York: Hawthorn Books.

Irons, Peter. 1983. *Justice at War: The Story of the Japanese Internment Cases.* Berkeley: University of California Press.

Kennett, Lee. 1985. *For the Duration: The United States Goes to War.* New York: Charles Scribner.

Kimmel, Husband E. 1955. *Admiral Kimmel's Story.* Chicago: Henry Regnery.

Levine, Ellen. 1995. *A Fence Away From Freedom: Japanese Americans and World War II.* New York: G.P. Putnam's Sons.

Lord, Walter. 1957. *Day of Infamy.* New York: Holt, Rinehart, and Winston.

McWilliams, Carey. 1944. *Prejudice: Japanese Americans: Symbols of Racial Intolerance.* New York: Little, Brown.

Millis, Walter. 1947. *This Is Pearl!* New York: William Morrow.

Millot, Bernard. 1970. *Divine Thunder.* New York: Pinnacle Books.

Morganstern, George. 1947. *Pearl Harbor.* New York: Devin-Adair.

Mosse, George L. 1990. *Fallen Soldiers: Reshaping the Memory of the World Wars.* New York: Oxford University Press.

Naito, Hatsuho. 1989. *Thunder Gods: The Kamikaze Pilots Tell Their Story.* New York: Dell.

Nam, Charles B. 1964. "Impact of the G. I. Bill on the Educational Level of the Male Population." *Social Forces* 43:26–32.

Neuman, William L. 1963. *America Encounters Japan: From Perry to MacArthur.* New York: Harper Colophon.

Prange, Gordon W. 1982. *At Dawn We Slept: The Untold Story of Pearl Harbor.* New York: Penguin Books.

Rhodes, Richard. 1986. *The Making of the Atomic Bomb.* New York: Simon and Schuster.

Rushbridger, James, and Eric Nave. 1992. *Betrayal at Pearl Harbor: How Churchill Lured Roosevelt into World War II.* New York: Touchstone Books.

Selden, Kyoto, and Mark Selden, eds. 1989. *The Atomic Bomb: Voices from Hiroshima and Nagasaki.* Armonk, NY: M.E. Sharpe.

Shibutani, Tamotsu. 1966. *Improvised News: A Sociological Study of Rumor.* Indianapolis: Bobbs-Merrill.

Smith, Bradford. 1948. *Americans from Japan.* Philadelphia: J.B. Lippincott.

Smith, C. Calvin. 1986. *War and Wartime Changes.* Fayetteville: University of Arkansas Press.

Tateishi, John. 1984. *And Justice for All: An Oral History of the Japanese American Detention Camps.* New York: Random House.

Terkel, Studs. 1984. *"The Good War": An Oral History of World War Two.* New York: Ballantine Books.

Theobald, Robert A. 1954. *The Final Secret of Pearl Harbor: The Washington Contribution to the Japanese Attack.* New York: Devin-Adair.

Toland, John. 1982. *Infamy: Pearl Harbor and Its Aftermath.* New York: Doubleday.

Vatter, Harold G. 1985. *The U.S. Economy in World War II.* New York: Columbia University Press.

Waller, George M. 1976. *Pearl Harbor: Roosevelt and the Coming of the War.* Lexington, MA: D.C. Heath.

Ward, Stephen R., ed. 1975. *The War Generation: Veterans of the First World War.* Port Washington, NY: Kennikat Press.

Wilson, John P. 1989. *Trauma, Transformation, and Healing.* New York: Brunner/ Mazel.

Wohlstetter, Roberta. 1962. *Pearl Harbor: Warning and Decision.* Palo Alto, CA: Stanford University Press.

Chapter 5

Adler, Les K. 1991. *The Red Image: American Attitudes Toward Communism in the Cold War Era.* New York: Garland.

Allison, Graham T., Albert Carnesale, and Joseph S. Nye Jr. 1985. *Hawks, Doves, and Owls.* New York: W.W. Norton.

Belfrage, Cedric. 1973. *The American Inquisition, 1945–1960.* Indianapolis: Bobbs-Merrill.

Beschloss, Michael R. 1991. *Kennedy Versus Khrushchev: The Crisis Years 1960–63.* Boston: Faber and Faber.

Bialer, Seweryn, and Michael Mandelbaum. 1988. *The Global Rivals.* New York: Alfred A. Knopf.

Blight, James G. 1992. *The Shattered Crystal Ball: Fear and Learning in the Cuban Missile Crisis.* Lanham, MD: Littlefield Adams Quality Paperbacks.

Blight, James G., and David A. Welch. 1990. *On the Brink: Americans and the Soviets Reexamine the Cuban Missile Crisis.* New York: Noonday Press.

Broadwater, Jeff. 1992. *Eisenhower and the Anti-Communist Crusade.* Chapel Hill: University of North Carolina Press.

Bundy, McGeorge. 1990. *Danger and Survival: Choices About the Bomb in the First Fifty Years.* New York: Vintage Books.

Caute, David. 1978. *The Great Fear: The Anti-Communist Purge Under Truman and Eisenhower.* New York: Simon and Schuster.

Ehrlich, Paul R., Carl Sagan, Donald Kennedy, and Walter Orr Roberts. 1984. *The Cold and the Dark: The World After Nuclear War.* New York: W.W. Norton.

Ewald, William Bragg. 1986. *McCarthyism and Consensus.* Lanham, MD: University Press of America.

Fehrenbach, T.R. 1963. *This Kind of War: A Study in Unpreparedness.* New York: Macmillan.

Fried, Richard M. 1990. *Nightmare in Red: The McCarthy Era in Perspective.* New York: Oxford University Press.

Garthoff, Raymond L. 1987. *Reflections on the Cuban Missile Crisis.* Washington, DC: Brookings Institution.

Grinspoon, Lester, ed. 1986. *The Long Darkness: Psychological and Moral Perspectives on Nuclear Winter.* New Haven, CT: Yale University Press.

Harris, John B., and Eric Markusen. 1986. *Nuclear Weapons and the Threat of Nuclear War.* New York: Harcourt Brace Jovanovich.

Hastings, Max. 1987. *The Korean War.* New York: Simon and Schuster.

Heale, M.J. 1990. *American Anticommunism: Combating the Enemy Within.* Baltimore: Johns Hopkins University Press.

Kull, Steven. 1988. *Minds at War: Nuclear Reality and the Inner Conflicts of Defense Policymakers.* New York: Basic Books.

Lifton, Robert Jay, and Eric Markusen. 1988. *The Genocidal Mentality: Nazi Holocaust and Nuclear Threat.* New York: Basic Books.

Mack, John E., and Roberta Snow. 1986. "Psychological Effects on Children and Adolescents." In *Psychology and Prevention of Nuclear War,* ed. Ralph K. White, pp. 16–33. New York: New York University Press.

McCrea, Frances B., and Gerald E. Markle. 1989. *Minutes to Midnight: Nuclear Weapons Protest in America.* Newbury Park, CA: Sage.

Paulson, Dennis, ed. 1986. *Voices of Survival in the Nuclear Age.* Santa Barbara, CA: Capra Press.

Porter, Jeffrey L. 1993. "Narrating the End: Fables of Survival in the Nuclear Age." *Journal of American Culture* 16:41–47.

Pratt, Ray. 2001. *Projecting Paranoia: Conspiratorial Visions in American Film.* Lawrence: University Press of Kansas.

Rovere, Richard H. 1970. *Senator Joe McCarthy.* New York: World.

Schrecker, Ellen. 1994. *The Age of McCarthyism: A Brief History.* Boston: St. Martin's Press.

Sherwin, Martin J. 1975. *A World Destroyed: The Atomic Bomb and the Grand Alliance.* New York: Alfred A. Knopf.

Smith, Jeff. 1989. *Unthinking the Unthinkable: Nuclear Weapons and Western Culture.* Bloomington: Indiana University Press.

Stouffer, Samuel A. 1955. *Communism, Conformity, and Civil Liberties.* Garden City, NY: Doubleday.

White, Ralph K., ed. 1986. *Psychology and the Prevention of Nuclear War.* New York: New York University Press.

Whitfield, Stephen J. 1991. *The Culture of the Cold War.* Baltimore: Johns Hopkins University Press.

York, Herbert F. 1987. *Making Weapons, Talking Peace: A Physicist's Odyssey from Hiroshima to Geneva.* New York: Basic Books.

Chapter 6

Brende, Joel O., and Erwin Parson. 1985. *Vietnam Veterans: The Road to Recovery.* New York: Plenum.

Bryan, C.D.B. 1976. *Friendly Fire.* New York: Putnam.

Caputo, Philip. 1977. *A Rumor of War.* New York: Ballantine Books.

Card, Josefina J. 1983. *Lives After Vietnam.* Lexington, MA: D.C. Heath.

Dershowitz, Alan M. 2004. *America on Trial: Inside the Legal Battles That Transformed Our Nation.* New York: Warner Books.

Edelman, Bernard, ed. 1985. *Dear America: Letters Home from Vietnam.* New York: W.W. Norton.

Fiddick, Thomas. 1989. "Beyond the Domino Theory: The Vietnam War and Metaphors of Sport." *Journal of American Culture* 12:79–88.

Gibson, James William. 1988. *The Perfect War: The War We Couldn't Lose and How We Did.* New York: Vintage Books.

Grossman, Dave. 1996. *On Killing: The Psychological Cost of Learning to Kill in War and Society.* Boston: Little, Brown.

Hendlin, Herbert, and Ann Pollinger Haas. 1984. *Wounds of War: The Psychological Aftermath of Combat in Vietnam.* New York: Basic Books.

Hendrix, Charles C., and Lisa M. Anneli. 1993. "Impact of Vietnam War Service on Veterans' Perception of Family Life." *Family Relations* 42:87–92.

Hess, Gary R. 1990. *Vietnam and the United States: Origins and Legacy of War.* Boston: Twayne.

Horowitz, Mardi J., and George F. Solomon. 1975. "A Prediction of Delayed Stress Response Syndromes in Vietnam Veterans." *Journal of Social Issues* 31:67–80.

Howell-Koehler, Nancy, ed. 1984. *Vietnam: The Battle Comes Home.* New York: Morgan and Morgan.

Karnow, Stanley. 1983. *Vietnam: A History.* New York: Viking Press.

Keegan, John. 1976. *The Face of Battle.* New York: Viking Press.

Kelly, William E., ed. 1985. *Post-Traumatic Stress Disorder and the War Veteran Patient.* New York: Brunner/Mazel.

Kelman, Herbert C., and Lee H. Lawrence. 1972. "Assessment of Responsibility in the Case of Lt. Calley." *Journal of Social Issues* 28, no. 1:177–212.

Kovic, Ron. 1976. *Born on the Fourth of July.* New York: McGraw-Hill.

Laufer, Robert S., M.S. Gallops, and Ellen Frey-Wouters. 1984. "War Stress and Trauma: The Vietnam Veteran Experience." *Journal of Health and Social Behavior* 25:65–84.

Lawson, Jacqueline E. 1989. "She's a Pretty Woman . . . for a Gook: The Misogyny of the Vietnam War." *Journal of American Culture* 12:55–66.

Lewis, Jerry M. 1971. "The Telling of Kent State." *Social Problems* 19:267–278.

Lifton, Robert J. 1973. *Home from the War.* New York: Simon and Schuster.

MacPherson, Myra. 1985. *Long Time Passing: Vietnam and the Haunted Generation.* New York: Signet.

McNamara, Robert S. 1995. *In Retrospect: The Tragedy and Lessons of Vietnam.* New York: Times Books.

Moskos, Charles C., Jr. 1975. "The American Combat Soldier in Vietnam." *Journal of Social Issues* 31, no. 4:25–38.

Ochberg, Frank M., ed. 1988. *Post Traumatic Therapy and Victims of Violence.* New York: Brunner/Mazel.

Scott, Grant F. 1990. "Meditations in Black: The Vietnam Veterans Memorial." *Journal of American Culture* 13:37–40.

Scruggs, Jan C., and Joel L. Swerdlow. 1985. *To Heal a Nation: The Vietnam Veterans Memorial.* New York: Harper and Row.

Shay, Jonathan. 1994. *Achilles in Vietnam: Combat Trauma and the Undoing of Character.* New York: Atheneum.

Sonnenberg, Stephen, Arthur S. Blank Jr., and John A. Talbot. 1985. *The Trauma of War: Stress and Recovery in Vietnam Veterans.* Washington, DC: American Psychiatric Press.

Wagner-Pacifici, Robin, and Barry Schwartz. 1991. "The Vietnam Veterans Memorial: Commemorating a Difficult Past." *American Journal of Sociology* 97:376–420.

Chapter 7

Banerji, Sanjukta. 1987. *Deferred Hopes: Blacks in Contemporary America.* New York: Advent Books.

Barbour, Floyd R. 1968. *The Black Power Revolt.* Boston: Porter Sargent.

Belin, David W. 1973. *November 22, 1963: You Are the Jury.* New York: Quadrangle.

Blumberg, Rhoda Lois. 1984. *Civil Rights: The 1960s Freedom Struggle.* Boston: Twayne.

Boxill, Bernard R. 1984. *Blacks and Social Justice.* Totowa, NJ: Rowman and Allanheld.

Branch, Taylor. 1988. *Parting the Waters: America in the King Years 1954–63.* New York: Simon and Schuster.

Brown, Thomas. 1988. *JFK: History of an Image.* Bloomington: Indiana University Press.

Buchanan, Thomas C. 1964. *Who Killed Kennedy?* New York: Putnam.

Canfield, Michael, and Alan J. Weberman. 1975. *Coup d'Etat in America: The CIA and the Assassination of John F. Kennedy.* New York: Third Press.

Cloward, Richard A., and Frances Fox Piven. 1975. *The Politics of Turmoil.* New York: Vintage Books.

Colaiaco, James A. 1993. *Martin Luther King, Jr.: Apostle of Militant Nonviolence.* New York: St. Martin's Press.

Downing, Frederick L. 1986. *To See the Promised Land.* Macon, GA: Mercer University Press. .

Dudley, William, ed. 1991. *Racism in America: Opposing Viewpoints.* San Diego: Greenhaven Press.

Epstein, Edward J. 1966. *Inquest: The Warren Commission and the Establishment of Truth.* New York: Bantam.

Farlie, Henry. 1973. *The Kennedy Promise: The Politics of Expectation.* Garden City, NY: Doubleday.

Fammonde, Paris. 1969. *The Kennedy Conspiracy: An Uncommissioned Report on the Jim Garrison Investigation.* New York: Meredith Press.

Friedly, Michael, and David Gallen. 1993. *Martin Luther King Jr.: The FBI File.* New York: Carroll and Graf.

Garrison, Jim. 1988. *On the Trail of the Assassins.* New York: Sheridan Square Press.

Greenberg, Bradley, and Edwin Parker, eds. 1965. *The Kennedy Assassination and the American Public.* Stanford, CA: Stanford University Press.

Grier, William H., and Price M. Cobbs. 1969. *Black Rage.* New York: Bantam Books.

Grunwald, Lisa. 1991. "Why We Still Care." *Life* (December): 34–46.

Halberstam, David. 1972. *The Best and the Brightest.* New York: Random House.

Hoskins, Lotte, ed. 1986. *"I Have a Dream": The Quotations of Martin Luther King, Jr.* New York: Grosset and Dunlap.

Josten, Joachim. 1964. *Oswald: Assassin or Fall Guy?* New York: Marzani and Munsell.

Kantor, Seth. 1978. *Who Was Jack Ruby?* New York: Everest House.

Kunhardt, Philip B., Jr. 1988. *Life in Camelot: The Kennedy Years.* New York: Time.

Lane, Mark. 1966. *Rush to Judgment.* New York: Holt, Rinehart, and Winston.

Manchester, William. 1967. *The Death of a President: November 20–25, 1963.* New York: Harper and Row.

Martin, Ralph G. 1983. *A Hero for Our Time: An Intimate Story of the Kennedy Years.* New York: Macmillan.

Oates, Stephen B. 1994. *Let the Trumpet Sound: The Life of Martin Luther King, Jr.* New York: Harper Perennial.

Pepper, William F. 1995. *Orders to Kill: The Truth Behind the Murder of Martin Luther King.* New York: Carroll and Graf.

Pettigrew, Thomas F. 1971. *Racially Separate or Together.* New York: McGraw-Hill.

Posner, Gerald. 1993. *Case Closed: Lee Harvey Oswald and the Assassination of JFK.* New York: Random House.

Powledge, Fred. 1991. *Free at Last? The Civil Rights Movement and the People Who Made It.* New York: Harper Perennial.

Schuyler, Michael. 1985. "The Bitter Harvest: Lyndon B. Johnson and the Assassination of John F. Kennedy." *Journal of American Culture* 8:101–109.

Sitkoff, Harvard. 1981. *The Struggle for Black Equality 1954–1980.* New York: Hill and Wang.

Summers, Anthony. 1980. *Conspiracy.* New York: McGraw-Hill.

Thompson, Josiah. 1967. *Six Seconds in Dallas: A Microstudy of the Kennedy Assassination.* New York: Bernard Geis Associates.
Warren Commission. 1964. *Report of the President's Commission on the Assassination of President John F. Kennedy.* Washington, DC: U.S. Government Printing Office.
Wilkinson, Doris Yvonne. 1970. "Tactics of Protest as Media: The Case of the Black Revolution." *Sociological Focus* 3:13–22.
Zelizer, Barbie. 1992. *Covering the Body: The Kennedy Assassination, the Media, and the Shaping of Collective Memory.* Chicago: University of Chicago Press.

Chapter 8

Bernstein, Carl, and Bob Woodward. 1974. *All the President's Men.* New York: Simon and Schuster.
Bok, Sissela. 1979. *Lying: Moral Choice in Public and Private Life.* New York: Vintage Books.
Chafe, William H. 1986. *The Unfinished Journey.* New York: Oxford University Press.
Dershowitz, Alan M. 1998. *Sexual McCarthyism: Clinton, Starr, and the Emerging Constitutional Crisis.* New York: Basic Books.
———. 2004. *America on Trial: Inside the Legal Battles That Transformed Our Nation.* New York: Warner Books.
Ervin, Sam J., Jr. 1980. *The Whole Truth: The Watergate Conspiracy.* New York: Random House.
Fields, Howard. 1978. *High Crimes and Misdemeanors.* New York: W.W. Norton.
Frost, David. *"I Gave Them a Sword": Behind the Scenes of the Nixon Interviews.* New York: Ballantine Books.
Hamilton, V. Lee. 1978. "Who Is Responsible? Toward a Social Psychology of Attribution." *Social Psychology* 41:316–327.
Katz, Jack. 1977. "Cover-Up and Collective Integrity: On the Natural Antagonism of Authority Internal and External to Organizations." *Social Problems* 25:3–17.
Kutler, Stanley I. 1990. *The Wars of Watergate: The Last Crisis of Richard Nixon.* New York: Alfred A. Knopf.
Lurie, Leonard. 1973. *The Impeachment of Richard Nixon.* New York: Berkeley Medallion Books.
Mankiewicz, Frank. 1975. *U.S. v. Richard M. Nixon: The Final Crisis.* New York: Quadrangle.
Mills, C. Wright. 1956. *The Power Elite.* New York: Oxford University Press.
Molotch, Harvey L., and Deirdre Boden. 1985. "Talking Social Structure: Discourse, Domination and the Watergate Hearings." *American Sociological Review* 50: 273–288.
Morton, Andrew. 1999. *Monica's Story.* New York: St. Martin's Press.
Reeves, Richard. 2002. *President Nixon: Alone in the White House.* New York: Touchstone.
Robinson, Douglas. 1985. "Nixon in Crisis-Land: The Rhetoric of 'Six Crises.'" *Journal of American Culture* 8:79–86.
Schudson, Michael. 1992. *Watergate in American Memory: How We Remember, Forget, and Reconstruct the Past.* New York: Basic Books.
Sirica, John J. 1979. *To Set the Record Straight: The Break-in, the Tapes, the Conspirators, the Pardon.* New York: Signet Books.

Sussman, Barry. 1992. *The Great Cover-up: Nixon and the Scandal of Watergate.* Arlington, VA: Seven Locks Press.
Thompson, Dennis F. 1980. "Moral Responsibility of Public Officials: The Problem of Many Hands." *American Political Science Review* 74:905–916.
Toobin, Jeffrey. 1999. *A Vast Conspiracy: The Real Story of the Sex Scandal That Nearly Brought Down a President.* New York: Touchstone.
White, Theodore H. 1973. *The Making of the President 1972.* New York: Bantam Books.
———. 1975. *Breach of Faith: The Fall of Richard Nixon.* New York: Atheneum.
Wicker, Tom. 1991. *One of Us: Richard Nixon and the American Dream.* New York: Random House.
Woods, John R. 1985. *Watergate Revisited.* Secaucus, NJ: Citadel Press.
Woodward, Bob, and Carl Bernstein. 1976. *The Final Days.* New York: Touchstone.

Chapter 9

Bach, Julie S., and Lynn Hall, eds. 1986. *The Environmental Crisis: Opposing Viewpoints.* St. Paul, MN: Greenhaven Press.
Brown, Harrison. 1954. *The Challenge of Man's Future.* New York: Viking Press.
Browne, Ray B., and Arthur G. Neal. 2001. *Ordinary Reactions to Extraordinary Events.* Bowling Green, OH: Bowling Green State University Popular Press.
Casti, John L. 1990. *Searching for Certainty: What Scientists Can Know About the Future.* New York: William Morrow.
Clarke, Lee. 1989. *Acceptable Risk? Making Decisions in a Toxic Environment.* Berkeley: University of California Press.
Davies, Christie. 1999. "Jokes on the Death of Diana." In *The Mourning for Diana,* ed. Tony Walter. New York: Oxford.
Douglas, Mary, and Aaron Wildavsky. *Risk and Culture: An Essay on the Selection of Technical and Environmental Dangers.* Berkeley: University of California Press.
Erikson, Kai T. 1976. *Everything in Its Path: Destruction of Community in the Buffalo Creek Flood.* New York: Simon and Schuster.
Freudenburg, William R., and Susan K. Pastor. 1992. "Public Responses to Technological Risks." *Sociological Quarterly* 33:389–412.
Fuller, John G. 1975. *We Almost Lost Detroit.* New York: Reader's Digest Press.
Gale, Robert Peter, and Thomas Hauser. 1988. *Final Warning: The Legacy of Chernobyl.* New York: Warner Books.
Gamson, William A., and Andre Modigliani. 1989. "Media Discourse and Public Opinion on Nuclear Power." *American Journal of Sociology* 95:80–95.
Goldberg, M. Hirsh. 1984. *The Blunder Book: Colossal Errors, Minor Mistakes, and Surprising Slipups That Have Changed the Course of History.* New York: William Morrow.
Keylin, Arleen, and Gene Brown, eds. 1976. "Hindenburg Burns in Lakehurst Crash." In *Disasters: From the Pages of the New York Times,* pp. 106–107. New York: Arno Press.
King, Margaret J. 1984. "Fear of Flying: Marketing Research and the Jet Crisis." *Journal of American Culture* 7:122–127.
Lawless, Edward W. 1977. *Technology and Social Shock.* New Brunswick, NJ: Rutgers University Press.

Morone, Joseph G., and Edward J. Woodhouse. 1986. *Averting Catastrophe: Strategies for Regulating Risky Technologies.* Berkeley: University of California Press.

Morrow, Patrick D. 1987. "Those Sick *Challenger* Jokes." *Journal of Popular Culture* 20 (spring): 175–184.

Norman, Donald A. 1988. *The Psychology of Everyday Things.* New York: Basic Books.

Pacey, Arnold. 1986. *The Culture of Technology.* Cambridge, MA: MIT Press.

Perrow, Charles. 1984. *Normal Accidents: Living with High-Risk Technologies.* New York: Basic Books.

Portmann, John. 2000. *When Bad Things Happen to Other People.* New York: Routledge.

Rhodes, Richard. 1999. *Visions of Technology.* New York: Simon and Schuster.

Sojka, Gregory S. 1984. "The Astronaut: An American Hero with 'The Right Stuff.'" *Journal of American Culture* 7, no. 2:118–121.

Stanley, Manford. 1978. *The Technological Conscience: Survival and Dignity in an Age of Expertise.* Chicago: University of Chicago Press.

Vaughn, Diane. 1996. *The* Challenger *Launch Decision: Risky Technology, Culture, and Deviance at NASA.* Chicago: University of Chicago Press.

Walsh, Edward J. 1981. "Resource Mobilization and Citizen Protest in Communities Around Three Mile Island." *Social Problems* 29:1–21.

Walsh, Edward J., and Rex H. Warland. 1983. "Social Movement Involvement in the Wake of a Nuclear Accident: Activists and Free Riders in the TMI Area." *American Sociological Review* 48:764–780.

Washington Post Staff. 1986. *Challengers: The Inspiring Life Stories of the Seven Brave Astronauts of Shuttle Mission 51–L.* New York: Pocket Books.

Westrum, Ron. 1991. *Technologies and Society: The Shaping of People and Things.* Belmont, CA: Wadsworth.

Zamora, Lois Parkinson. 1982. *The Apocalyptic Vision in America.* Bowling Green, OH: Bowling Green University Popular Press.

Chapter 10

Allen, James, ed. 2000. *Without Sanctuary: Lynching Photography in America.* Santa Fe, NM: Twin Palms.

Beck, Aaron T. 1999. *Prisoners of Hate: The Cognitive Basis of Anger, Hostility, and Violence.* New York: HarperCollins.

Bock, Alan W. 1996. *Ambush at Ruby Ridge.* Berkeley, CA: Berkeley Publishing Group.

Crothers, Lane. 2003. *Rage on the Right: The American Militia Movement from Ruby Ridge to Homeland Security.* Lanham, MD: Rowman and Littlefield.

Dyer, Joel. 1998. *Harvest of Rage: Why Oklahoma City Is Only the Beginning.* Boulder, CO: Westview Press.

Grier, William H., and Price M. Cobb. 1969. *Black Rage.* New York: Bantam Books.

Hewitt, Christopher. 2003. *Understanding Terrorism in America from the Klan to Al Qaeda.* New York: Routledge.

Hudson, Rex A. 1999. *Who Becomes a Terrorist and Why.* Guilford, CT: Lyons Press.

Kimball, Charles. 2002. *When Religion Becomes Evil.* New York: HarperCollins.

Koppelman, Susan. 2001. "The Oklahoma City Bombing: Our Responses, Our Memories." In *Ordinary Reactions to Extraordinary Events,* ed. Ray B. Browne and

Arthur G. Neal, pp. 102–121. Bowling Green, OH: Bowling Green State University Popular Press.

Landsberg, Alison. 2004. *Prosthetic Memory.* New York: Columbia University Press.

Levitas, Daniel. 2002. *The Terrorist Next Door: The Militia Movement and the Radical Right.* New York: Thomas Dunne Books.

Linedecker, Clifford L. 1993. *Massacre at Waco, Texas.* New York: St. Martin's Press.

Markovitz, Jonathan. 2004. *Legacies of Lynching: Racial Violence and Memory.* Minneapolis: University of Minnesota Press.

Nickols, Caroline. 2004. *Monument to Sentiment: The Discourse of Nation and Citizenship at the Oklahoma City National Memorial.* Paper presented at the annual meeting of the Popular Culture Association, San Antonio, Texas.

Poole, W. Scott. 2004. *Never Surrender: Confederate Memory and Conservatism in the South Carolina Upcountry.* Athens: University of Georgia Press.

Reavis, Dick J. 1995. *The Ashes of Waco: An Investigation.* New York: Simon and Schuster.

Smit, Christopher R. 2001. "Columbine: An Exploration of the Hyperreal in Televisual Chaos." In *Ordinary Reactions to Extraordinary Events*, ed. Ray B. Browne and Arthur G. Neal, pp. 88–101. Bowling Green, OH: Bowling Green State University Popular Press.

Snow, Robert L. 1999. *Terrorists Among Us: The Militia Threat.* New York: Perseus.

Stern, Jessica. 2003. *Terror in the Name of God: Why Religious Militants Kill.* New York: HarperCollins.

Vetter, Harold J., and Gary R. Perlstein. 1991. *Perspectives on Terrorism.* Pacific Grove, CA: Brooks/Cole.

Vidal, Gore. 2002. *Perpetual War for Perpetual Peace: How We Got to Be So Hated.* New York: Thunder's Mouth Press.

Walter, Jess. 2002. *Ruby Ridge: The Truth and Tragedy of the Randy Weaver Family.* New York: Regan Books.

Chapter 11

The 9/11 Commission Report. 2004. *Final Report of the National Commission on Terrorist Attacks upon the United States.* New York: W.W. Norton.

Altheide, David L. 2002. *Creating Fear: News and the Construction of Crisis.* New York: Aldine deGruyter.

Barber, Benjamin R. 2003. *Fear's Empire: War, Terrorism, and Democracy.* New York: W.W. Norton.

Bellah, Robert N. 1975. "Civil Religion in America." In *Life Style Diversity in American Society*, ed. Saul D. Feldman and Gerald W. Thielbar, pp. 16–34. Boston: Little, Brown.

Berkowitz, Bruce. 2003. *The New Face of War: How War Will be Fought in the 21st Century.* New York: Free Press.

Brown, Cynthia, ed. 2003. *Lost Liberties: Ashcroft and the Assault on Personal Liberties.* New York: New Press.

Brown, Roger, and James Kulik. 1977. "Flashbulb Memories." *Cognition* 5:73–99.

Browne, Ray B., and Arthur G. Neal. 2001. *Ordinary Reactions to Extraordinary Events.* Bowling Green, OH: State University Popular Press.

Cassel, Elaine. 2004. *The War on Civil Liberties.* Chicago: Lawrence Hill Books.

Crotty, William, ed. 2004. *The Politics of Terror: The U. S. Response to 9/11.* Boston: Northeastern University Press.

Dershowitz, Alan M. 2002. *Why Terrorism Works: Understanding the Threat, Responding to the Challenge.* New Haven, CT: Yale University Press.

Edkins, Jenny. 2003. *Trauma and the Memory of Politics.* New York Cambridge University Press.

Etzioni, Amitai, and Jason H. Marsh, eds. 2003. *Rights and Public Safety After 9/11: America in the Age of Terrorism.* New York: Rowan and Littlefield.

Florini, Ann. 2003. *The Coming Democracy: New Rules for Running the World.* Washington, DC: Island Press.

Fukuyama, Francis. 1992. *The End of History and the Last Man.* New York: Free Press.

———. 1995. *Trust: The Social Virtues and the Creation of Prosperity.* New York: Free Press.

Furedi, Frank. 1997. *The Culture of Fear.* Washington, DC: Cassell.

Glasner, Barry. 1999. *The Culture of Fear: Why Americans Are Afraid of the Wrong Things.* New York: Basic Books.

Griffin, David R. 2004. *The New Pearl Harbor.* Northhampton, MA: Olive Branch Press.

Himmelfarb, Gertrude. 2004. *The Road to Modernity.* New York: Alfred A. Knopf.

Huntington, Samuel P. 1997. *The Clash of Civilizations and the Remaking of World Order.* New York: Touchstone.

Jewett, Robert, and John Shelton Lawrence. 2003. *Captain America and the Crusade Against Evil: The Dilemma of Zealous Nationalism.* Grand Rapids, MI: William B. Eerdmans.

King, Gilbert. 2004. *Dirty Bomb: Weapon of Mass Destruction.* New York: Penguin.

Landsberg, Alison. 2003. "Prosthetic Memory: The Ethics and Politics of Memory in an Age of Mass Culture." In *Memory and Popular Film,* ed. Paul Grainge. Manchester, UK: University of Manchester Press.

Laqueur, Walter. 1987. *The Age of Terrorism.* Boston: Little, Brown.

Lifton, Robert Jay, and Eric Markusen. 1988. *The Genocidal Mentality: Nazi Holocaust and Nuclear Threat.* New York: Basic Books.

Lowenthal, David. 1985. *The Past Is a Foreign Country.* New York: Cambridge University Press

Meyers, Sondra, ed. 2002. *The Democracy Reader.* New York: International Debate Educational Association.

Morrow, Lance. 2003. *Evil: An Investigation.* New York: Basic Books.

Naito, Hatsuho. 1989. *Thunder Gods: The Kamikaze Pilots Tell Their Story.* New York: Dell.

Neal, Arthur G. 1998. *National Trauma and Collective Memory: Major Events in the American Century.* Armonk, NY: M.E. Sharpe.

Perrow, Charles. 1984. *Normal Accidents: Living with High Risk Technologies.* New York: Basic Books.

Revel, Jean-François. 2002. *Anti-Americanism.* Trans. Diarmid Cammell. San Francisco: Encounter Books.

Rosenbaum, Ron. 2002. "Degrees of Evil." *Atlantic Monthly* (February): 63–68.

Schuetz, Alfred. 1971. *Collected Papers I: The Problem of Social Reality.* The Hague: Martinus Nijhoff.

Scruton, Roger. 2002. *The West and the Rest: Globalization and the Terrorist Threat.* Wilmington, DE: Intercollegiate Studies Institute.

Stern, Jessica. 2003. *Terror in the Name of God: Why Religious Militants Kill.* New York: HarperCollins.

Sullivan, Andrew. 2001. "This Is a Religious War." *New York Times*, October 7.
Tirman, John, ed. 2004. *The Maze of Fear: Security and Migration After 9/11*. New York: New Press.
Tuan, Yi-Fu. 1979. *Landscapes of Fear*. Minneapolis: University of Minnesota Press.
Turner, William W. 2004. *Mission Not Accomplished*. Roseville, CA: Penmarin Books.
Williams, Jessica. 2004. *50 Facts That Should Change the World*. New York: Disinformation Company.
Worth, Robert F. 2002. "A Nation Defines Itself by Its Evil Enemies." *New York Times*, February 25.
Zelizer, Barbie. 1992. *Covering the Body: The Kennedy Assassination, the Media, and the Shaping of Collective Memory*. Chicago: University of Chicago Press.

Chapter 12

Alexander, Jeffrey C. 2004. "On the Social Construction of Moral Universals: the 'Holocaust' from War Crime to Trauma Drama." In *Matters of Culture: Cultural Sociology in Practice*, ed. Roger Friedland and John Mohr. New York: Cambridge University Press.
Appleby, Joyce, Lynn Hunt, and Margaret Jacob. 1994. *Telling the Truth About History*. New York: W.W. Norton.
Ben-Amos, Dan, and Liliane Weissberg, eds. 1999. *Cultural Memory and the Construction of Identity*. Detroit: Wayne State University Press.
Bengston, Vern L. 1970. "The Generation Gap: A Review and Typology of Social Psychological Perspectives." *Youth and Society* 2:7–32.
Bennett, W. Lance, and Martha S. Feldman. 1981. *Reconstructing Reality in the Courtroom*. New Brunswick, NJ: Rutgers University Press.
Berger, Peter. 1969. *The Sacred Canopy*. Garden City, NY: Anchor.
Berger, Peter, Brigitte Berger, and Hansfried Kellner. 1974. *The Homeless Mind: Modernization and Consciousness*. New York: Vintage Books.
Boorstin, Daniel J. 1961. *The Image: A Guide to Pseudo-Events in America*. New York: Harper Colophon Books.
Brown, Roger, and James Kulik. 1977. "Flashbulb Memories." *Cognition* 5:73–99.
Browne, Ray B., and Arthur G. Neal. 2001. *Ordinary Reactions to Extraordinary Events*. Bowling Green, OH: Bowling Green State University Popular Press.
Cantril, Hadley. 1965. *The Pattern of Human Concerns*. New Brunswick, NJ: Rutgers University Press.
Casey, Edward S. 1987. *Remembering: A Phenomenological Study*. Bloomington: Indiana University Press.
Chomsky, Noam. 1989. *Necessary Illusions: Thought Control in Democratic Societies*. Boston: South End Press.
Dixon, Wheeler Winston. 1999. *Disaster and Memory: Celebrity Culture and the Crisis of Hollywood Cinema*. New York: Columbia University Press.
Eber, Dena E., and Arthur G. Neal, eds. 2001. *Memory and Representation: Constructed Truths and Competing Realities*. Bowling Green, OH: Bowling Green State University Popular Press.
Edkins, Jenny. 2003. *Trauma and the Memory of Politics*. New York: Cambridge University Press.
Elder, Glen H., Jr. 1974. *Children of the Great Depression*. Chicago: University of Chicago Press.

Fehrenbach, T.R. 1963. *This Kind of War.* New York: Macmillan.
Feurer, Lewis S. 1969. *The Conflict of Generations.* New York: Basic Books.
Grainge, Paul, ed. 2003. *Memory and Popular Film.* New York: Manchester University Press.
Halbwachs, Maurice. 1992. *On Collective Memory,* ed. Lewis A. Coser. Chicago: University of Chicago Press.
Huber, Joan, ed. 1991. *Macro-Micro Linkages in Sociology.* Newbury Park, CA: Sage.
Kertzer, David L. 1983. "Generation as a Sociological Problem." *Annual Review of Sociology* 9:125–149.
Kramer, Jane. 1996. *The Politics of Memory.* New York: Random House.
Kuiken, Don, ed. 1991. *Mood and Memory.* Newbury Park, CA: Sage.
Landsberg, Alison. 2004. *Prosthetic Memory: The Transformation of American Remembrance in the Age of Mass Culture.* New York: Columbia University Press.
Lowenthal, David. 1985. *The Past Is a Foreign Country.* New York: Cambridge University Press.
MacCannell, Dean. 1976. *The Tourist: A New Theory of the Leisure Class.* New York: Schocken Books.
Mannheim, Karl. [1928] 1952. "The Problem of Generations." In *Essays on the Sociology of Knowledge,* pp. 276–322. London: Routledge and Kegan Paul.
Mico, Ted, John Miller-Monzon, and David Rubel, eds. 1995. *Past Imperfect: History According to the Movies.* New York: Henry Holt.
Mosse, George L. 1990. *Fallen Soldiers: Reshaping the Memory of the World Wars.* New York: Oxford University Press.
Power, Samantha. 2002. *The Problem from Hell: America and the Age of Genocide.* New York: Perseus Books.
Pratt, Ray. 2001. *Projecting Paranoia: Conspiratorial Visions in American Film.* Lawrence: University Press of Kansas.
Schudson, Michael. 1992. *Watergate in American Memory: How We Remember, Forget, and Reconstruct the Past.* New York: Basic Books.
Schuman, Howard, and Cheryl Rieger. 1992. "Historical Analogies, Generational Effects, and Attitudes Toward War." *American Sociological Review* 57:315–326.
Schuman, Howard, and Jacqueline Scott. 1989. "Generations and Collective Memories." *American Sociological Review* 54:359–381.
Schwartz, Barry. 1982. "The Social Context of Commemoration: A Study in Collective Memory." *Social Forces* 61:374–402.
Simon, William, and John H. Gagnon. 1976. "The Anomie of Affluence." *American Journal of Sociology* 82:356–378.
Wagner-Pacifici, Robin, and Barry Schwartz. 1991. "The Vietnam Veterans Memorial: Commemorating a Difficult Past." *American Journal of Sociology* 97:376–420.
Ware, Susan. 1982. *Holding Their Own: American Women in the 1930s.* Boston: Twayne.
Wertsch, James V. 2002. *Voices of Collective Remembering.* New York: Cambridge University Press.
Zelizer, Barbie. 1992. *Covering the Body: The Kennedy Assassination, the Media, and the Shaping of Collective Memory.* Chicago: University of Chicago Press.

Index

Abortion clinics, 166
Activism. *See* Demonstrations
Afghanistan, 183–85, 188–89
African Americans
    church burnings, 169
    civil rights movement, 115–23
    Great Depression, 49–50, 51
    historical reporting, 213
    lynching, 168–69
    racial terrorism, 160–61, 163, 167–70
        racism, 115, 116, 117–23
        slavery, 160–61, 167
Agnew, Spiro, 129
AIDS virus, 3, 4, 12, 158
Alabama National Guard, 118, 121
Aldrin, Buzz, 144
Alfred P. Murrah Federal Building (Oklahoma
    City). *See* Oklahoma City bombing (1995)
American Revolution
    national identity
        development of, 21–23
        disturbance of, 29–30
    terrorism, 160
Arkansas National Guard, 118
Arlington Cemetery, 108–9, 204, 205
Armstrong, Neil, 143, 144
Army of God, The, 166
Assassinations. *See* Kennedy, John F.; King,
    Martin Luther, Jr.; Lincoln, Abraham

Bay of Pigs invasion, 33–34, 133
Bernstein, Carl, 125–26, 137
Bin Laden, Osama, 183–84, 185
Bioterrorism, 186–87
Bork, Robert, 128
Bowling for Columbine, 165
Branch Davidians (Waco, Texas), 15, 171,
    172–73, 175–76
Brown, John, 160–61
Bureau of Prisons, 79
Bush, George H.W., 139
Bush, George W., 105–6, 146, 185–86, 187,
    189, 191
Butterfield, Alexander, 128

Calley, William, Jr., 95
Canada, 22, 23, 24, 189
Capitalism, 39, 43–45, 51, 52, 77
Carnegie, Dale, 50
Carter, Jimmy, 154
Castro, Fidel, 33–34, 133
Causal explanations
    collective memory, 197, 199, 201–2, 208,
        209–12
    collective trauma, 12, 14–15
    news media, 12, 14, 15
    terrorism, 15, 160, 161, 162, 163–76,
        182–85, 189–94
    See also Communism; Conspiracy
        theories; National security;
        Religion
Central Intelligence Agency (CIA), 33–34,
    114, 126, 127, 135–36, 138, 211–12
Challenger explosion (1986), 9, 15, 18, 34,
    142, 144–46, 147
Chernobyl (Soviet Union), 156–57
China
    Korean War (1950), 75, 76
    World War II, 57, 58, 59, 69
China Syndrome, The, 155
Christian Identity, 170, 171
Churchill, Winston, 61
Civil Rights Act (1964), 116
Civil rights movement
    collective memory, 123
    demonstrations, 115, 117, 118–19, 120–23
    discussion questions, 123
    freedom rides, 122
    generational effects, 200–1
    leadership, 115–23
    Montgomery bus boycott, 117, 118, 120
    national identity disturbance, 32
    news media, 122, 123
    nonviolent resistance, 116, 120–23
    segregation, 117, 118, 122–23
    social disruption, 117–23
    trusteeship, 118–20, 121–22
    violence, 9, 116, 118–20, 121, 122
    voting rights, 121

About the Author

Arthur G. Neal, formerly Distinguished University Professor of Sociology at Bowling Green State University in Ohio, now has adjunct appointments with the Center for Population Research and the Sociology Department at Portland State University in Oregon. He is the author or coauthor of nearly twenty books and research monographs and numerous research articles. He has taught a wide variety of graduate seminars in sociology and in American culture studies. His recent books include *Memory and Representation* (with Dena Eber), *Intimacy and Alienation in Female/Male Relationships* (with Sara Collas), and *Ordinary Reactions to Extraordinary Events* (with Ray B. Browne).